Lynching in American Literature and Journalism

Lynching in American Literature and Journalism

Edited by Yoshinobu Hakutani

LEXINGTON BOOKS
Lanham • Boulder • New York • London

Published by Lexington Books
An imprint of The Rowman & Littlefield Publishing Group, Inc.
4501 Forbes Boulevard, Suite 200, Lanham, Maryland 20706
www.rowman.com

86-90 Paul Street, London EC2A 4NE

Copyright © 2022 by The Rowman & Littlefield Publishing Group, Inc.

All rights reserved. No part of this book may be reproduced in any form or by any electronic or mechanical means, including information storage and retrieval systems, without written permission from the publisher, except by a reviewer who may quote passages in a review.

British Library Cataloguing in Publication Information Available

Library of Congress Cataloging-in-Publication Data Available

ISBN: 978-1-66690-907-4 (cloth)
ISBN: 978-1-66690-908-1 (electronic)
ISBN: 978-1-66690-909-8 (pbk.)

Contents

Acknowledgments	vii
Introduction	1
Chapter One: The "Girl Reporter" Confronts the Lynch Mob: Miriam Michaelson's *A Yellow Journalist* Debbie Lelekis	5
Chapter Two: Theodore Dreiser's "Nigger Jeff": The Development of an Aesthetic Donald Pizer	21
Chapter Three: Theodore Dreiser's "Nigger Jeff," Richard Wright's "Big Boy Leaves Home," and Lynching Michael Sanders	31
Chapter Four: Lynching as an American Tragedy in Theodore Dreiser's Literary Works Kiyohiko Murayama	47
Chapter Five: Faulkner on Lynching Neil R. McMillen and Noel Polk	61
Chapter Six: Lynching in Richard Wright's "Big Boy Leaves Home" Toru Kiuchi	73
Chapter Seven: Lynching in Modern American Short Stories and Sexual Crime in Classic Myth Yoshinobu Hakutani	91
Chapter Eight: The Southern Ritual of Lynching in Faulkner's *Light in August* and Ellison's *Three Days before the Shooting* Robert Butler	103

Chapter Nine: The Electric Execution of Bigger Thomas in
   Wright's *Native Son*   113
   Yoshinobu Hakutani

Chapter Ten: Lynching as Surrealism: Leon Forrest's "The Vision"   137
   Keith Byerman

Chapter Eleven: Lynching in African-American Poetry   151
   Toru Kiuchi

Chapter Twelve: Depictions of Racial Violence in the Work of Paul
   Laurence Dunbar   167
   Debbie Lelekis

Index   181

About the Contributors   191

Acknowledgments

I would like to thank Toru Kiuchi for making an index and Yoshiki Hakutani for editorial and technical support.

I also acknowledge:

Chapter 2, Donald Pizer, "Theodore Dreiser's 'Nigger Jeff': The Development: The Development of An Aesthetic" is reprinted with permission from *American Literature*, Vol. 41, No. 3 (Nov., 1969), pp. 331–41.

Chapter 4, Kiyohiko Murayama, "Lynching in Theodore Dreiser's Literary Works" is reprinted with permission from *Mississippi Quarterly*, Vol. 70/71, No. 2 (Spring 2017/2018), pp. 163–79.

Chapter 5, Neil R. McMillen and Noel Polk, "Lynching on Faulkner" is reprinted with permission from *The Faulkner Journal*, Vol. 8, No. 1 (Fall 1992), pp. 3–14.

Introduction

The primary goal of the project is to investigate the history and development of writing about lynching in American journalism and literature. Contemporary historians and literary critics view lynching as an American tragedy and the ugliest element of national character. Like the Holocaust, lynching, which is antithetical to the principles of democracy, is a national shame. According to the Tuskegee Institute, 4,743 people were lynched between 1882 and 1968 in the United States, including 3,446 African Americans and 1,297 European Americans. More than 73 percent of the lynchings in the post-Civil War period occurred in the Southern states. Lynching attacks on African Americans, especially in the South, increased dramatically in the aftermath of Reconstruction, after slavery had been abolished and free men gained the right to vote. The peak of lynching occurred in 1882, after Southern white Democrats had regained control of state legislators.

The racialization of lynching, the exclusive targeting of African Americans for punishment by white vigilante mobs, took place during the era of Reconstruction. White men's sexual relationship or alleged rape, unlike alleged black men's rape of white women, was not illegal. Between the Revolutionary War and the Civil War, lynching encompassed the corporal punishments (lashings, far and feathering, riding the rail) of white men by semiregular public authorities in frontier areas. Such practice continued during Reconstruction. As Theodore Dreiser noted in his article "Delaware's Blue Laws," he was appalled that while black offenders has no chance to lessen their punishment, the white offenders who had a high standing in their community and could afford to offer their possessions and leave the state escaped this public punishment. Dreiser concluded his study: "It is the man with conscience and feeling upon whom this relic of an older order of civilization weighs unjustly. The hardened criminal whom it is supposed to reach does not suffer at all, and is not corrected thereby" (*Ainslee's* 7: 56). Racial prejudice underlying the practice of corporal punishment and lynching originated in slavery and persisted during Reconstruction. Civil War and

Reconstruction led to much violence and lynching in the nineteenth century as extremist whites turned to vigilante groups to carry out punishment for those accused of a crime and alleged rape, in particular, without the due process of law, and often this led to mobs hunting down the victims and lynching them. The practice of lynching gained momentum during Reconstruction when viable black towns sprang up across the South and African Americans began to make political and economic inroads by registering to vote, establishing businesses, and running for public office. Many white people—landowners and poor whites—felt threatened by this rise in black prominence. These people were obsessed with a fear of sex between the races. Some white people espoused the idea that black men were sexual predators and desired integration in order to be with white women.

Ida B. Wells, an African-American journalist, distinguished herself in bringing up this national shame to the attention of the public with the publication of *Southern Horrors* in 1892. She argued, "At the very moment . . . civilized whites were announcing their determination 'to protect wives and daughters'" from black male sexual predators, white men stalked black women fearlessly because as Wells angrily observed, "when the victim is a colored woman it is different" (*Southern Horrors* 26). A year later, Theodore Dreiser, another journalist to become an eminent novelist with *Sister Carrie* (1900) and *An American Tragedy* (1925), published a newspaper article, "A Negro Lynched," in *St. Louis Republic*. Dreiser then created a short story entitled "Nigger Jeff" out of the article and published it in *Ainslee's Magazine* in 1901. This conversion of a newspaper article to a work of fiction exemplifies American realists' creative activities in the twentieth century. As a result, modern American fiction made social and political issues in journalism into major themes in literature with artistic and structural devices. Novelists like Faulkner, Hemingway, and others followed Dreiser's lead and produced works of fiction that contributed to social reform. Their works intensified the social realities and inspired the reader to attain one's conscience.

American modernists in fiction and poetry made social and political phenomena reported in journalism intensive and vivid. In defining the difference between journalism and literature, Henry James argued: "What a man thinks and what he feels are the history and character of what he does; on all of which things the logic of intensity rests. Without intensity where is vividness, and without vividness where is presentability?" (*The Art of the Novel* 66). The limits of traditional journalism, which often excluded reporting of lynching, often failed to inspire readers to think for themselves. Since these limitations were apparent to creative writers like Dreiser and Paul Laurence Dunbar, it was in their fiction and poetry that they most effectively drew attention to and moved beyond those boundaries, producing texts intended to engage the reader's thoughts and emotions. In Dreiser's "Nigger Jeff," for instance, a technical device displayed is the contrast in the images of man and nature. Although in the beginning the reporter is convinced that Jeff is guilty, he grows increasingly less certain. Even before he reaches the site of the lynching, Davies takes notice of "the whiteness of the little house, the shimmering beauty of the little creek you had to cross in going from the depot. At the one main corner a few men [a part of the mob] were gathered about a typical village barroom." As the mob hurries on with the horror impending, the "night was exceedingly beautiful. Stars were already beginning to shine. . . . The air was fresh and tender. Some pea fowls were crying afar off and east promised a golden moon." Again, a contrast of light and dark is maintained in Dreiser's depiction of the scene. As Davies watches the limp body plunging down and pulling up with the sound of a creaking rope, in "weak moonlight it seemed as if the body were struggling, but he could not tell. Only the black mass swaying in the pale light, over the shiny water of the stream seemed wonderful. . . . The light of morning began to show as tender lavender and gray in the east. Still he sat. Then came the roseate hue of day, to which waters of the stream responded, the white pebbles beautifully at the bottom. Still the body hung black and limp, and now a light breeze sprang up and stirred it visibly" (*Ainslee's* 8: 366–74). The images of dark, "the struggling body," "the dark mass," and "the body hanging black and limp," are poignantly contrasted with those of light, "weak moonlight," "pale light," "the shiny water of the stream," "the light of morning," "tender lavender and gray in the east," "the roseate hue of day," "the white pebbles shining beautifully at the bottom." The images of dark and light are intermingled in Davies's mind. At the end of the story, David is overwhelmed not only by the remorse he feels for the victim but also by his compassion for the victim's bereft mother sitting in the dark corner of the room. Such a depiction of the tragedy makes great impact on the reporter's conscience and on the sense of urgency in which the protagonist is compelled to act as a reformer. Not only is literature a work of art, it functions as social reform.

Chapter One

The "Girl Reporter" Confronts the Lynch Mob

Miriam Michaelson's A Yellow Journalist

Debbie Lelekis

Miriam Michelson's 1905 collection of stories entitled *A Yellow Journalist* is notable not only for its featuring of a young female journalist named Rhoda Massey who fits within the "girl reporter" tradition established in popular fiction of the nineteenth and early twentieth centuries, but also for its exploration of racial violence. Massey's bold reporting style allows the character to have access to people and situations that normally wouldn't be open to her. While the title of the collection is an obvious nod to the type of sensationalist journalism that these stunts can lead to, some scholars have suggested an additional racialized meaning. Many of Massey's adventures take place in San Francisco's Chinatown, and Lori Harrison-Kahan and Karen E. H. Skinazi argue that the title of the collection is also a reference to Massey's evolving views of her identity as a racial outsider during the brief insider's view her reporting allows her to obtain of the ethnic enclave (12). Michelson's own unique background as a Jewish woman on the multiethnic west coast of nineteenth-century America likely contributed to the shaping of her views regarding gender, race, and class. These factors led to the creation of a character who is aligned most often with the Other rather than the dominant white power. *A Yellow Journalist* chronicles Massey's assignments as a reporter for the San Francisco based *News* where she frequently goes beyond the call of duty, disguising herself as a Chinese slave girl in a Chinatown brothel in the story "In Chy Fong's Restaurant," maneuvering her way into a wagon for an exclusive interview with an accused murderer that leads to an attempted lynch mob where a bullet grazes her cheek in "Honors Are Easy," and crossing gender lines by dressing as a Chinese boy in "The Fascination of Fan Tan" where she uncovers a gambling ring and inadvertently exposes police corruption. Rather than having Massey directly analyze and criticize these situations, particularly in the case of the lynch mob, we see her initial emotional responses and her contrasting detachment in her schemes to cover the news stories. As Harrison-Kahan and Skinazi contend, *A Yellow Journalist* uses stunt reporting to "upend the relationship between cultural insiders and outsiders," creating a unique position for Massey within the narrative (17). Since Michelson herself was both an insider and outsider due to her gender and Jewish heritage, she was able to give voice to characters on the margins.

Michelson was a popular writer in the early 1900s, but her work had fallen out of favor by the end of the century. However, over the last decade and a half, a few scholars have begun recovery efforts. She is mentioned by Nina Bayam in *Women Writers of the American West, 1833–1927* (2011) and by Jean Marie Lutes in *Front-Page Girls* (2006), and more extensive work was done on her by Lori Harrison-Kahan and Karen E. H. Skinazi in two articles and an edited collection and in a chapter of my own book *American Literature, Lynching, and the Spectator in the Crowd: Spectacular Violence* (2015). Harrison-Kahan and Skinazi point out that compared to the writing of Jack London and Stephen Crane, Michelson's work was often misconstrued as pop culture entertainment, despite the fact that all three authors published in the same mass-circulated magazines.

Like the fictional Massey, Michelson learned her craft in the newsrooms of San Francisco. The Michelson family made their way out west after a brief stop in New York when they arrived in the United States from Poland in the mid-nineteenth century.[1] Her brother Charles helped her get her start in 1895 at the *San Francisco Call*, the same paper that launched Mark Twain's career over thirty years earlier. First Michelson wrote theater criticism, and this led to the position of dramatic editor. During her time at both the *San Francisco Call* and the *San Francisco Bulletin* reporting on crime and politics, she challenged gender barriers. Michelson covered the conditions of Chinese girls and women in Chinatown. Harrison-Kahan and Skinazi point to Michelson's article "The Terror of Quarantine to an Unsophisticated Chinese Lady" (1900) as a prime example. Despite the fact that Michelson did not consider her family to be very religious, their Jewish heritage did mark them as different to others, and as Harrison-Kahan and Skinazi assert in their article "Miriam Michelson's Yellow Journalism and the Multi-Ethnic West," the Jewish press recognized her work, and her religion could account for the ethnic variety in much of her fiction that came later. Irish immigrants are particularly prevalent in her writing, featured most prominently in her novel, *The Madigans* (1904), and some believe that Rhoda Massey is of Irish descent even though it is never explicitly stated in the text.

The West Coast proved to be fertile ground for women reporters, and in addition to Michelson herself, there are several other possible real-life inspirations for the fictional Massey. Patricia Bradley highlights the achievements of female reporters like Winfred Sweet, who wrote under the name Annie Laurie as a stunt reporter for the *San Francisco Examiner*, Mabel Craft of the *San Francisco Chronicle*, and Marjorie Driscoll of the *Los Angeles Examiner* (117). The foundation out of which Michelson's Rhoda Massey came from can be traced back to these pioneering women. Sari Edelstein argues that American women's writing arose out of a "dynamic, often critical, relationship with mainstream journalism," and in both "form and content, women's writing registers a dual impulse" to employ journalistic methods while at the same time being critical of journalism's "representational biases, oversights, and ideological premises" (2). This accounts for the ways in which women's writing intertextualizes and reflects the influences of journalistic practices in women's creative writing. Furthermore, Karen Roggenkamp contends that the 1890s was the height of the period in which journalism and American fiction were linked. There was an expectation that reporters would possess the narrative skills and literary techniques necessary to effectively mold both factual and manufactured material into the news stories they produced. As a result, reporters sometimes became part of their stories. This became even more prevalent in the case of female reporters. Harrison-Kahan and Skinazi examine the ways in which Michelson did this specifically in an 1897 article on the Hawaiian Patriotic League's anti-annexation views after she visited the island as a correspondent for the *San Francisco Call*. Her fictional reporter, Massey, also inserts herself into the action frequently, and the potentially dangerous consequences of this are seen most clearly in the lynch mob scene in the story I analyze in this essay. Harrison-Kahan and Skinazi see these literary and journalistic techniques as crucial to the development of the era's journalistic narratives, which "blurred the lines between fiction and nonfiction" (2).

In the early years of the twentieth century, Michelson turned to fiction writing and published magazine stories and five novels. Her first book, *In the Bishop's Carriage* (1904), was a best-seller. She followed that with a series of stories about Rhoda Massey that were first published in *The Saturday Evening Post* and later collected as *A Yellow Journalist*. Overall, her writing is difficult to classify because she experimented with a variety of genres ranging from science fiction to utopian fiction and historical romances, in addition to her nonfiction writing. This diversity adds much to our understanding of women writers of that period, and as Harrison-Kahan and Skinazi argue, the interplay between her journalism and fiction "enriches the turn-of-the-twentieth-century canon in terms of gender, ethnicity, and cross-racial representations"

(3). Michelson creates unconventional female protagonists and Massey is one of her best. Both author and character helped to actively create a new public space for women within the realm of print culture. As Alice Fahs describes in her book about newspaper women, this new territory was staked out by female reporters who we now know relatively little about, with the exception of pioneers like Nellie Bly (Elizabeth Jane Cochrane) or the "sob sisters" who covered notorious murder trials.[2] As newspapers evolved during the 1890s, and the sensational tactics of yellow journalism became more prevalent, there were new opportunities for women writers. Fahs argues that these changes made it increasingly more feasible for women to take on a larger variety of newspaper work, although many of those female writers still worked predominantly on the section known as the woman's page; this was understandably frustrating for those who wished to branch out beyond the more traditionally feminine topics. According to Fahs, it was practically unachievable for a female writer to "avoid the woman's page entirely over the course of her newspaper career—even if she was hired as an 'all around' reporter or as a 'stunt' reporter" (5). In Michelson's stories, Massey appears to be a fictional example of a female reporter who *has* been able to take on a more expansive role as a reporter, although it is possible that part of her assignment was to get the "woman's angle" even if it wasn't explicitly spelled out by the characters.

While Massey is not described officially as being employed by her newspaper as a stunt reporter, she frequently engages in behavior that reflects some of the most well-known daring feats of real women reporters at the turn of the century. Maurine H. Beasley and Shelia J. Gibbons recount how women reporters "ascended in balloons, descended in diving bells, dressed up like beggars and waifs, feigned madness, and posed as servants in the homes of society figures to pursue exciting and scandalous tidbits for their readers" (64). These activities sound strikingly similar to some of Massey's own capers. Part of Massey's success might be due to her ability to challenge the stereotypes that kept many female reporters tied to the gossip columns or society news sections. Readers see her take on her male competition head on with triumphant results. She follows in a tradition that Beasley describes in her study "Recent Directions For the Study of Women's History in American Journalism," which examines female reporters who helped expand the meaning of journalism beyond the traditional notions of reporting on conflicts and controversies that were of primary interest to men; furthermore Beasley contends that "Widening our concept of journalism allows us to take into account more fully the way women have participated in all areas of the field, whether oriented to the presentation of 'hard' (front-page) or 'soft' (feature) news" and it also leads us to consider the work of women in literary journalism or alternative presses, and even women who transitioned away from journalism into the fiction genre ("Recent Directions" 209).

Fahs asserts that female stunt reporters produced writing that was part of a "new articulation of modern life in which newspaper women became performative public figures" (6–7). Their work helped to shape a new connection between women and public life that was concentrated around active participation and observation. According to Fahs, the newspaper work that women engaged in during this era demanded new modes of seeing and observing (8). In my book chapter on Michelson in *American Literature, Lynching, and the Spectator in the Crowd: Spectacular Violence* (2015), I examined the tensions between the role of the reporter as observer and the responsibilities of a person who witnesses violence. By examining the nature of spectatorship, I argue that Michelson is critiquing the public's consumption of violence in popular fiction and highlighting the complicity of all witnesses, including those who are paid to watch and write about what they observe.

Lutes has pointed out the ways in which girl reporters simultaneously generated serious attention and invited ridicule, because they were frequently willing to benefit from their shock value.[3] They were often featured more prominently than the actual news stories that they produced, and this seems to be the case with Michelson's Rhoda Massey in *A Yellow Journalist*. Due to this link between a female journalist's bodily experience as a primary source of news and the emphasis placed on emotional responses, a figure like Massey becomes a complicated spectator of violence.

Massey, like her literary ancestors from Henry James's Henrietta Stackpole on, is characterized chiefly by her forthright manner, freedom, and confidence. The anxiety that she felt while covering her first big story away from the home office in "The Pollexfen Story" has disappeared by the second piece in *A Yellow Journalist*. Her rivalry with Ted Thompson of the *Times-Record* fuels Massey's actions in all of the stories, but particularly in "Honors are Easy," which I focus on here as a prime example in the collection of her complex role as a reporter of racial violence. The competition between Thompson and Massey goes back to the opening lines of "The Pollexfen Story," when they are sent to cover the same story for their respective newspapers and she notes his sardonic smile and the fact that "Everyone knows that [he] doesn't consider a newspaper woman a foeman worthy of his steel" (1). At one point, Massey refers to herself as a "wretched little local-room prodigy, full of envy and ambition" and she vows to be a valued reporter like Thompson who can pick and choose his assignments (15). This incites Massey's burning desire to beat him to the story and that rivalry is still alive at the beginning of "Honors are Easy." Massey uses her natural talent for manipulating others, as well as her keen sense of observation, to put herself at the forefront of the action in the pivotal lynch mob scene and the subsequent encounters where she unravels the accused man's situation before the other reporters.

As the narrative opens, Massey is interrogating and berating her newspaper's local correspondent in San Isidro for his incompetence. The man who has blown the newspaper's chance at being the first to report on the story about the unfolding murder case of Thad Demling is comically named Blewett, and Massey doesn't even attempt to hide her disgust for him. In the most unflattering terms, Blewett is portrayed as "the picture of fat, self-satisfied dullness," with clothes too tight, a skull too thick, and "vanity too dense for disgust to penetrate" (25). It's Massey's job now to take the potential news story out of the inept correspondent's hands. Before Massey's arrival Ted Thompson has already produced an initial story for his paper by writing a report ahead of time, including a fake interview with the prisoner, and then monopolizing the telegraph office operator by filing his report near midnight. It's clear that the "lumbering" and "blundering" Blewett is overmatched by Thompson who is characterized by his "cool, audacious quickness" (27). In response to Blewett's mismanagement of the coverage for the *News*, Massey has been sent to rectify the situation and she takes the opportunity to chastise the local reporter for not getting word to the newspaper office about Thompson's report. It is apparent that Massey possesses the same sense of cunning as her rival, but unfortunately for her newspaper, the dim-witted Blewett didn't even consider the notion of trying to contact the paper from the telegraph office in the neighboring town of Grafton. This further infuriates the clever and ambitious Massey, but her plan to get even with Thompson is met "stiffly" by Blewett. Even though it is his fault that Massey has to take up the story herself, Blewett gives a strong impression of silent disapproval for what he most likely sees as her un-ladylike aggressiveness. She is described as speaking to him in a furious and explosive manner, and she smugly points out that his only chance of keeping his job is dependent on him helping her.

Even though her emotions are high as she fumes over Blewett's incompetency and Thompson's gloating, Massey is able to quickly and calmly assess the accused man Demling who has been charged with the murder of his family, the burning of his house, and the masked robbery of a stagecoach. She reserves judgment and shows signs of journalistic objectivity before she meets with and interviews Demling herself. Initially she plans to convince Demling's lawyer to grant her an interview, but before she can do so, Blewett alerts her to the plan of the townspeople of Grafton, where the prisoner is going to be transported. She learns that they intend to take Demling from the sheriff and lynch him. Massey questions whether the townspeople would really carry out their threat of the lynch mob and Blewett warns her that they are "all aflame with indignant and outraged public spirit" (30). The prisoner, who is described as a "thin-lipped, rat-eyed young man," arrives in a wagon with the sheriff and deputy sheriff, Pennoyer (31). Massey suggests that Blewett ride with them to Grafton, but she knows that he lacks the courage to pursue the story. Unsurprisingly, Blewett declines, and Massey instantly springs into action, sending Blewett on the train to Grafton to get the reaction of the crowd while she makes plans to ride with the prisoner in the wagon. Due to her clever manipulation of Blewett and the sheriff, she gains exclusive access to the main story. When she jumps into the wagon, she becomes part of the spectacle herself as her presence incites a "murmur of amazement that broke into a laugh and swelled into a cheer" as the crowd watches her (32).

It is at this point in the story when Massey's actions are most clearly aligned with the tradition of the girl reporter. She fits neatly into Lutes's description of the "hybrid of emotional 'soft news' and tough-minded 'hard news,'" which made these female journalists the heroines of their own stories by using their bodies "not just as a means of acquiring the news but as the very source of it" (14). Massey is depicted in the true reporter-heroine fashion of popular fiction as brave, clever, compassionate, and resourceful. As Lutes asserts, the reporter-heroine is a source of humor for her readers, but she is also a memorable and powerful figure (103).

Even though Massey feels a sense of glee at her triumph over Thompson when she secures the only seat left in the wagon, she does still have a momentary sensation of being "yellow" and a blush rises in her cheeks as she turns away from the crowd and sets her gaze straight ahead. Her behavior gains a "roar of appreciation" from the deputy Pennoyer who laughs at her sly questioning of the possibility of Thompson following them on other horses borrowed from people in the town. The sheriff eases her anxiety and assures her that she's "got the whole works" to herself and that "Thompson can't get a thing on four legs that'll get him to Grafton" sooner than them (32). Massey's success in securing her position in the wagon over Thompson is clearly due to her ability to charm the deputy and sheriff, which she acknowledges when she silently admires the sheriff's "susceptib[ility] to woman's wiles" (33). Michelson's depiction of Massey as possessing the qualities of the female stunt reporter in unmistakable in this scene, as she relies on outlandish tricks and spunk, in addition to her status as a young woman, to successfully pursue the story she is after.

Michelson constantly highlights Massey's cleverness, which is certainly an important trait for a reporter, but the emphasis on her conniving strategies does at times undercut the seriousness of the situation, particularly when the vigilante group defies the traditional legal process afforded to all who are accused of a crime. Before she enters the wagon to ride with the prisoner, Massey discussed the impending lynch mob with Blewett, and she impatiently interrupted him when he tried to elaborate on how the populace was aroused by a "mighty sentiment" (30). Massey's annoyance is troubling, causing the reader to doubt whether she even stopped to consider the motivations of the lynch mob and the emotions behind their actions.

When she is introduced to the prisoner in the back of the wagon, Massey's supposed "innocence and simplicity" is contrasted against his "swift, suspicious glance" from sharp eyes above lips tightly shut (33). This description is strange and uncharacteristic of Massey, and it appears to be included merely for effect; since she is always trying to work an angle to manipulate the situation to her best advantage, it seems that in this instance it is to her advantage to play the innocent female in order to gain the information she wants. In this sense, Massey's actions can be read as a performance that reveals the social construction of gender. This performance is effective as it allows her to win the admiration of the sheriff and the trust of the prisoner. In one of the story's best lines, the sheriff describes Massey in this light, saying, "Oh! these girl reporters have got grit all right" (33). The deputy and sheriff are amused by her, yet it is clear that they still have a sense of respect for the cleverness she displays. Both of them have been charmed by her and it is their intervention that enables her to block Thompson from "checkmating" her. The sheriff praises her for being the only reporter in town to figure out that they were going to move the prisoner by wagon rather than on the train. Even though Thompson had offered to pay the price of the rig for a seat, the sheriff had refused because the seat was already promised to Massey, and he believed that she the reporter most deserving of the opportunity. Massey is acutely aware of her powers and uses them without regret to gain an advantage. However, she always sees herself first and foremost as a reporter, not just a female reporter, and it is clear that her skills as a listener, observer, and communicator are driven by an inquisitiveness that compels her to get to the bottom of whatever mystery she is confronting at the moment.

Despite her intense desire to interview the prisoner right away while he is without a lawyer and they are stuck in the wagon for a two-hour ride, she utilizes a more indirect strategy for gathering information. The prisoner is anxious and desperately appeals to Massey as a reporter to share her opinion about the rumors regarding the lynch mob that could be potentially pursuing them. This plays right into her scheme, as she seems to be trying to gain his trust in the hopes that he will be more likely to talk to her without having to pry the story out of him. This is conveyed in her wittiest line: "Oh, to have your fish ask you to please be so good as to bait a hook for him! The silly fish—he didn't know that the man who asks an interviewer a question is lost" (34). Massey's strategy proves to be effective because Demling talks during the entire trip to Grafton. Although there is no direct discussion of the specifics of the murder accusation, Massey uses this chance to learn a lot about Demling, including "his hobby, his vanities, his tastes, his prejudices . . . his weak, hard face . . . his mannerisms [and] his peculiarities of speech" (34). This allows her to collect potentially significant details about the accused man and formulate a sense of how she will depict him and the events that unfold later in her news story.

As they get near the town of Grafton, Massey suddenly finds herself in the middle of the lynch mob: "When the men came up, and where they came from, I don't know to this day. There was a score of them on horseback, and they rode fiercely at us" (35). Her status as a female reporter and her direct participation in the action draws attention. Initially, when the lynchers see her in the wagon, they are confused and they temporarily turn away, "check[ing] their horses suddenly [as they] dash frantically down a cross street" (35). The appearance of the mob startles Massey so much that she is at first unable to speak. The sheriff notices her quizzical gaze and answers it by explaining, "'They must have seen you, miss, an' thought they'd made a mistake. They'll be back, of course; but that's so much time lost'" (35). The wagon is eventually overtaken by the crowd after they gallop up the main street, and men were "clambering up on the wheels" and yelling at the sheriff to hand over the prisoner (36). Massey's presence causes some of the men to fall back again in disbelief. It's not until the mob is caught between the fire of shots from the sheriff in the wagon and the guards at the jail that they are actually obstructed, and this gives Pennoyer the chance to shove the reigns into Massey's hands as he wildly whips the horses and speeds forward toward the jail.

This leads to the climactic scene in the story when, in the midst of the frantic action, Massey "felt something swift fly across [her] cheek" (36). This turns out to be a bullet that grazes her before hitting the deputy's shoulder, and it is at this point in the narrative where the outcome of her aggressive reporting style is most apparent. She is momentarily stunned into silence, and her shaking almost necessitates that she be carried inside by the others. Massey's emotional response is further conveyed by the compassion she displays toward the distraught prisoner as she observes "the mark of the sheriff's boot-heel on [Demling's] face," and she is "so nauseated that [she] broke into shivering cries" (37). Her emotional reaction to the sight of the violence and the terror it inspires in the prisoner clashes with the more calculating reporter persona that she manages to maintain throughout the majority of the story.

For a different perspective, the reader is provided with Thompson's reaction to Massey's involvement in the mob scene and it is comprised of a mixture of awe and criticism: "It was a bold, bad beat. . . . No *lady* would have done it, even if Blewett is a coward; it was purely masculine business. You deserved to get shot—how good it is that young women seldom get what they deserve!" (38). Echoing Blewett's earlier disapproval of Massey's aggressive style, Thompson's condescending critique also insinuates that Massey's exploits are distasteful because she is a *woman*, not because her motives are questionable or her actions dangerous. Thompson's taunt doesn't prevent him from asking Massey out to lunch the next afternoon following the session in the courtroom, and this can be seen as a sign of their good-natured rivalry, foreshadowing the romantic relationship that eventually forms between them in subsequent stories in *A Yellow Journalist*.

The Grafton townspeople show a similar mix of interest and disdain when they encounter Massey. She views the general response to the presence of the reporters in town as one of fascination, comparable to the intrigue and spectacle a visiting circus would cause. Since Massey is a female reporter, she arouses a "delightful compound of curiosity and patronizing interest" like the bearded lady at the circus (38). They watch her every move, commenting on her eating habits and her attire, much to the amusement of her fellow (male) reporters. Massey becomes both spectator and spectacle in this instance, and the controversy over her presence at the mob scene and subsequent trial proceedings illustrates the ways in which most newspaper women were treated during this time period. As Lutes describes, participatory journalism was one of the few ways that a woman could get noticed and move beyond the women's pages of the paper. Consequently, Massey's reporting style contributed to her success and the position she has attained at her newspaper in the early stories of the collection.

In "Honors are Easy," a contrast is set up between the terror and fast pace of the lynch mob scene and the long, drawn-out courtroom drama that Massey witnesses. While the trial is in session, Thompson slips out and later sends a note to Massey breaking their lunch date. This mysterious absence is explained the next morning when Massey discovers his front-page interview with Demling's girlfriend Ella Harris in the *Times-Record*, accompanied by sketches and a signed statement. Massey's frustration with Thompson's exclusive access to Harris is compounded as he churns out a series of stories for the *Times-Record* while all of the other reporters wait out the trial in Grafton. His scheme of keeping Harris away from Grafton and out of potential communication with other reporters angers Massey.

Michelson's descriptions of Massey's reactions to the court scenes versus the vigilante scene create a more complex picture of the way she views justice and violence in the narrative. The significance of the attempted lynch mob for Massey is connected to the opportunity she gained for exclusive access to the prisoner and the subsequent scene that she could include in her eventual news story. The courtroom scenes, by contrast, are depicted as boring and ineffectual even though that's where the legitimate legal activity occurs. Massey appears to be a reporter focused on the sensational but her role in the story proves to be more multilayered than that.

Rather than make Massey a conventional heroine who directly confronts the injustice of the vigilante scene, Michelson draws upon the traditions of the girl reporter to insert Massey into the action in ways that would be impossible for other female characters. Due to her single-minded focus on proving her talents as a reporter and beating her competition, Massey witnesses a key scene of violence that threatens the legal and democratic methods established for dealing with a person accused of a crime. The combination of her emotional responses to the violence and to Demling, along with her detached methods as a reporter, creates a unique, indirect critique of vigilantism and lynching in the narrative.

Her keen observational skills tell her that Thompson has faked much of his reports with Harris, since "every idea in the girl's stupid little head must have given out days ago," and Massey is able to "see what was Thompson and what was real" because she has studied his style (42). She is therefore able to glean useful information about Demling's character from Thompson's writing and she devises a scheme based on what she learns. Her plan to get the truth out of Demling begins when she ensures that he overhears her telling the sheriff that she thinks there is a possibility that he is innocent. This prompts Demling to want to speak with her, and this scene once again highlights Massey's proficient use of her well-practiced techniques of persuasion. When Massey meets with Demling in his cell, she can still see the effects of the terror of the mob on him, in addition to his subsequent week of "slow torture [and] the crumbling of every hope" during the unfolding court case mounting against him (46). Briefly she feels "sheer pity for the wretch" with his "haggard, unshaven face [and] his restless, frightened eyes," (46) but her calculating logic and powers of observation quickly outweigh her fleeting emotions. This is part of a pattern of initial emotional responses by Massey which are overpowered by her reporter qualities of observation and objectivity. Massey's emotions are presented as personal reactions, separate from her actions as a reporter and her intended news story.

Even though she generally has a detached approach to the gathering of information for her story, she does express a view of Demling which is mixed with animalistic imagery when she describes his "latent strength" and views his "great hulking mass of muscles bending over the table as an animal over the food it tears" (47). This depiction of Demling is quite different from the terrified young man who was hiding under the wagon seat during the mob scene. She cautiously confronts the "wickedness [that] stared brutally at [her]," noting that all traces of weakness seemed to be gone from his face, and she begins her scheme to draw the truth out of him with her advice that he confess about the man he is protecting who is really the guilty party (47). Demling interprets her words to mean that she is already aware that his father is truly the murderer, and he confirms Massey's speculations as she launches into her theory of how the murders happened. She posits that the impetus for the crime was the father's reaction to being found out by his son to be the one who stole the money from the stagecoach the month prior. Demling praises Massey for being the only reporter smart enough to figure out the truth and he urges her to print the story. However, it is not entirely clear whether the reader is meant to believe that this is really the truth or if Demling just sees it as a good defense to use in his favor. Massey appears hesitant at his enthusiastic response, and she notices how he paces in his cell "almost gaily, his evil young face alight with the braggart's confidence" (51). With a journalistic "matter-of-fact tone," she steers the conversation back to a potentially contradictory point about the hypothetical story. This point involves what happened to Demling's little brother, who is described as "half-witted," and Massey soon confirms her suspicion that he is "the one tender spot in this brute's life" (52). The reader is left questioning whether Demling is really protecting someone else or if he is actually guilty and whether or not his little brother's death was an accident as he claims. The answers to these questions are never definitively answered.

Massey triumph over obtaining the prison interview with Demling and writing her news story based on it is short-lived when she is once again thwarted by her rival Thompson who has already made sure that both the telegraph and telephone in town are being monopolized, making it impossible for her to send it to her newspaper office in San Francisco. However, Massey is too clever to be obstructed by his antics a second time, and she quickly devises a plan that involves tricking the court stenographer onto the train so she can complete her coverage of the case and send off the entire story from the next town. This is yet another example of how Michelson keeps the focus on Massey's cleverness as a reporter over the actual news story itself. A portion of her plan hinges on Massey's ability to convince the train conductor to help her, which she does in part by appealing to his "natural nose for news [and] taste for a fight" (56). As she has done before in the story, Massey successfully manipulates a male in power into assisting her and giving her the advantage over her rival reporters. Her power of persuasion extends to the stenographer, Miss Ely, as Massey manages to flatter and coerce her into giving up all of the notes from the court proceedings. As the train speeds off carrying Massey and Ely toward San Isidro, the prim stenographer is charmed into reading her notes aloud "peaceable as a lamb" while the reporter "clicked it all off on the typewriter" (57). At the end of the narrative there is no further mention of the prisoner and his guilt or innocence. Instead, the focus is on Massey who feels "mad with delight" over her accomplishment (57). The news story itself is not given any real attention. The final lines of the story return the reader to the competitive relationship between Massey and Thompson with a gloating message that she sends to him stating, "We'll have that lunch in the city. The Demling case is done brown, and honors are easy. (Signed) One of the Cooks" (57).

Massey's role as a spectator and journalist that actively works to uncover the truth and convey significance in her news story at times seems to be overshadowed by her desire to beat the other reporters and prove her own cleverness. However, this is not surprising when examined within the context of Massey's connections to the stunt reporter tradition, which often included many female reporters known for "formulaic and unreflective" writings that showed little "deliberation and depth" (Lutes 3). This does not mean that the story Massey produced necessarily lacked depth or had no significant influence; as Lutes argues, the new role for newspapers at the turn of the century included addressing a rapidly growing and diverse readership that eagerly responded to the drama of these female reporters' writing, which was often aligned with sensational journalism.

The image of the girl reporter in popular fiction clearly helped to shape the American perception of women writers. Lutes suggests that real and fictional female reporters cultivated controversial new models of "self-reflexive authorship" that involved not just reporting the news but "*becoming* the news" (5). Massey's status as a female reporter makes her an especially complex figure because, as Lutes describes, women's newspaper reportage was "anchored in the physical, defined by its appeal to the masses [and] distinguished by its failure to transcend its moment and its obvious entanglement in anxieties about sex, class and race" (5). Furthermore, many of the articles written by women during this time became increasingly and more overtly a commentary on themselves and their reporting style, which supported a deeply personal way of reporting the news through a format that was otherwise developing in a more impersonal manner.

This helps account for the lack of attention that is paid to the actual news story that Massey produced and contributes to the reason why the story ends with a focus on her instead of her writing. This is not to suggest that her role as a reporter and spectator had no meaning in the story though. It is crucial to take into consideration how, as Lutes asserts, newspaper women established a lively tradition of journalism that highlighted the sensational and used their own bodies as "conduits for the news," which propelled these women into their stories and into their readers' minds (6).

Massey is a notable figure because her role as a reporter is connected to her ability to serve as a mediator between her readers and the violence. Lutes contends that girl reporters often deliberately put themselves in situations in which the "female body was likely to be viewed as suspect, oversexed, out of control" and as a result they tended to "cultivate the position of an intensely interested spectator" rather than a purely objective one (36). Due to this position of the girl reporter, Massey is able to transmit the significance of the situation through her first-person narration of the events more effectively than through her actual news story. Massey's act of inserting herself into the action and putting herself at risk, allows her to provide a way for the readers to confront the danger of the lynch mob through her and gain a greater sense of meaning from the event.

Female reporters (both real and fictional) frequently appeared to be less concerned with documenting a reality that occurred independent of themselves than with conveying their own experiences, and "inventing and circulating stories that became 'news' simply because they were being made public" (Lutes 120). Since newspaper women were not always valued for their objectivity, their emphasis was more often on the display of their passion and physical engagement in their news writing, Fahs's work highlights the ways in which female journalist shaped public lives and public spaces in vital ways through this active engagement. Massey's ambition and commitment to her writing is presented as almost inseparable from her rivalry with male reporter Ted Thompson, but it is meant to be a way of challenging her to become a better and more successful reporter; when comparing herself to Thompson early in the collection, she asserts, "Oh, I'll do it all and be it all myself some day!" (16). In a later story, "The List of Bassett's," Thompson questions when she is going to give up newspaper work, and she replies, "Never! Fancy me with nothing doing day after day and year after year; with nothing to find out and nothing to crow over . . . like a well-trained fire horse, I'd run away from home at the signal of a story" (143). By the end of *A Yellow Journalist*, Thompson has joined her paper as the News Editor and Massey is promoted to City Editor. Massey is aware of how rare her success is, and she explicitly acknowledges the magnitude of her accomplishment, when she says, "Do you know that for one woman who gets to the City Editor's desk nine hundred and ninety-nine go down to death and obscurity in the Woman's Page?" (173).[4]

Massey complicates the notion of journalistic objectivity, particularly in situations where racial violence is occurring because she asserts her power through her sensational tactics and personal involvement in the story that she is covering. Edelstein contends that the concepts of objectivity and sentiment became "freighted with gendered meanings over the course of the century" and women writers "anticipated the overvaluation of objectivity long before the term and concept became articulated as a journalistic standard" because they "recognized the inadequacies and limitations of purely empirical modes of assessing social reality" (7–8). Massey is seen as acting outside traditional gender roles, and by using her as the lens through which we view vigilantism, Michelson gives us indirect commentary on the role of violence as a counter to legal and democratic processes. This is further complicated when Massey becomes as much of a spectacle as her sensationalist news stories.

While Michelson does not provide the reader with a direct analysis and critique of the lynch mob scene or the interactions that follow, a pattern of Massey's initial emotional responses is established and set in contrast to her detached coverage of the news story. As Harrison-Kahan and Skinazi contend, *A Yellow Journalist* uses Massey's methods of reporting to uniquely position her in a role not commonly available to women at the time, and as a result, Michelson's writing "complements and provides alternatives to that of the best-known women writers of her era [Wharton, Gilman, Chopin] by offering a less constricted and more optimistic view of women's place in mass culture and the publishing sphere" (17). In this sense Massey functions within Edelstein's concept of a woman writer who adopts and revises the "major representational techniques of the press" in order to "intervene in political conversations, stage dissenting points of view, and comment on the forms of public discourse" (4). The opportunities and limitations of newspaper work for female writers are apparent in both the fictional depiction of Rhoda Massey and in the lived experiences of her creator, Miriam Michelson. I argue that Massey operates as a conduit between the lynch mob and the reader, describing the scene vividly and transmitting Michelson's analysis of vigilantism in regards to justice and violence. Michelson, as a reporter-turned-novelist, is able to engage with gender and ethnic issues most effectively through the lens of her most compelling protagonist and female reporter Rhoda Massey. Michelson's work brings attention to the important ways in which figures of popular culture, including the girl reporter, contribute to our perceptions and understanding of racial violence at the beginning of the twentieth century.

WORKS CITED

Baym, Nina. *Women Writers of the American West, 1833–1927.* Urbana: University of Illinois Press, 2011.

Beasley, Maurine. "Recent Directions for the Study of Women's History in American Journalism." *Journalism Studies* 2.2 (2001): 207–20.

Beasley, Maurine H. and Shelia J. Gibbons. *Taking Their Place: A Documentary History of Women and Journalism.* State College, PA: Strata Publishing, 2003.

Bradley, Patricia. *Women and the Press: The Struggle for Equality.* Medill School of Journalism. Evanston: Northwestern University Press, 2005.

Edelstein, Sari. *Between the Novel and the News: The Emergence of American Women's Writing.* Charlottesville: University of Virginia Press, 2014.

Fahs, Alice. *Out on Assignment: Newspaper Women and the Making of Modern Public Space.* Chapel Hill: University of North Carolina Press, 2011.

Harrison-Kahan, Lori, editor. *The Superwoman and Other Writings by Miriam Michelson.* Wayne State University Press, 2019.

Harrison-Kahan, Lori and Karen E. H. Skinazi. "Miriam Michelson's Yellow Journalism and the Multi-Ethnic West." *MELUS* 40.2 (2015): 1–26.

Lelekis, Debbie. *American Literature, Lynching, and the Spectator in the Crowd: Spectacular Violence.* Lexington Books, 2015.

Livingston, Dorothy Michelson. *The Master of Light: A Biography of Albert A. Michelson.* New York: Scribner, 1973.

Lutes, Jean Marie. *Front-Page Girls: Women Journalists in American Culture and Fiction, 1880–1930.* Ithaca: Cornell University Press, 2006.

Michelson, Miriam. *A Yellow Journalist.* New York: D. Appleton, 1905.

Roggenkamp, Karen. *Narrating the News: New Journalism and Literary Genre in Late Nineteenth-Century American Newspapers and Fiction.* Kent: Kent State University Press, 2005.

Skinazi, Karen E. H. and Lori Harrison-Kahan. "Miriam Michelson, American Jewish Feminist Literary Star of the Western Frontier." *Tablet Magazine* Nextbook Inc., 24 Nov. 2014.

Whitt, Jan. *Women in American Journalism: A New History.* Urbana: University of Illinois Press, 2008.

NOTES

1. Miriam Michelson's family history is discussed in *The Master of Light: A Biography of Albert A. Michelson* (1973) by Dorothy Livingston. She was one of seven children, including one brother, Albert, who won the Nobel Prize in Physics, and another brother, Charles, who worked as a journalist and eventually served as publicity director for the Democratic National Committee during the time of Franklin D. Roosevelt.

2. In her book *Out on Assignment: Newspaper Women and the Making of Modern Public Space* (2011), Fahs chronicles the women who developed new styles of newspaper writing, including celebrity interviews, advice columns, and suffrage writing. They notably generated a "rich set of public conversations within the public spaces of the newspaper" which often reached a national audience (2).

3. Lutes's book *Front-Page Girls* covers a wide scope in the history of the newswoman from the stunt journalism phenomenon, including a discussion of stunt reporter Nellie Bly to the anti-lynching crusade of Ida B. Wells, a section on "sob sisters," and the careers of three journalists-turned-writers (Edna Ferber, Willa Cather, and Djuna Barnes).

4. According to Bradley, the federal census shows that between 1880 and 1890, there was an increase of fulltime women journalists from 288 to 1888, and this number continued to rise at the turn of the twentieth century (115).

Chapter Two

Theodore Dreiser's "Nigger Jeff"

The Development of an Aesthetic

Donald Pizer

Thanks to the work of Robert H. Elias and W. A. Swanberg, we are beginning to have an adequate sense of Dreiser's life. But many aspects of Dreiser the artist remain relatively obscure or unexplored—in particular, his aesthetic beliefs and fictional techniques at various stages of his career. An excellent opportunity to study Dreiser's developing aesthetic lies in the existence of several versions of his short story "Nigger Jeff." The extant versions of this story reveal with considerable clarity and force Dreiser's changing beliefs concerning the nature of fiction.

Dreiser's first attempt to write a story about the lynching of a Missouri Negro is preserved in an unpublished University of Virginia manuscript called "A Victim of Justice."[1] Although "A Victim of Justice" is clearly a work of the 1890s, it is difficult to date its composition precisely. The narrator of the story begins by noting that he has recently spent "a day in one of Missouri's pleasant villages." While visiting a Potter's Field, he recalls a rural Missouri lynching that he had witnessed "several years since." This opening situation is the product of a number of events of the mid-1890s. Dreiser was a reporter on the *St. Louis Republic* in the fall of 1893, and it was during this period that he observed the lynching on which the story is based.[2] In addition, on July 23, 1894, Dreiser wrote for the Pittsburgh *Dispatch* an article entitled "With the Nameless Dead" in which he described an Allegheny County Potter's Field. A few weeks later he visited his fiancé, Sallie White, who lived in a small town near St. Louis.[3] Dreiser's only attempts at fiction before the summer of 1899 occurred in the winter and spring of 1895 when he wrote several stories after leaving the New York *World* and before becoming editor of *Ev'ry Month*.[4] In view of these facts, it is possible to speculate that Dreiser wrote "A Victim of

Justice" in early 1895 and that he combined in the story his memory of the 1893 lynching, his July, 1894, article (from which he quoted several passages verbatim), and his visit to Missouri in the summer of 1894.

The next extant version of the story is a manuscript in the Los Angeles Public Library entitled "The Lynching of Nigger Jeff." This manuscript served, with minor changes, as the text for the November, 1901, publication of "Nigger Jeff" in *Ainslee's Magazine*. Encouraged by his friend Arthur Henry, Dreiser had begun writing stories in earnest during the summer of 1899, and he later recalled that "Nigger Jeff"—that is, the Los Angeles Public Library—*Ainslee's* version—dates from this period.[5] The fourth version of the story is Dreiser's revision of the *Ainslee's* version for inclusion in his *Free and Other Stories*, published in August, 1918. Since the changes in this last version are primarily additions to the *Ainslee's* text, and since this added material is not in the Los Angeles Public Library manuscript, the revision can be attributed to the period shortly before the appearance of *Free*, when Dreiser collected and revised his stories for republication.[6]

There are thus three major versions of "Nigger Jeff." Although none of these versions can be dated exactly, each can be associated with an important segment of Dreiser's career. The Virginia manuscript of the mid-1890s reflects the Dreiser depicted in *A Book About Myself*, the young journalist who was viewing much of the tragic complexity of life but understanding little of it. The *Ainslee's* publication represents the Dreiser of *Sister Carrie*. The story has been rewritten by an author with a characteristic vision of life and with a distinctive fictional style. The 1918 publication suggests a writer whose ideas have become increasingly self-conscious and polemical, the Dreiser of the essays of *Hey Rub-a-Dub-Dub* (1920) and the Dreiser who was eventually to devote a large portion of his later career to philosophical inquiries. The three versions, in short, span the principal periods of Dreiser's career, and their differences can tell us much about Dreiser's developing aesthetic.

Although the three versions of "Nigger Jeff" differ in several important ways, all have the same basic outline. A young man is sent in early spring to investigate reports of a possible lynching in a rural Missouri community.[7] He discovers that a farmer's daughter has been attacked by a Negro and that the farmer and his son are in pursuit of the Negro in order to lynch him. The Negro is apprehended by a local peace officer, however, and is taken to another village for safekeeping until the arrival of reinforcements. A mob gathers, overpowers the peace officer, and returns with the Negro to its own community, where he is hanged from a bridge. The following day the investigator visits the home of the Negro and views his body.

Dreiser's earliest version of this story, "A Victim of Justice," is told in the first person and uses a frame device. The story opens with the unidentified narrator visiting a Potter's Field near a small Missouri town. After much soulful lament over the "strange exigencies of life" that have brought the denizens of the graveyard to their mournful fate, the narrator is disturbed by the "grieving orisons" of an elderly woman. Before he can question her, she departs. But she has stimulated still further his moody reflections on the "wounding trials of life," and it is on this note that he introduces his recollections of the lynching. He begins by explaining that he was "commissioned to examine into the details" of the incident, but he does not identify himself as a reporter. Nor do we have a sense of his involvement in the action of the story. His narrative "voice" is principally an omniscient authorial voice, telling us about the lynching (often in summary form) but devoid of personal participation. The story concludes with the second half of the frame device. The narrator describes the Negro's lonely grave on a hillside, a burial place marked by a wooden cross. "Day after day it stands, bleak, gray, desolate, a fitting emblem of the barren life now forgotten, wasted as sparks are wasted on the night wind." Again, the narrator broods over the vicissitudes of life, though his melancholy is lightened somewhat by the thought that nature is ever-beautiful even in this forsaken spot.

"A Victim of Justice" has three major themes. The first is suggested by the ironic title of the story and by several authorial comments. The Negro (named Jim in this version) is the victim of the "hasty illegalities" and "summary justice" of the mob. The second theme involves a more generalized sorrow over the fate of most men, a theme which arises out of the narrator's "meditations" in the graveyard. Dreiser's lugubrious exploitation of the conventional rhetoric of injustice and melancholy suggests that both themes have their source in the traditional literature of sentiment. Jim is a "poor varlet," and the graveyard scene echoes the diction and sentence structure of a Hawthorne or an Irving. Life is sad, Dreiser says, and he asks us to share this sentiment by imitating the prose of writers known for their ability to evoke melancholic moods. The third theme of the story is that of the powerful human emotions that arise out of the lynching itself—the quest for vengeance by the father, the resoluteness of the peace officer, the terror of the Negro. In a sense these emotions constitute a suppressed or unacknowledged theme, since they are extraneous to the explicit themes imposed upon the story by the narrator. The peace officer could have been a coward and Jim brave and unflinching, and the narrator would still have been able to enclose the story within his reflections on injustice and melancholy. These reflections may be apt responses to a lynching, but Dreiser's failure to integrate them into the account of the lynching itself implies that he has indeed imposed them on his response. His "true" response is "buried" within the narrative of the lynching, for Dreiser at this point was unable to articulate his response—that is, he was unable to recognize what moved him in the lynching. Thus, though he depicted the lynching as a moving event, he confused the nature of his response with those "deep" emotions readily available to him in traditional literary forms.

The *Ainslee's* version of "Nigger Jeff" omits the frame sections. The story, now told in the third person, focuses on the experiences of a young reporter, Eugene Davies,[8] who has been sent to look into a possible lynching. It is a beautiful spring day, and the insouciant, self-confident Davies undertakes his assignment with relish. Arriving in Pleasant Valley, he is drawn into the events of the lynching as he pursues his story. Davies is at first a passive observer of these events. But when the blubbering, terrified Jeff is seized by the mob, the reporter uncontrollably "clapped his hands over his mouth and worked his fingers convulsively."[9] "Sick at heart" (p. 373), he accompanies the mob back to Pleasant Valley. The hanging itself stuns him into a deep torpor. By the close of the story, when he encounters Jeff's weeping mother, he has viewed a wide range of character and emotion—the competent, strong-willed sheriff, the cowardly mob, the father intent on vengeance, and above all the terrified Jeff and his heartbroken mother.

In "A Victim of Justice" Dreiser mentioned the grieving mother early in the narrative but not afterward. In "Nigger Jeff" he reserved introducing her grief until the final, climactic scene of the story, a scene which is present only in a brief summary form in the earlier version. As Davies views Jeff's body, he hears a noise in the room. Greatly disturbed, he hesitated, and then as his eyes strained, he caught the shadow of something. It was in the extreme corner, huddled up, dark, almost indistinguishable crouching against the cold walls.

> "Oh, oh, oh," was repeated, even more plaintively than before.
> Davies began to understand. He approached lightly. Then he made out an old black mammy, doubled up and weeping. She was in the very niche of the corner, her head sunk on her knees, her tears falling, her body rocking to and fro. (p. 375)

On leaving the cabin, Davies "swelled with feeling and pathos.... The night, the tragedy, the grief, he saw it all.

> "'I'll get that in,' he exclaimed, feelingly, 'I'll get it all in'" (p. 375).

Dreiser has thus shifted the axis of the story. Unlike "A Victim of Justice," in which the narrator presents us with a response to a lynching, "Nigger Jeff" dramatizes a growth in emotional responsiveness by the principal viewer of the action. The narrative is now primarily an initiation story—the coming into knowledge of the tragic realities of life by the viewer. And since the viewer is a reporter who will attempt to "get it all in," the story is also the dramatization of the birth of an aesthetic.

Briefly, the conception of the theme and form of art symbolized by the "it" in the last sentence of "Nigger Jeff" contains three major elements, each rendered in dramatic form within the story. These are: a belief that two emotions in particular pervade all life; a belief that these emotions are often found in moral and social contexts which lend them a special poignancy; and a belief that these emotions adopt a certain pattern in life and therefore in art. Let me discuss each of these beliefs more fully, beginning with the central emotions of life as Dreiser depicts them in this story.

One such emotion is sexual desire. It is the first flush of spring, and Jeff, a poor, ignorant Negro, attacks a white girl—a girl who knows him and whom he meets in a lane. "'Before God, boss, I didn't mean to. . . . I didn't go to do it,'" he cries to the mob (p. 372). Although sexual desire may not lead to the destruction of such figures as Frank Cowperwood, it is nevertheless a dominant, uncontrollable force in almost all of Dreiser's principal male characters. Hurstwood, Lester Kane, Eugene Witla, and Clyde Griffiths are at its mercy. In addition, the "it" of the final sentence includes the unthinking love and loyalty which exists within a family and particularly between a mother and a child. When Davies arrives at Jeff's home after the lynching, he asks the Negro's sister why Jeff had returned to his cabin, where he had been captured by the waiting sheriff.

> "To see us," said the girl.
> "Well, did he want anything? He didn't come just to see you, did he?"
> "Yes, suh," said the girl, "he come to say good-by." Her voice wavered.
> "Didn't he know he might get caught?" asked Davies.
> "Yes, suh, I think he did."
> She stood very quietly, holding the poor battered lamp up, and looking down.
> "Well, what did he have to say?" asked Davies.
> "He said he wanted tuh see motha.' He was a-goin' away." (p. 374)

The son come back to say goodbye to the mother, the mother mourning over the son's body—here is emotion which in its overpowering intensity parallels the sex drive itself. It is the force which binds the Gerhardt family together, which is the final refuge of Clyde Griffiths, and which creates the tragic tension of Solon Barnes's loss of his children. In "Nigger Jeff" this force appears not only in the relationship between Jeff and his mother but also in the figure of the assaulted girl's father. Although Dreiser depicts the mob as cowardly and sensation-seeking, he respects the motives of the father. Both victim and revenger are caught up in the same inexplicable emotional oneness which is a family.

"Nigger Jeff" thus contains two of the most persistent themes in all of Dreiser's work—the power of desire and the power of family love and loyalty.

Davies's awakening to their reality can be interpreted as Dreiser's declaration of belief in the dominance of these emotions in human affairs. Indeed, in his later autobiographies Dreiser depicted these emotions as two of the principal inner realities of his own youth. His ability to identify himself with these emotions as early as "Nigger Jeff" is revealed by a sentence omitted in *Ainslee's* but present in the Los Angeles Public Library manuscript of "The Lynching of Nigger Jeff." Immediately following "The night, the tragedy, the grief, he saw it all," there appears in "The Lynching of Nigger Jeff": "It was spring no less than sorrow that ran whispering in his blood." The sensuality of youth, the family love taking its shape in sorrow—these appear in Dreiser's work as complementary autobiographical themes until they coalesce most fully and powerfully both in *Dawn* and in *An American Tragedy*.

The second major aspect of Dreiser's aesthetic contained in the final "it" involves the moral and social context in which these emotions are found. Like most of Dreiser's characters, the principal figures in "Nigger Jeff" have little of the heroic about them. Even the sheriff loses his potential for such a role once he is easily tricked by the mob and complacently accepts its victory. Jeff himself is described at the moment of his capture by the mob as a "groveling, foaming brute" (p. 372). But the major figures in "Nigger Jeff," despite their often-grotesque inadequacies, feel and suffer, and the young reporter comes to realize the "tragedy" of their fate. To Dreiser, tragedy arises out of the realities that nature is beautiful, that man can desire, and that a mother or father can mourn.

These realities do not lend "nobility" to Dreiser's figures; like Jeff, they are often weak and contemptible despite their fate. But their capacity to feel combined with their incapacity to act wisely or well is to Dreiser the very stuff of man's tragic nature. The realization which the young reporter must "get in" thus involves not only the truths of lust and of mother love but also the truth that the experience of these emotions gives meaning and poignancy to every class and condition of man.

The third aspect of the aesthetic symbolized by the final "it" concerns the pattern assumed by the two principal emotions of the story. Most of Dreiser's novels involve a seeker or quester—sometimes driven by desire, sometimes by other motives—who finds at the end of the novel that he has returned to where he started: Carrie still seeking beauty and happiness; Jennie once again alone despite her immense capacity to love; Cowperwood's millions gone; Clyde still walled in; Solon returning to the simplicity of faith. It is possible to visualize Dreiser's novels as a graphic irony—the characters believe they are pushing forward but they are really moving in a circle. Dreiser occasionally makes this structural principle explicit by a consciously circular symbol, such as the rocking chair in *Sister Carrie* and the street scene in *An American Tragedy*. "Nigger Jeff" contains a rough approximation of this pattern. The passions which have driven the narrative forward in its sequence of crime and punishment are dissipated, and Jeff returns to where he has started both physically and emotionally. That is, the bleak room in which he rests and his mother keening over his body represent the permanent realities of his life and his death. He, too, has come full circle.

Despite his reputation as stylistically inept, Dreiser was capable of a provocative and moving verbal symbolism. This quality appears in his use of "beauty" in connection with Carrie at the close of *Sister Carrie* and in his use of "life" in the next to last paragraph of *The Bulwark* ("I am crying for *life*"). These otherwise banal abstractions represent the complexity and depth of experience depicted in the novels concerned, and they are therefore powerfully evocative. The word "it" at the close of "Nigger Jeff" has some of the same quality. The word symbolizes a deeply felt aesthetic which Dreiser never explained as well elsewhere, just as he never discussed "beauty" and "life" in his philosophical writings as well as he dramatized their meaning for him in his novels.

The *Free* version of "Nigger Jeff" omits almost nothing from the *Ainslee's* text. Aside from stylistic revisions, the changes in the *Free* version consist of additions, many of which merely flesh out particular scenes. Some of the additions, however, extend the themes of the story in two significant ways.

One such extension is revealed in Dreiser's addition to the first sentence of the story (here and elsewhere the added material appears in brackets):

> The city editor was waiting for one of his best reporters, Elmer Davies [by name, a vain and rather self-sufficient youth who was inclined to be of that turn of mind which sees in life only a fixed and ordered process of rewards and punishments. If one did not do exactly right, one did not get along well. On the contrary, if one did, one did. Only the so-called evil were really punished, only the good truly rewarded—or Mr. Davies had heard this so long in his youth that he had come nearly to believe it.][10]

By the next to last paragraph of the story, Davies has come to realize that "[it was not always exact justice that was meted out to all and that it was not so much the business of the writer to indict as to interpret]" (p. iii). In these and similar additions Dreiser has extended the nature of Davies's initiation. In the *Ainslee's* version, Davies's growth is above all that of his awakening to the tragic nature of human experience. The *Free* version associates this awakening with his conscious awareness that moral absolutes are based on naïveté or inexperience and are inapplicable to the complex realities of life. In a sense even "A Victim of Justice" contains an aspect of this theme, since Dreiser in that version noted the injustice of the "summary justice" of mob rule. But in the *Free* "Nigger Jeff" this theme is both more overt and more central. Its presence in this enlarged and emphatic form suggests Dreiser's increasing tendency throughout the later stages of his career (beginning about 1911) to associate the function of art with the explicit inversion of conventional moral and social beliefs. It is during this period that Dreiser the polemicist (as revealed in *Hey Rub-a-Dub-Dub*) and Dreiser the novelist combine to produce *An American Tragedy*, in which the putative reader is placed in the position of Davies. Like the naïve beliefs of Davies, the reader's faith in the American dream of success and in the workings of justice is destroyed by encountering the reality of a tragedy.

A second major extension of theme in the *Free* "Nigger Jeff" occurs in the scenes following the capture of Jeff by the mob. As Davies accompanies the mob on its way to hang Jeff, he reflects that

> [both father and son now seemed brutal, the injury to the daughter and sister not so vital as all this. Still, also, custom seemed to require death in this way for this. It was like some axiomatic, mathematic law—hard, but custom. The silent company, an articulated, mechanical and therefore terrible thing, moved on. It also was axiomatic, mathematic.] (p. 103)

After the hanging, Davies sits near the bridge and muses: "[Life seemed so sad, so strange, so mysterious, so inexplicable]" (p. 105). These additions reflect two of the principal areas of Dreiser's philosophical speculation during the last half of his career.

On the one hand, he believed that every phase of life is governed by law. During the period from approximately 1910 to the late 1920s he often, as in the *Free* "Nigger Jeff," associated this law with the harsh extermination of the weak. Dreiser the mechanist called this law an "equation inevitable" in *Hey Rub-a-Dub-Dub*. But by the end of his career Dreiser the quasi-pantheist had come to call it "design" in *The Bulwark* and to associate it primarily with beauty and with cosmic benevolence. His particular conception of law at various stages of his later career, however, is perhaps less important than his enduring search for a principle of meaning which would encompass the cruelty and the beauty, the destructiveness and the continuity, which he found in life.

On the other hand, Dreiser affirmed throughout his later career a belief in the essential mystery at the heart of life. Both attitudes—the search for meaning and the belief in mystery—are present in *Hey Rub-a-Dub-Dub*, in which the often-doctrinaire mechanistic philosophizing is counterbalanced by the subtitle of the work: "A Book of the Mystery and Terror and Wonder of Life." And both are present in *The Bulwark*, in which Solon's discovery of the principle of design is inseparable from his discovery of the mystery of life. In his *Free* version of "Nigger Jeff" Dreiser has thus expanded his aesthetic to include not only an explicit ironic reversal of moral certainties but also a dramatization of the vast philosophical paradoxes underlying all life. Davies's discovery of what art must do—"[to interpret]"—now has a conscious philosophical element which was to play an ever increasing role in Dreiser's career.

The various versions of "Nigger Jeff" which I have been discussing incorporate Dreiser's principal beliefs about the nature of art. From the imposed sentimentality of "A Victim of Justice" to the moral polemicism and incipient philosophizing of the *Free* "Nigger Jeff," the three versions reflect much that is central in Dreiser's thought and in his practice as a writer. No doubt there is room for qualification of some of the generalizations about Dreiser's developing aesthetic which I have drawn from this study of the three versions of "Nigger Jeff." Nevertheless, there is much to be said for the attempt to deduce a writer's beliefs about art directly from a creative work dealing with the nature of art rather than from his literary criticism. For Dreiser, there is a special need for this kind of attempt, since most of his overt comments about art are either vague or overpolemical. Moreover, we are coming to realize that "Dreiser is not only a writer of stature (as Alfred Kazin has maintained) but also of finesse (as Ellen Moers believes)."[11] He is a writer, in other words, whose stories and novels in their various revisions can often be explored for the complex intertwining of permanence and change characteristic of the creative work of a major literary figure.

*Reprinted from *American Literature*, vol. 41, no 3 (November 1969), 331–41, by permission of the author and the journal.

NOTES

1. I wish to thank the Curator of the Clifton Waller Barrett Library of the University of Virginia Library for permission to examine the manuscript and Mr. Harold J. Dies for permission to quote.

2. Dreiser told Richard Duffy, an editor of *Ainslee's Magazine*, that "Nigger Jeff" derived from a lynching he had seen during his St. Louis days. (Recalled by Duffy in a conversation with Robert H. Elias, November 23, 1944. I wish to thank Professor Elias for making his notes available to me.) In *A Book About Myself* (New York, 1922), p. 325, Dreiser placed the lynching in the fall of 1893. At that time, he was a reporter for the *St. Louis Republic*, and in the *Ainslee's* version of "Nigger Jeff" he identified his newspaperman protagonist as a *Republic* reporter. He specified the date of the lynching as April 16, however, a date on which he was still working for the St. Louis *Globe-Democrat*. He seems to have shifted the date of the lynching for thematic reasons (see below) but to have maintained the Republic as the "correct"

newspaper. I have not been able to find an account of a lynching resembling that of "Nigger Jeff" in either the *Globe-Democrat* or the *Republic*.

3. W. A. Swanberg, *Dreiser* (New York, 1965), p. 58. Relying on Dreiser's account in *A Book About Myself*, Swanberg dates this trip as July. The chronology of Dreiser's contributions to the *Dispatch*, however, suggests early August as a more probable date.

4. Notes on Dreiser's lecture at Columbia University, November 9, 1938 (in the possession of Robert H. Elias). See also Elias, *Theodore Dreiser: Apostle of Nature* (New York, 1949), pp. 88, 317 n. 1.

5. Dreiser to H. L. Mencken, May 13, 1916, in *Letters of Theodore Dreiser*, ed. Robert H. Elias (Philadelphia, 1959), 1, 212–13.

6. Swanberg, in *Dreiser*, p. 229, comments on Dreiser's extensive revision in the spring of 1918 of the stories making up the *Free* collection. It is of interest to note that critics have often quoted significant passages from the Free version and attributed them to the Dreiser of 1899 without realizing that these passages do not appear in the *Ainslee's* version. See, for example, F. O. Matthiessen, *Theodore Dreiser* (New York, 1951), pp. 53–54.

7. The *Free* version contains a weak attempt to disguise the state. Pleasant Valley, Mo., becomes Pleasant Valley, Ko.

8. The name Eugene Davies has autobiographical implications, since Dreiser later used Eugene as the name of his autobiographical protagonist in *The "Genius."* In the *Free* "Nigger Jeff" Dreiser revised the reporter's name to Elmer Davies. *The "Genius"* had been published in 1915, which perhaps led Dreiser, in 1918, to consider Eugene as too explicitly autobiographical.

9. *Ainslee's Magazine*, VIII, 372 (Nov. 1901). Further citations will appear in the text.

10. *Free and Other Stories* (New York, 1918), p. 76. Further citations will appear in the text. Permission to quote from this version of "Nigger Jeff" has been granted by the World Publishing Company, which has republished the story in *The Best Short Stories of Theodore Dreiser* (Cleveland, 1956).

11. *The Stature of Theodore Dreiser*, ed. Alfred Kazin and Charles Shapiro (Bloomington, Ind., 1955) and Ellen Moers, "The Finesse of Dreiser," *American Scholar*, XXXIII, 109–14 (Winter, 1963–1964).

Chapter Three

Theodore Dreiser's "Nigger Jeff," Richard Wright's "Big Boy Leaves Home," and Lynching

Michael Sanders

Emerson's concept of transcendental beauty posits that "there is no object so foul that intense light will not make it beautiful" ("Nature" 9), and "Nigger Jeff" can be seen as Dreiser's attempt to examine it in a realistic context.[1] His inability to fully come to terms with Emerson's ideal may in fact be confirmation of the ultimate futility of the initial premise. Transcendental beauty envisions natural beauty as an ameliorating force; Emerson explains, "To the body and mind which have been cramped by noxious work or company, nature is medicinal and restores their tone" ("Nature" 9–10). Yet for Elmer Davies, the protagonist of "Nigger Jeff," consciousness of nature does not lead to physical and mental healing; instead, it constitutes an escape from the brutal reality of American culture, more specifically, the racial prejudice that had intensified in the wake of the Civil War and the ensuing Reconstruction.[2] The young Dreiser had been influenced by a romantic vision of American culture, particularly Emerson's optimistic transcendentalism.

When Dreiser began his journalistic career in confronting the lynching of a black man in Missouri, he was torn between a romantic and realistic vision of American life, and ultimately related the incident in a 1901 magazine article. Over his entire career, Dreiser produced nothing like the romantic *Adventures of Huckleberry Finn* or even the bitter social criticism of the region in Twain's *Pudd'nhead Wilson*. Instead, in describing the fate of an innocent African-American man, Dreiser directly confronted the reality of American life. Unlike most of his early short stories, "Nigger Jeff" became his first attempt to describe a reality in American life. This short story suggests that throughout his career Dreiser encountered American romanticism as well as American realism; "Nigger Jeff" is a superb example of the latter.

Donald Pizer proposes that there are actually three major versions of "Nigger Jeff," and "each can be associated with an important segment of Dreiser's career" (122).[3] He adds that the final version, the one that appears in *Free and Other Stories*, represents the final stage of Dreiser's "developing aesthetic," and "suggests a writer whose ideas have become increasingly self-conscious and polemical . . . the Dreiser who was to eventually devote a large portion of his later career to philosophical inquiries" (122). Pizer goes on to describe Dreiser as an author "whose stories and novels in their various revisions can often be explored for the complex intertwining of permanence and change characteristic of the creative work of a major literary figure" (130). In this context, we can see this particular account as a product of the mature Dreiser, a writer aware of his transcendentalist influences embarking on a period when his writing adopts a more philosophical/spiritual approach in its analysis of American culture.[4]

"Nigger Jeff" brings to the forefront the racial issues that indirectly permeate "McEwen of the Shining Slave Makers." Jeff Ingalls, while ostensibly the subject of the story, takes a backseat to Elmer Davies, a reporter sent to cover Ingalls's pursuit, whose self-involvement and ambivalence toward the scene he ultimately witnesses make him the focus of Dreiser's story.[5] Davies finds himself repulsed by the idea of the lynching, yet finds himself fascinated by it and actually, through his inaction, becomes an indirect participant. Hiding behind a façade of amoral objectivity, Davies deplores the brutality he witnesses, yet ultimately objectifies Ingalls just as the lynch mob had.[6] While he eventually realizes the humanity of his "subject" in the end, he still views his participation as part of "doing his job."

In addition, Davies becomes defined by his ability to assimilate himself, ultimately adopting the ethos and language of those surrounding him.[7] Not only does he ingratiate himself with the lynch mob, riding with them as one of the boys, he is able to make an ally of Seavey, the postmaster, who helps to reinforce his emotional removal from the scene itself and to encourage his flight into objectivity. Through Seavey, he sees the lynching primarily in terms of being physically repulsive, overlooking the larger, more horrific moral questions. As Seavey remains apart from the scene, limiting his participation to what he can observe, interacting only through his transmittal of Davies's story, Davies uses their relationship to reinforce his "safe" role, that of the reporter.

Our initial impression of Davies comes through the eyes of the city editor, who sees him as a vain and rather self-sufficient youth who was inclined to be of that turn of mind which sees in life only a fixed and ordered process of rewards and punishments. If one did not do exactly right, one did not get along well. On the contrary, if one did, one did. Only the so-called evil were really punished, only the good truly rewarded—or Mr. Davies had heard this so long in his youth that he had nearly come to believe it. (76)

Davies's reactions are fixed by this limited worldview. After reading the details of the situation, his response is consistent with the editor's estimation: "What a terrible crime! What evil people there were in the world! No doubt such a creature ought to be lynched, and that quickly" (77). Davies embodies the nascent 1890's transcendentalist, his Emersonian self-reliance tempered by his vanity and his inability to progress beyond quasi-Puritanical conceptions of good and evil. Although "the world was going unusually well with him. It seemed worth singing about," it is primarily a product of his simplistic binary worldview (76). In essence, his inexperience and the resulting lack of awareness confine him, leaving him unprepared and unable to cope with the vicious reality he is about to face.

Davies dreads his assignment, and "The mere thought of an approaching lynching troubled him greatly, and the farther he went the less he liked it" (78). It is not, however, the lynching itself that troubles him; in fact, he appears to overlook it altogether, deciding instead, "if all were well, or ill, as it were, he could just gather the details of the case and the—aftermath—and return" (78). Ingalls's actions constitute the "crime"; the societal/cultural reaction is euphemized with the vagueness of "—aftermath—," almost as if Davies cannot conceive of it in any other way. He alleviates his discomfort by noting "the whiteness of the little houses, [and] the shimmering beauty of the small stream one had to cross in going from the depot" (78). This is not the last time Davies is to escape direct involvement by "doing his job." In fact, denial becomes his primary coping mechanism.

After Ingalls is captured by the sheriff, the lynch mob takes off in pursuit. Davies finds himself distractedly riding to the scene "through as pleasant a country as one would want to see, up hill and down dale, with charming vistas breaking upon the gaze at every turn" (83). Although he is "so disturbed" that he "scarcely noted the beauty that was stretched before him," he finds himself compelled "to note that it was so" (83). His involvement in the incident, although limited, is morally distasteful, yet he remains aware, perhaps to further ameliorate the inevitable, and eagerly anticipated, brutality.

As the posse learns that the sheriff has taken Ingalls into custody and is transporting him to Pleasant Valley, the pursuit continues:

> The company started off on another excited jaunt, up hill and down dale, through the lovely country that lay between Baldwin and Pleasant Valley
> [...] By contrast with the horror impending, as [Davies] now noted, the night was so beautiful that it was all but poignant. Stars were already beginning to shine. Distant lamps twinkled like yellow eyes from the cottages in the valleys and on the hillsides, the air was fresh and tender. Some pea-fowls were crying afar off, and the east promised a golden moon. (88–89)

Davies, unable (and perhaps subconsciously unwilling) to focus on and comprehend the stark reality of the scene and "the horror impending," is distracted by the sublimity of his surroundings. Although these are assuredly things he has seen before, albeit in different contexts, he seems to notice, and perhaps appreciate, them now for the first time, and achieves a sense of temporary inner peace. Dreiser is careful to intermingle both natural and culturally constructed images here to reinforce the grave reality of the situation. This juxtaposition emphasizes that humanity is inextricably part of nature and subject to natural law, despite apparent attempts and behaviors that tend to lessen and nearly destroy the vital connection.

After Ingalls is captured by the mob, he is taken to be lynched, and Davies's attention remains elsewhere, and his sole observation that "the moon was still high, pouring down a wash of silvery light" is further evidence of his removal from the reality of the situation (102). At this point, Davies realizes that although the "whole procedure seemed so unreal, so barbaric that he could scarcely believe it [...] he was a part of it" (102–3). This realization brings denial as he envisions himself "resting in his own good bed back in K—!" the following day, after the ordeal is over (103). His horror is evident as he can

> scarcely realize that he, ordinarily accustomed to the routine of the city, its humdrum and at least outward social regularity, was part of this. The night was so soft, the air so refreshing. The shadowy trees were stirring with a cool night wind. Why should anyone have to die this way? Why couldn't the people of Baldwin or elsewhere have bestirred themselves on the side of the law before this, just let it take its course? (103)

Here, he is unable to reconcile the transcendent natural beauty of the scene with his guilt over his own inertia. Finding himself compelled toward complicity in the unfolding tragedy, the serenity of the trees and the wind bring little solace and, if anything, deepen his confusion.

As the captured Ingalls is taken to be lynched, Davies's ambivalence becomes more pronounced. Admitting the mob's actions are "a ghastly, murderous thing to do," he finds himself unable to act on his convictions, and he once again finds solace in the natural scene as he followed, past fields lit white by the moon, under dark, silent groups of trees, through which the moonlight fell in patches, up low hills and down into valleys, until at last a little stream came into view, the same little stream, as it proved, which he had seen earlier to-day and for a bridge over which they were heading. Here it ran now, sparkling like electricity in the night. (104)

The trees, now silent, take on an ominous aspect while the stream is relatively innocuous, yet remains significant as it reminds him of the recent past, a time when he was much more balanced in the way he envisioned the world. He finds himself alone, unable to condone the mob's actions and his own involvement, "leaving him quite indifferently to himself and his thoughts. Only the black mass swaying in the pale light over the glimmering water seemed human and alive, his sole companion" (105).

Shocked, he begins to return to his previous way of thinking: "He sat down upon the bank and gazed in silence. Now the horror was gone. The suffering had ended. He was no longer afraid. Everything was summery and beautiful. The whole cavalcade had disappeared; the moon finally sank" (105). He has returned to "vain and rather self-sufficient youth" that had embarked on the quest. The horror, suffering and fear were his alone, and after they abate, he is left with the natural imagery he has relied on all along to deny his complicity:

> the light of morning broke, a tender lavender and gray in the east. Then came the roseate hues of dawn, all the wondrous coloring of celestial halls, to which the waters of the stream responded. The white pebbles shone pinkily at the bottom, the grass and sedges first black now gleamed a translucent green. Still the body hung there black and limp against the sky, and now a light breeze sprang up and stirred it visibly. (105–6)

In Davies's mind, Ingalls's corpse has become part of the natural setting, an object affected by the breeze and the sunny day, its gruesomeness incorporated into nature itself. Although he still feels somewhat affected by the tragic events, he goes back to his business, settling his bill with the liveryman and "idling about" the town, ameliorating his guilt with the sundry details surrounding the event. Again, the brutal images are secondary to the natural beauty of the rural setting. For Davies, nature becomes a buffer, even an escape, as the horrifying events are somehow mollified by pastoral beauty and mild weather.

His removal from the scene is complete as "It was sundown again before he remembered that he had not discovered whether the body had been removed. Nor had he heard why the negro came back, nor exactly how he was caught" (107). Davies has completely objectified Ingalls at this point, refusing even to give him the distinction of a name, referring to him simply as "the negro."

This objectification "balances" Davies, and his new attitude is apparent as he makes his way out to Ingalls's cabin:

> The negro's cabin was two miles out along a pine-shaded road, but so pleasant was the evening that he decided to walk. En route, the last rays of the sinking sun stretched long shadows of budding trees across his path. It was not long before he came upon the cabin, a one-story affair set well back from the road and surrounded with a few scattered trees. By now it was quite dark. The ground between the cabin and the road was open, and strewn with the chips of a woodpile. The roof was sagged, and the windows patched in places, but for all that it had the glow of a home. Through the front door, which stood open, the blaze of a wood-fire might be seen, its yellow light filling the interior with a golden glow. (107)

In effect, Davies sees exactly what he wants to see. The tragedy itself is muted by the pastoral setting and the imposed images of domesticity. The dilapidated structure does not become a sign of a life brutally cut short; instead, it becomes "background" for the story he is determined to write.

Inside the cabin, Davies finds himself fascinated, yet repulsed by the scene. Although he finds himself "greatly disturbed," he persists and approaches Ingalls's grieving mother. At this point, Davies "began to understand," yet he remains torn as he "approached slowly, then more swiftly desired to withdraw" (110). Finally, he sees the situation only in terms of the story he has to write. His journalistic objectivity prevents him from becoming "involved," yet he has as much to gain as the rest. They are able to satisfy their bloodlust while he can get the story that will elevate him in the eyes of his editor.

Davies realizes that "before such grief his intrusion seemed cold and unwarranted. The guiltlessness of the mother—her love—how could one balance that against the other?" (111). Davies finds himself consumed by "the cruel instinct of the budding artist that he already was, he was beginning to meditate on the character of the story it would make—the color, the pathos [. . .] it was not so much the business of the writer to indict as to interpret" (111). His final words destroy the moment of epiphany: "'I'll get it all in!' he exclaimed feelingly, if triumphantly at last. 'I'll get it all in!'" (111).[8] Yet the callousness of his remark may also indicate a flight to the cover of objectivity as well. Objectivity, in this case, allows Davies to completely dissociate himself from any sort of responsibility in the lynching, hence providing him with access to the moral high ground. Besides the irony of the word "feelingly" (if anything, he has removed himself from any emotional attachment at this point), the idea that he considers any of the activities (and his role in them) triumphant indicate a total corrosion of his character evidenced by his eagerness to exploit Ingalls's mother's anguish to further his professional goals.

According to Emerson, "Every heroic act is also decent, and causes the place and bystanders to shine" ("Nature" 11). Yet the incident and the final scene of "Nigger Jeff" are bathed in shadow and darkness. The heroic actor becomes the mother as Davies succumbs to relative safety in his position of distanced objectivity. Emerson proposes that "Truth, and goodness, and beauty, are but different faces of the same All. But beauty is not ultimate. It is the herald of inward and eternal beauty, and is not alone a solid and satisfactory good" ("Nature" 14). As an indicator, the concept of transcendental beauty is present in "Nigger Jeff," but it indicates nothing more than potential as it becomes a diversion from the brutality of the situation. Dreiser's tacit condemnation of Davies can be delineated exclusively in terms of his inability to live up to the transcendental ideal.

Dreiser's influence on Richard Wright is unmistakable. "The first great American novelist I came across," Wright admits, "was Theodore Dreiser. Thanks to him, I discovered a very different world in America" (*Conversations* 214). Wright's outrage over the injustice of American culture certainly arose from his personal experiences, yet his social vision can be seen as a result of Dreiserian influence. In a 1938 *New York Post* interview, Wright stated: "I wanted to show exactly what Negro life in the South means today.... I think the importance of any writing lies, in how much felt life is in it" (*Conversations* 4).[9] As a result, Wright's dedication to the Communist ideal, as presented in the second half of *Native Son*, allowed him "to render the life of their race in social and realistic terms. For the first time in Negro history, problems such as nationalism in literary perspective, the relation of the Negro writers to politics and social movements were formulated and discussed" (qtd. Fabre, *Quest* 129). Wright's early writing, in this case, *Uncle Tom's Children*, represent Wright's efforts to express this sense of protest and anger through literature.[10] Wright's reading of Dreiser, particularly "Nigger Jeff," had an obvious influence on "Big Boy Leaves Home," the first story in the 1938 and 1940 editions *of Uncle Tom's Children*, which, like "Nigger Jeff," explores the violence inherent in the Jim Crow South.

Edmund Burke, whose definition of the sublime in *Philosophical Enquiry into the Origin of our Ideas of the Sublime and Beautiful* essentially established its Romantic incarnation, emphasizes that the sublime encompasses "Whatever is fitted in any sort to excite the ideas of pain and danger, that is to say, whatever is in any sort terrible, or is conversant about terrible objects, or operates in a manner analogous to terror, is a source of the *sublime*; that is, it is productive of the strongest emotion which the mind is capable of feeling" (34). Burke goes on to explain:

> But as pain is stronger in its operation than pleasure, so death is in general a much more affecting idea than pain; because there are very few pains, however exquisite, which are not preferred to death: nay, what generally makes pain itself, if I may say so, more painful, is, that it is considered as an emissary of this king of terrors. When danger or pain press too nearly, they are incapable of giving any delight, and are simply terrible; but at certain distances, and with certain modifications, they may be, and they are, delightful, as we every day experience. (55)

It is within this traditional paradigm that Dreiser moves away from his early transcendental inclinations and provides the link to literary realism, not as an abandonment of the previous principles, rather, as an extension of them. This tendency is amplified in Wright's "Big Boy Leaves Home," where the concepts are merged through the juxtaposition of the natural and the tragic.

In his discussion of the evolution of "Nigger Jeff," Donald Pizer sees the three versions of the story as evidence of Dreiser's "enduring search for a principle of meaning which would encompass the cruelty and the beauty, the destructiveness and the continuity, which he found in life" (129). Pizer sees the revisions as evidence of Dreiser's progression from "the young journalist who was viewing much of the tragic complexity of life but understanding little of it," to "an author with a characteristic vision and with a distinctive fictional style," to his final incarnation as "a writer whose ideas have become increasingly self-conscious and polemical" (122). The first two versions, told in the first person are characterized as "melancholy" and as "a more generalized sorrow over the fate of most men" (123). The final version, told in the third person, "dramatizes a growth in emotional responsiveness by the principal viewer of the action. The narrative is now primarily an initiation story—the coming into knowledge of the tragic realities of life," hence, the connection to Wright's more modern, realistic approach (125). The goals of Wright and Dreiser merge through the connections in the stories: "Like the naïve beliefs of Davies, the reader's faith in the American dream of success and in the workings of justice is destroyed by encountering the reality of tragedy" (128).

Hakutani sees this convergence revealed in the spatial narrative of "Big Boy." Like "Nigger Jeff," "Big Boy" ends by presenting "signifiers of hope" emerging over "those of despair" (Hakutani 32). According to Hakutani, protest fiction "becomes successful literature only if it is endowed with a universal sense of justice," and Davies's purpose, to "get it all in," certainly satisfies this requirement (33). "Big Boy," however, complicates this qualification with its ambiguous ending. Whereas Davies remains free to follow his conscience (and presumably become a successful journalist in the process), Big Boy's future is much more tenuous. He does escape the lynch mob, but at the same time, his future is bleak. He will arrive in Chicago undereducated, young, without connections or marketable skills—a recipe for disaster in the big city. Big Boy has merely moved from one life-threatening situation to another, emphasizing the suggestion that "human beings have failed to see 'transcending beauty' and 'unity of nature,' which are merely illusions to them, and that they have imitated only the cruel and the indifferent which nature appears to signify" (Hakutani 32–33). Hence, Dreiser straddles the chronological and philosophical divide between Burke and Wright, enabling Wright's modernist/realist vision to establish itself as a continuation of literary tradition.

For Elmer Davies, nature, as a source of solace, comfort, and reassurance, allows him to maintain his objectivity. What he observes is anything but sublime (even in its most terrifying forms. Ingalls's lynching is horrific and devoid of beauty in any form), and his contact with the natural world in effect "saves" him from the horror he has witnessed, and his determination at the close of the story becomes a reaffirmation of his humanity.

Nature for Big Boy, on the other hand, is a destructive, dangerous force to be struggled with and overcome. The initial scene is indicative—the boys are "laughing easily" in the natural setting, but that sense of ease is disrupted by their "Beating tangled vines and bushes with long sticks," despite their overt sense of security: "Ah kin feel tha ol sun goin all thu me" (17, 18). Although the ground itself feels "warm," nurturing, and "Jus lika bed," the sound of the train becomes disruptive. The boys, however, celebrate it: "Boun fer up Noth, Lawd, boun fer up Noth," emphasizing the "Boun fo Glory" aspect of their chant. Shortly thereafter, the scene erupts into violence as the boys wrestle, and Big Boy almost breaks Bobo's neck, foreshadowing the lack of cooperation that characterizes the later parts of the story.

The specter of Old Man Harvey hovers over their swimming, first as a reason not to, then as a hypothetical. Just before they see the woman, Bertha, serene natural images dominate the scene: a butterfly hovers, a bee drones, and sparrows twitter amid "the sweet scent of honeysuckles" (28). When the woman appears, there is a moment of Edenic self-consciousness as "They stared, their hands instinctively covering their groins" (29). The natural sounds are replaced by silence, Big Boy speaks in "an underbreath," and the woman, "her eyes wide, her hand over her mouth," is struck mute (29, 30). The silence is broken by her screams and the subsequent gunfire. As Buck dies, "sending up a shower of bright spray to the sunlight. The creek bubbled," the previously comforting images assume a sinister connotation (31). As Big Boy and Bobo flee, they run into barbed wire, the final imposition of disruption on the natural scene. Even after climbing the fence, "vines and leaves switched their faces," a continuation of the threat imposed by the barbed wire (33). This comingling is complete when they finally leave the forest: "They hung back, afraid. The thick shadows cast from the trees were friendly and comforting. But the wide glare of the sun stretching out over the fields was pitiless" (33).

Big Boy's flight to the kilns completes the transformation, as he finds himself "fearing every clump of shrubbery, every tree" (45). Nature becomes a primary threat in the absence of the approaching lynch mob. Facing the menacing snake, Big Boy's earlier playful violence assumes a brutal urgency, as he "was upon him, pounding blows home, one on top of the other. He fought viciously, his eyes red, his teeth bared in a snarl. He beat till the snake lay still; then he stomped it with his heel, grinding its head into the dirt" (47). The now cold, damp ground brings thoughts of regret, perhaps a final disavowal of the peace and serenity nature, and even previous (much more joyful) trips to the kilns, had provided. The women in the lynch mob sing, a distorted echo of the singing the boys had done earlier, and nature reacts: "cricket cries" that "cut surprisingly across the mob song," and the howling of the dog at the top of the hill (55). The natural sounds, however, remain secondary, overwhelmed by the scene of Bobo's mutilation that follows shortly thereafter.

The final section of the story opens with Big Boy in the puddle of rainwater. The light is described as brackish, as is the water. Pain shoots up his legs, his vision is blurred, but he has survived. His salvation, Will's truck, continues the disrupted nature that informs the story as a whole. The floor is made of steel, but "bits of sawdust danced with the rumble of the truck," completing the juxtaposition. Even as he tries to steady himself with the wooden boxes (yet another disruption of nature/the sublime), he hears the crow of a rooster, yet "It all seemed unreal now" (60). Big Boy's world has been changed, and the transformation is complete. The "golden blades of sunshine" that conclude the story no longer function as reminders of the past. Rather, they become predictors of his uncertain future.

In "Nigger Jeff," Davies maintains his objectivity (he witnesses the lynching, yet doesn't respond) until he meets Ingalls's mother, which changes him. The victim, in this case, Ingalls, regains subjectivity, which Wright expands upon in "Big Boy." Big Boy observes the lynching of Bobo in much the same manner, yet Wright's focus remains narrowly personal. Big Boy fails to react because he cannot—Davies because he will not, as he retreats into the role of reporter, thinking about the lynching only in terms of the story and its potential effect on his career. In this way, Big Boy resists objectivity—he is irrevocably affected by what he has observed. The conclusions of both stories reflect this disparity—Big Boy is doomed, while Davies will survive, even prosper. Big Boy's becomes a totally subjective experience, but his actions remain inevitably futile; whereas Davies's ability to objectivize the experience becomes a source of potential and effective action. While both authors leave the endings of the stories open, merely intimating what the future might hold, the lack of true closure in both cases leaves open any number of possibilities while closing off others.

In a country seemingly committed to simultaneously renouncing and reconstructing the memory of its segregationist past and the inextricably connected violent legacy, it's not surprising to see where art, with its ambiguity and metaphor, is the best medium to consider a topic in terms of what Jacqueline Goldsby calls "cultural logic." According to Yoshinobu Hakutani, "great social fiction can be created not so much with the artistry the writer can put into it . . . as with the writer's moral space and perspective required by the subject matter" (33). For Goldsby, "literature is particularly responsive to historical developments we cannot bear to admit shape the course of our lives" (6), and because of its unspeakable cruelty and moral degeneracy, lynching becomes understandable primarily through the indirect means that art provides, even as the viewer/artist may be guilty of a "vicarious act of complicity" in the spectacle itself (15).

Goldsby's proposition that lynching flourished because "the death toll of African-American lynch victims could be both shocking and ordinary, unexpected and predictable, fantastic and normal, horrifying and banal" (27) serves to set the stage for her critique of the practice and the society that enabled it. The encroaching modernity of the twentieth century represented a threat to an agrarian culture committed to retaining traditional social structures, and for Goldsby, "modernity requires violence, specifically the violence directed at cultural others, as the price of its achievement" (140). Essentially, as the world changed, African Americans, the most marginalized segment of American society, became the scapegoat for white frustration.

Goldsby cites the example of Samuel Burdett, an anti-lynching activist, who stumbles upon "a carefully planned display of the newest technology America had to offer in 1893"—photographs and phonograph recordings documenting the Paris, Texas lynching of Henry Smith (13). Ultimately, Burdett's horror of lynching becomes complicated by his simultaneous identification with the Seattle viewers who considered the display to be entertainment, leading to Burdett's confusion: "Was viewing the simulation a way to protest the lynching, or did watching amount to a vicarious act of complicity with the southern mob?" (15). Dreiser, finding himself in a similarly morally ambiguous situation around the same time, expresses his confusion in the short story "Nigger Jeff." Jeff Ingalls, the nominal subject of the story, takes a back seat to Elmer Davies (a thinly veiled version of Dreiser), a reporter sent to cover the Ingalls case. Davies' self-absorption and ambivalence toward the scene he ultimately witnesses make him the true focus of the story. Davies is both repulsed and fascinated by the idea of the lynching, and, through his inaction, becomes an indirect participant. Hiding behind a façade of objectivity which allows him to refuse to take a moral stance, Davies deplores the brutality he witnesses, yet ultimately objectifies Ingalls just as the lynch mob had. While he eventually realizes the humanity of his "subject," he still defines his participation as that of a reporter required to maintain objective distance, commodifying the experience by using it to earn his living. According to Jerome Loving, Dreiser uses "Nigger Jeff" to "articulate—perhaps apologize for—the 'cruel instinct of the budding artist,' and state that it 'was not so much the business of the writer to indict as to interpret,'" and "the story as a whole does condemn by indirection, the way art should, but somehow Dreiser felt the need to apologize here for being an artist instead of a political activist" (138).

Burdett, unlike Dreiser/Davies, "remained firm in his refusal to profit from the sale of his memoir [published eight years later, in 1901], suggesting that the very act of writing about the murder placed him in a complex moral dilemma" (38). Commodifying his experience would make him guilty of the same exploitative motivation as the creators of the "entertainment" of the original display of Smith's lynching. As a result, Burdett concludes *A Test of Lynch Law* "with a short story that fictionalized Smith's murder, to imagine an outcome that could restore his own and his readers' faith in democratic justice" (qtd. in Goldsby 39). Burdett deemphasizes the brutality of the lynching and focuses on the pursuit and indictment of the mob leaders; however, Goldsby asserts that while the alteration provides a sense of "moral relief" for Burdett and his readers, his interruption of the story also confuses things in that it appears to "countermand the memoir's ethics in significant ways" by promising to complete the story in a future installment—essentially turning it into a serial novel (qtd. in Goldsby 39). *A Test of Lynch Law* was published with Burdett's own funds and relied on donations to recoup costs. The subsequent installment would be sold for a dollar. While Burdett's intentions may have been purer than Dreiser's Davies, Burdett ultimately encounters the same problem: how does one report on, inform others of, make public, the facts and horror of lynching—in order to stop it—without also "entertaining" the readers and viewers and making a profit for oneself?

Even Stephen Crane's *The Monster*, a novella that avoids any direct mention of lynching at all. After all, what would a white author, writing in a genre (realism) that eschews metonymy and symbolism in favor of detailed representation, in a setting (Port Jervis, New York) far removed from the archetypal southern/midwestern roots of the phenomenon, and depicting a scene of heroism rather than deviance, have to do with the most sensitive and taboo topic of the era? In fact, Crane's work, according to Goldsby, contradicts so many of our literary assumptions when she compares Henry Johnson's monsterization and subsequent ostracism, a form of cultural death, to lynching. Goldsby's reinterpretation of the work, moving it literally into the tradition of Ida B. Wells and James Weldon Johnson, exemplifies the difficulty of any sort of a direct discussion of the topic.

For Goldsby, "lynching calls into question . . . why we presume modernity necessarily means 'progress' that promotes human liberty and happiness" (286). Ultimately, lynching "challenge[s] the meaning of modernity; how to value black death as central to our processes for building a nation" (287). Goldsby seems to suggest that if we continue to revise our past, as Billie Holiday tried to do with the authorship of "Strange Fruit," we run the risk of a dangerous sanitizing, eliminating the ugly and brutal and repulsive in order to imagine ourselves as the glorious city on the hill with nothing to hide. America has become what it is because of its history. Despite our attempts at historical revision, these images, and lynching, as a part of that history, has contributed to who and what we are right now. For Dreiser and Wright, both prominent literary voices during the height of Jim Crow, fiction, closely modeled on real-world experience and observation, represented both a reminder of the horrific present and a move toward the future that would inevitably move beyond its violent history.

WORKS CITED

Burke, Edmund. *A Philosophical Inquiry into the Origin of Our Ideas of the Sublime and Beautiful.* 1457. London: Cartright, 1824. Print.

Dreiser, Theodore. "Nigger Jeff." *Free and Other Stories.* New York: Modern Library, 1918. 76–111. Print.

Emerson, Ralph Waldo. "Nature." *The Complete Essays and Other Writings of Ralph Waldo Emerson.* Ed. Brooks Atkinson. New York: Modern Library, 1940. 3–42. Print.

Goldsby, Jacqueline. *A Spectacular Secret: Lynching in American Life and Literature.* Chicago: U of Chicago P, 2006. Print.

Hakutani, Yoshinobu. *Cross-Cultural Visions in African American Modernism: From Spatial Narrative to Jazz Haiku.* Columbus: Ohio State UP, 2006. Print.

———. *Young Dreiser: A Critical Study.* Rutherford, NJ: Fairleigh Dickinson UP, 1980.

Loving, Jerome. *The Last Titan: A Life of Theodore Dreiser.* Berkeley: U of California P, 2005.

Pizer, Donald. *The Game as It Is Played: Essays on Theodore Dreiser.* New York: Peter Lang, 2013. Print.

Wright, Richard. "Big Boy Leaves Home." *Uncle Tom's Children.* 1940. New York: Harper Perennial, 2008. 17–61. Print.

———. *Conversations with Richard Wright*, Ed. Keneth Kinnamon and Michel Fabre. Jackson, MS: University Press of Mississippi, 1993.

———. "How 'Bigger Was Born." *Native Son.* 1940. New York: HarperPerennial, 1993. 503–40. Print.

NOTES

1. Elmer Davies, a young reporter for a small Missouri newspaper, is sent to cover the pursuit and capture and potential lynching of Jeff Ingalls, an African American accused of raping a white woman. Davies is initially swept away by the passion and enthusiasm of the posse but becomes increasingly horrified by its behavior. After the posse kidnaps Ingalls and lynches him, Davies regrets his minor role in the incident (basically one of omission: he does nothing to stop the proceedings, covering himself with the cloak of journalistic objectivity), and questions his own reactions when his moral beliefs were put to the test. He sees the human consequences of the incident during a visit to Ingalls's mother and realizes the inhumanity he has observed, yet somewhat ironically, remains unable to comprehend his own role in the episode.

2. Dreiser, in fact, emphasizes Edmund Burke's foundational concept of the sublime in that "Indeed terror is in all cases whatsoever, either more openly or latently, the ruling principle of the sublime" (55).

3. Pizer lists the three versions as "A Victim of Justice" (1895 unpublished), "The Lynching of Nigger Jeff" (1901 in *Ainslee's Magazine*), and "Nigger Jeff" (1918 in *Free and Other Stories*).

4. Hakutani supports this as well, claiming "'Nigger Jeff,' in disclosing true social conditions, can be construed as a powerful expression of Dreiser's hope for the better in American society. And it is quite reasonable to suppose that all this time there was in Dreiser as much optimism in viewing life as a struggle for Utopia as there was pessimism" (*Young Dreiser* 165).

5. While Pizer cannot definitively date the lynching itself, he does make it apparent that Davies is based on Dreiser in his newspaper writing days in the early 1890s (331–32).

6. Emerson claims that "Every man discriminates between the voluntary acts of his mind and his involuntary perceptions, and knows that to his involuntary perceptions a perfect faith is due" ("Self-Reliance" 156). Yet Davies's "involuntary perceptions" (i.e., his reaction to the horror of the scene and his sympathy for Ingalls) lead directly to his inability to make an individual stand.

7. Similarly, Dreiser's attempts to come to terms with his own disillusionment can be seen in the increasing coarsening of the story's title the stories as it is revised. Initially the first manuscript is titled "A Victim of Justice," the second "The Lynching of Nigger Jeff," and the final (published) version "Nigger Jeff." The final version more accurately reflects the spiritual/moral horror of the incident and Dreiser's reaction to it. In effect, by adopting the discourse of the community, he includes himself.

8. Hakutani adopts a much more positive view, seeing this as a "proclamation of [Davies's] new ambition and hope not only for himself as an artist but for all men" (*Young Dreiser* 154).

9. The interviewer stated: "From reading Mencken in Memphis, Richard Wright branched out in Chicago to Henry James and Dostoievsky, to Hemingway, Malraux, Faulkner, Sherwood Anderson and Dreiser, writers of 'the more or less naturalistic school,' although he lays no claims to being, or even wanting to be a 'naturalistic' writer" (*Conversations* 4).

10. Wright himself came to doubt the effectiveness of his attempt to create "a richer illusion of reality," admitting, "I realized that I had made an awfully naïve mistake. I found that I had written a book which even bankers' daughters could read and weep over and feel good about" ("How 'Bigger' Was Born 537, 531).

Chapter Four

Lynching as an American Tragedy in Theodore Dreiser's Literary Works

Kiyohiko Murayama

Much as the tragedy as a term is used in the writings of Theodore Dreiser, it seems that serious attention to this predilection of has seldom been adequately recognized by critics. This essay is an attempt to explore where his idea of the tragedy came, and what significance it had to his development as a writer. Of Dreiser's awareness of lynching, I would like to suggest here, that might have instigated him to conceive a tragic vision of life. From this standpoint, "Nigger Jeff," one of the earliest short stories by Dreiser, comes to assume a particular importance as a result of his literary endeavor to deal with lynching.

"Nigger Jeff" begins as a young reporter, Elmer Davies, is sent to cover the possible lynching in the rural community of Pleasant Valley, in a state abbreviated as Ko., a thinly disguised name for Missouri where Dreiser himself worked as a young newspaperman. Davies discovers that a farmer's daughter, Ada Whitaker, allegedly has been attacked by a black man and that her father, Morg Whitaker, and brother, Jake, are leading a mob in pursuit of the suspect in an attempt to lynch him.

Davies, to carry out his assignment as a reporter, has to follow the hastily collected posse as if he himself were "(perforce) one of a lynching party—a hired spectator" (82) as he puts it in his mind. That he is concerned about his own complicity in the lynching should be remarkable, because in those days lynchings became spectacles attracting many people, and, as Jonathan Markovitz notes, "[i]n important ways, the power of spectacle lynchings actually increased as their frequency declined, since modern communication technologies made it possible for images and narratives of lynching to be disseminated to ever-larger audiences" (xxvii). Markovitz continues, "[b]ecause representations of lynching worked to extend and magnify the surveillant functions and the terror of the mob, they should be understood not as entirely separate entities from lynchings themselves but as key components of the power of the practice" (loc. cit.). After the incident, Davies is again depicted as being anxious: "The whole procedure seemed so unreal, so barbaric that he could scarcely believe it—that he was a part of it" (102–3).

The black man, Jeff Ingalls, however, is apprehended by a local sheriff, Mathews, who wants to protect him until legal measures can be taken. The mob gathers in front of the sheriff's cottage, threateningly demanding Jeff, but, led only by young Jake is in due time driven off by Mathews. Davies is pleased to find that he has got "the story of a defeated mob" with the sheriff being "his great hero" (93).

The mob, however, now joined and led by Morg, who is much more determined than his son, eventually overpowers the sheriff and succeeds in hanging Jeff from a bridge. Davies is shocked at the white men's atrocities inflicted upon the black man. As Davies observes,

> The crowd gathered about now more closely than ever, more horror-stricken than gleeful at their own work. None apparently had either the courage or the charity to gainsay what was being done. . . . As Davies afterwards concluded, they were not so much hardened lynchers perhaps as curious spectators, the majority of them, eager for any variation—any excuse for one—to the dreary commonplaces of their existences. (102)

The psychological impact of the incident upon the reporter is brought into focus toward the end of the story, as Davies puzzles,

> Why should any one have to die this way? Why couldn't the people of Baldwin or elsewhere have bestirred themselves on the side of the law before this, just let it take its course? Both father and son now seemed brutal, the injury to the daughter and sister not so vital as all this. Still, also, custom seemed to require death in this way for this. (103)

Seeing Mathews later, he notes that the sheriff "[takes] his defeat . . . philosophically. There [is] no real activity in that corner later. He [wishes] to remain a popular sheriff, no doubt" (106–7). Davies's sorrow and exasperation culminate in meeting Jeff's family in their cabin and viewing Jeff's body. Told by Jeff's sister that he has come back home to say goodbye, Davies is overwhelmed by the lamentation of his mother.

It is from his own experience as a newspaperman in St. Louis that Dreiser drew the subject matter for "Nigger Jeff." Once during his working there, he had to witness and report the lynching of a black man. He mentions this experience in his autobiography, *A Book About Myself* published in 1922, if only sarcastically contrasting with frivolity of his own infatuation with Sara White, his future wife, stating: "A negro in an outlying country assaulted a girl, and I arrived in time to see him lynched, but walking in the wood afterward, away from the swinging body, I thought of her—and life contained not a single ill. Such is infatuation" (271).

The newspaper article Dreiser is supposed to have written about this lynching case, however, remained unidentified for a long time. It is T. D. Nostwich who established that the two news stories in the *St. Louis Republic*, January 17 and 18, 1894, were what Dreiser wrote, and includes them in his edition of collected newspaper writings by Dreiser, *Journalism*. There are significant differences, though, between Jeff Ingalls in the short story and John Buckner in the newspaper accounts. About the differences Nostwich writes in "The Sources of Dreiser's 'Nigger Jeff,'": "Students of Dreiser's narrative technique will be interested in how he altered elements of the original version to suit his fictional ends, making Jeff a more sympathetic figure than Buckner, enlarging the roles of some of the people who were involved, diminishing those of others, and omitting virtually every trace of the racist rhetoric that disfigures his *Republic* account but that seems to have been almost obligatory in 1890 news stories about such cases" (176–77). By making the victim of the lynching more sympathetic, Dreiser succeeds in transforming a sensational report into a tragic work of fiction.

Although the victims of the summary, extralegal executions by vigilantes were neither limited to African-American males, nor the allegations against the victims were limited to rape, black men suspected of rape were the stock targets of lynching. Such a rape myth was perhaps the effect of what Jacqueline Goldsby in *A Spectacular Secret* calls "lynching's 'cultural logic'" (5) set in American modernity after the Reconstruction. In the developing modernism between 1880 and 1920 in the United States, in which "the violence was part of a cultural milieu" (24), as Goldsby contends, "white men could recover their lost sense of authority through violence" (56). Dreiser confronted such a cultural malady of American society by composing the short story, which first appeared in *Ainslee's* No. 8 (November 1901), and later was revised to be collected in *Free and Other Stories* published in 1918.

In the closing passage of "Nigger Jeff," a new awareness of "the business of writer" (111) that dawns on Davies is delineated, as he realizes: "The night, the tragedy, the grief, he saw it all" (111). The "grief" here means "the cruel sorrow of [Jeff's] mother" (111) Davies witnesses in his family's cabin. Interestingly, the black man's mother is mentioned also in the newspaper account of the lynching of John Buckner, if only briefly: "Through the broken panes of a miserable window the pale, cloud-broken moonlight cast its sheen and shadow on the gaunt form of the dead, while near it, in a dark corner, wept the mother of the erring boy alone" (*Journalism*, 253). The weeping mother is an important element of a formula both in balladry and journalism that traditionally served as a device for coping with horrible crimes.

Moreover, the word "tragedy" or "tragic" is used to denote lynching in the short story as well as the news report. While, in one part of the newspaper article, lynching is referred to as "the tragic enactment of unwritten moral law" (252), in "Nigger Jeff" the word appears no less than 5 times. The notion of tragedy had long been a familiar contrivance employed in the titles of ballads about sex-related crimes such as "The Berkshire Tragedy" and news stories about sexual crimes. Dreiser evidently resorted to such a venerable convention of the working-class culture in conceiving the short story.

Although certain scholars complain that the vernacular habit of using the word "tragedy" as a synonym for disaster has muddled the concept of tragedy as a literary form, its popular sense cannot be too strictly differentiated from its classical sense, as Raymond Williams in *Modern Tragedy* argues: "[We do not need] to be impatient and even contemptuous of what they regard as loose and vulgar uses of 'tragedy' in ordinary speech and in the newspaper. [Instead, we must ask,] what actual relations are we to see and live by, between the tradition of tragedy and the kinds of experience, in our own time, that we ordinarily and perhaps mistakenly call tragedy?" (14–15).

After seeing and writing about the lynching he encountered in the 1890s, Dreiser's concern about lynching continued to manifest itself not only in "Nigger Jeff" but also in other later writings. It might well seem to him that the helplessness of the victims of lynching, particularly the targets of the populace's anger aroused by alleged sexual crimes, takes on the sense of inevitability that tragedy might generate.

A revealing passage is found in *A Hoosier Holiday*, a book about an automobile journey to his home state Indiana published in 1916. During this trip, Dreiser came to know about the lynching of a young Jew Leo Frank in Georgia, who was charged with attempted rape and subsequent murder of a thirteen-year-old girl. While today it is believed that Frank was wrongly convicted because of anti-Semitism rampant in the region, he was kidnapped from prison by a group of armed men and lynched. The case attracted national press, and the news that reached Dreiser in travelling gave him occasion to raise an outspoken criticism of the lynching mob, stating in part: "[T]his sort of thing always strikes me as a definite indictment of the real native sense of the people" (237).

Since lynching was a form of extreme terrorism, any allegation against the lynched would have been basically irrelevant. It did not matter whether those victims of lynching actually committed an offense or what offense was committed. "Although the impression was widely held that most of the

Negroes lynched had been accused of raping white women," as John Hope Franklin in *From Slavery to Freedom* observes, "the records do not sustain this impression" (323). Insofar as lynching is the white men's practice of exercising the sexual as well as racial domination, the rape myth is likely to be connected with it.

"Racial violence," however, as Dora Apel contends, "was rooted in both race and gender anxieties that criminalized sexual relations between black men and white women and feared the enfranchisement and education of African Americans that might further such relations and destabilize the white-dominated power structure" (2). Therefore, as Stephen Whitfield suggests, "[a]mong the ideals that were to be questioned [for an incisive critique of lynching entangled with race and sex] was the need of males to protect females from the dark temptations of sexuality outside the sanctity of matrimony" (109–10). The need to "protect" females also implies the need to control them.

While race and sex were closely linked in lynching, the focal point of Dreiser's concerns about it, possibly prompted by the sense of difficulties in his own marriage and sex life, seems to have been gradually shifting from its nature as racial oppression to its associations of sexual crimes. Sensational media coverage exploited people's lurid curiosity, stressing the lynching mob's ribald indulgence in violence and mutilation of corpse. Anomalous curiosity about sex crimes can be construed as a projection of the general public's own fears and obsession. In regard to fascination with the fate of sex criminals, Dreiser might seem to share the morbid propensity with the public, but his concerns were perhaps based on his awareness that the rise of consumer hedonism and popular culture was closely tied with the emerging recognition of the power of sexuality.

The Hand of the Potter, a play published in 1919, is another product of Dreiser's fascination with the sexually as well as racially oppressed. According to the entry about this play by Frederic Rusch in *A Theodore Dreiser Encyclopedia*, "Dreiser based much of the action and many of the characters in *The Hand of the Potter* on newspaper accounts of the murder of twelve-year-old Julia Connors by twenty-four-year-old Nathan Swartz in the Bronx in 1912, the behavior of Swartz's family before the Grand Jury called to bring an indictment against him and the circumstances surrounding Swartz's suicide while police were searching for him" (177–78). The composition of the play is detailed in "Introduction" to *The Collected Plays of Theodore Dreiser* edited by Keith Newlin and Frederic Rusch, who, making it clear that "Dreiser began work on the play in the fall of 1916" (xx), states, "Precisely why Dreiser began thinking about the Swartz-Connors case at this time is unknown" (xxii). The inception of the play, however, chronologically coincides largely with the publication of *A Hoosier Holiday* and the revision on "Nigger Jeff" to be included in *Free and Other Stories*, both of which have reference to sexual crimes.

From the standpoint of H. L. Mencken, the timing should never have been so detrimental as Dreiser's actual course of trying to write, publish, and put on the stage this drama of a sexually perverted man, because, as Newlin-Rusch elucidate, at that time Mencken was working very hard to help Dreiser to fight the censorship of *The "Genius"* on a charge of obscenity. If *The Hand of the Potter* was published, Mencken was afraid all his efforts would come to nothing, so he wrote a letter of vehement objection to Dreiser when he was privately shown the draft by Dreiser. Nevertheless, Dreiser persisted in completing the work, defending the play in a reply of December 18, 1916, in the following terms:

> A poor weak pervert, defended or tolerated and half concealed by a family for social reasons commits a sex crime—not shown on the stage—and thereby entails a chain of disaster which destroys the home and breaks the spirit of the father and mother. What pray is there about this that is so low and vulgar? You proceed to recite a litany of vulgarities or obscenities in this. I have attempted a tragedy. To you it is not tragic—technically a botch. . . . You write as if you thought I were entering on a defense of perversion—trying to make it plausible or customary. If you would look at the title page you would see it labeled *a tragedy*. What has a tragedy ever illuminated—unless it is the inscrutability of life and its forces and its accidents[?] What has one ever sought to teach or inculcate[?] (Riggio 1:283–84)

The protagonist of the play, Isadore Berchansky, is a young Jew out of work, whose self-hate makes him insist to his brother, "But I'm not goin' to use that name Isadore any more. It's a kike name. People laugh at it. I'm Irving from now on" (195). His perversity causes him to assault and murder a young girl. Held at bay by the police in a hiding place of a room of a tenement house, cowering not unlike Jeff Ingalls in the short story who "cower[s] and chatter[s] in the darkest corner of the cellar [of the sheriff's cottage]," (91), Isadore, deranged, blurts out:

> I can't stand it! It's the red ones [meaning some sort of hallucinations that Isadore has in a fit]. It ain't my fault—it's theirs. I can't help myself no more. They make me do it. [*He grows savage, vigorous. His shoulder jerks.*] Well, I won't die, either. [*Throws down the tubing.*] Why should I? It ain't my fault. I ain't done nothin' much, have I? I couldn't help it, could I? I didn't make myself, did I? (262)

For all his self-defense denouncing unfairness and delusion of newspapers, police, and the public at large, he commits suicide in the room by gassing himself. In addition, after his death, he has Dennis Quinn, a reporter, speak in his defense, by arguing in part that "People judge these fellies solely by their acts, when as a matter ave fact they aaht to take into account the things which make up their natures and dispositions. This felly could no more help bein' what he was than a fly can help bein' a fly an' naht an elephant" (275).

In Act III the case is laid before the grand jury to decide whether Isadore is guilty or not. The process of taking testimonies is at some length represented, at the last stage of which Isadore's father, Aaron Berchansky, is called to witness and interrogated severely by Miller, the Assistant District Attorney. He not only confesses, "My son did it. He killed her!" but also admits, "I told him vot to do! He should kill himself, I told him!" (257). From his words, "Dey try an' teach us. Dey say ve are old fashion'—vot dey call 'not up to date'" (210), Isadore's parents can be assumed to be pious Jews, so the possibility that sexual repression afflicting Isadore is related with parental religious rigidities is suggested. By his own experiences with his father, Dreiser knew how oppressive a pious father could be.

In *The Bulwark*, the novel Dreiser had been working on since 1914, though it was not published until 1946 posthumously, Stewart's involvement in a sex crime entailing his suicide in the local jail that is depicted as a result of his resentment at the restrictions placed by his Quaker father, Solon Barnes. As Newlin-Rusch argue, in 1914,

> [Dreiser] wrote the scene where Solon is alone with the body of his son after Stewart has committed suicide "when I first thought of the idea of *The Bulwark*, to see if it had the germ of a great tragedy in it. After I wrote this, I felt that it did." As Dreiser studied newspaper accounts of Nathan Swartz's father at the indictment hearing, he must have been struck by the similarity between him and Solon Barnes. Like Solon, Samuel Swartz was a good man, who, along with his family, was suffering deep sorrow and despair over the actions of his son. Here, too, was a tragedy. (xxiv–xxv)

In the published version of the novel, Stewart facing the judicial investigation, though not subject to racial discrimination, is no less helpless than Isadore "because of public opinion, which [is] always violently aroused by crimes of this character" (293) as well as due to his fear of his father. Just before killing himself, Stewart is delineated: "So oppressed was he by these thoughts that he could see no way. Let a jury decide what it might, he could never escape the jury of his own mind, of his father's mind: the judgment of the Inner Light" (293–94). The concern about the jury which enters into the picture in *The Bulwark* as well as *The Hand of the Potter* echoes back to an earlier essay Dreiser wrote as editor of *E'vry Month*.

E'vry Month was the piano music monthly edited by Dreiser whom Howley, Haviland, and Company, one of the most successful Tin Pan Alley publishers, hired in the mid-1890s owing to his brother Paul's recommendation. For this magazine Dreiser as "The Prophet," which, as Nancy Barrineau observes, was one of the many pseudonyms he created "[i]n order to disguise the fact that he was the magazine's only writer" (xx). He wrote "Reflections," the long column about the general topics featured in every issue, of which the installment of July 1896 includes in part a critique of the jury system in the American judiciary:

> They are constantly working to reform and improve the jury system, when, as a matter of fact, the system cannot be improved. It is old and established, and has reached the limit of its usefulness, so that the only thing to do in the matter is not to reform but to abolish. Never was there another relic of the feudal ages so fortunate in retaining the blind, unreasoning support of the people, nor was there ever anything so utterly subversive of the rights it was invoked to maintain. The jury system, as exemplified in actual daily practice throughout the United States, in courts of every degree of decorum, is a rank and outrageous mockery. It is the most expensive appendage of our judicial system, and its results are the most worthless. It is above all things a breeder of bribes, a refuge of ignoramuses, a castle from which to work in safety any sort of injury—a useless, idiotic, malice-infected, and ghost-supported pest. (118)

Dreiser's hostility to the jury system was so longstanding that disparaging depictions of it occasionally cropped up in his works. His anxiety about the judicial system is not unfounded. If the jury is composed by the whites only, for instance, a black defendant, as numerous examples have shown, would have an enormous difficulty in obtaining a verdict "not guilty" in a criminal court case which could turn into a "legal lynching." More of which will be touched upon later.

Another publication that exhibits a similar interest in sexual crimes is *Hey Rub-A-Dub-Dub*, an extraordinary salmagundi by Dreiser published in 1920. An essay in it, "Some Aspects of Our National Character," offers his observation that "[a]lmost daily [the black man] is burned alive somewhere in America, and for all but indifferent crimes" (43). Another essay in the book, "Neurotic America and the Sex Impulse," is a diagnosis of the "deep-seated neurosis relating to [sex]" (126) affecting the American nation, and cites the examples of the symptom including "[t]he profound and even convulsive interest in any case involving a sex crime or delusion (Thaw, Leo Frank, Billy Brown, Carlisle Harris, Nan Patterson, Durant; or any negro rape case in the South)" (126). It is notable how closely lynching, sex crimes, and American national characteristics are related in Dreiser's mind.

In due course, Dreiser's endeavor to weave a narrative of an oppressed young man who commits a sexual crime only to be treated unfairly by society, at last reached a culmination in his major novel, *An American Tragedy* in 1925. Clyde Griffiths is accused as a murderer of his sweetheart though his guilt is highly problematic. When he is taken into custody by the police, "a crowd of at least five hundred—noisy, jeering, threatening" (616) assembles around an upstate county jail, as is depicted:

> There had been hard and threatening cries of "There he is, the dirty bastard! You'll swing for this yet, you young devil, wait and see!" This from a young woodsman not unlike Swenk in type—a hard, destroying look in his fierce young eyes, leaning out from the crowd. And worse, a waspish type of small-town slum girl, dressed in a gingham dress, who in the dim light of the arcs, had leaned forward to cry: "Lookit, the dirty little sneak—the murderer! You thought you'd get away with it, didnja?" (616–17)

Although the attempt by the mob to lynch him is balked, Clyde cowers to hearing those cries in the jail, "thinking: Why, they actually think I did kill her! And they may even lynch me!" (617)

While Clyde is not racially marked like Jeff Ingalls or Isadore Berchansky, he is no less impoverished, a feature emphasized because of the contrast with his rich cousin, Gilbert, who ironically looks just like Clyde. Even if Clyde's parents are neither Jews like Isadore's nor Quakers like Stewart's, they are no less pious, being self-designated missionaries preaching on the streets, presenting another conflict between the parental religious rigor and the filial sexual repressions. Nevertheless, Clyde is representative of the average American people, "true to the standard of the American youth, or the general American attitude toward life" (26), though his limitations are played up:

> For to say the truth, Clyde had a soul that was not destined to grow up. He lacked decidedly that mental clarity and inner directing application that in so many permits them to sort out from the facts and avenues of life the particular thing or things that make for their direct advancement. (189)

Notably, Dreiser speaks explicitly on behalf of an ordinary youth executed as a perpetrator of the sex crime, Chester Gillette, the model for Clyde created a sensation because of its similarity to the plot of *An American Tragedy*. As Dreiser observes,

> Not Chester Gillette . . . planned this crime, but circumstances over which he had no control—circumstances and laws and rules and conventions which to his immature and more or less futile mind were so terrible, so oppressive, that they were destructive to his reasoning powers. . . . And yet in spite of these conditions

and circumstances which were plainly to be seen by anyone who could see, the boy was fearfully denounced, tortured with public obloquy and even hatred. It was suggested that he be lynched, and once the case was given to the jury he was quickly convicted of murder and sentenced to death. (12)

Such a type of crime, Dreiser contends:

> Seemed to spring from the fact that almost every young person was possessed of an ingrowing ambition to be somebody financially and socially. In short, the general mental mood of America was directed toward escape from any form of poverty. This ambition did not imply merely the attainment of comfort and the wherewithal to make happy one's friends, but rather the accumulation of wealth implying power, social superiority, even social domination. (5)

From Dreiser's point of view, in America where "[f]ortune-hunting became disease" (6), an ordinary young man like Chester Gillette or Clyde, if possessed not by "anti-social dream" but *"pro-social* dream" (10), should not be executed. Deiser argues that "In part I blame America and its craze for social and money success" (7), and subsequently avows: "I wanted to ferret out . . . the untoward and possibly unjustifiable compulsions of society and life itself which came upon him through the medium of the conventions, notions and taboos of the region in which he dwelt, compulsions which possibly brought out through him a crime of which he was more the victim than the perpetrator" (17).

Denying that the American judiciary and the jury system in particular is equal to passing judgment on young transgressors, Dreiser declares:

> [T]he murder was not one which could either wisely or justly be presented to an ordinary conventional, partly religious, and morally controlled American jury and be intelligently passed upon. Rather I concluded that there were too many elements of a social and economic, as well as moral and religious, character to permit a jury (themselves the representatives, one might even say the victims, of these same financial conditions and social taboos) to judge fairly the guilt or innocence of the alleged murderer. (9)

In the concluding passage, he writes: "Actually the law in regard to love situations of all kinds should be altered. Instances such as this should not come before twelve calm ordinary men and women out of the streets of life, who themselves at the time are not such victims. It is not equity" (73–74).

This is perhaps why *An American Tragedy* gives a detailed delineation of how the jury for the trial of Clyde Griffiths is selected with "five entire days consumed" (688) for it. As I have suggested above, if what verdict a defendant is to receive depends on a jury composed of members selected from the local population liable to employ vigilantism, a court trial would be futile, degenerating into what the civil rights activists often called a "legal lynching." This is examined methodically by Timothy V. Kaufman-Osborn in "Capital Punishment as Legal Lynching?" and other new abolitionists contributing to *From Lynch Mobs to the Killing State*, and vivid examples of which are illustrated in detail, for instance, by George C. Wright in "By the Book: The Legal Executions of Kentucky Blacks."

As Rebecca Hill in *Men, Mobs, and Law* demonstrates, the concept of the "legal lynching" was built up by the ILD (International Labor Defense, a Communist front) to enable them to fight the Scottsboro case. In 1931, at the court of Scottsboro, Alabama, young black men were convicted for raping white women by an all-white jury and sentenced to death. Vehement protests arose both nationally and internationally, in the midst of which Dreiser, chairman of the National Committee for the Defense of Political Prisoners, a subordinate organization of the ILD, contributed to an ILD pamphlet on the Scottsboro case titled *Dreiser on Scottsboro*. It denounced the "Alabama lynch terrorists" (qtd. in Hill 232). In "an 1100-word statement that traced the history of racism in the South," Dreiser set forth the argument, as Richard Lingeman explicates:

> The death penalty for rape was "definitely aimed at the Negro male" rather than the white equivalent, "who miscegenates without serious opposition. But mixing the blood of a white man with that of a Negro woman is certainly the same as mixing the blood of a black man with that of a white woman." He closed by urging a "general broadening and humanizing of the universal treatment and condition of the Negroes, especially in the South." (348–49)

The significance of Scottsboro was that it brought about a major turnaround in the history both of anti-lynching movement and labor-defense, as Hill maintains:

> [T]he party's official position was that lynching was a part of capitalist class justice, and most ILD publications argued that lynching was a capitalist phenomenon. Therefore, this case should be fought by the ILD. This analysis of lynching as class justice, and the idea that the case should be fought by an interracial working class, made the ILD's Scottsboro project different from progressive era anti-lynching activism. It was, in other word, a case of "legal lynching," making the actions of the state and the "respectable community" rather than "mob violence" the target of attack. The "legal lynching" concept allowed the Scottsboro activists to point to the connections between lynch mobs and the institutions of law. These aspects of the case put it outside the traditional "anti-mobbism" of the progressive anti-lynching movement but within the logic of the radical "police-mob continuum" identified by Ida B. Wells and taken up

most programmatically by the NAACP in the Arkansas, Tulsa, and Houston riot cases of the First World War era. (230)

In *An American Tragedy*, the judiciary which convicts Clyde is depicted as dubious. This is reflected by the "police-mob continuum" noticeable in the lynch mob thronging to the jail Clyde is put in, the lengthy process of the selection of the jury, the sensational treatment of the case by newspaper, and the political and personal bias both Orville Mason, the District Attorney, and Alvin Belknap, the counsel for the defense. In short, the court trial Clyde has to undergo is close to a "legal lynching." His discontent about unfairness of the whole process of the trial could never be wiped away. His feeling at the last stage is narrated:

> There was a system—a horrible routine system—as long since he had come to feel it to be so. It was iron. It moved automatically like a machine without the aid or the hearts of men. These guards! They with their letters, their inquiries, their pleasant and yet really hollow words, their trips to do little favors, or to take the men in and out of the yard or to their baths—they were iron, too—mere machines, automatons, pushing and pushing and yet restraining and restraining one—within these walls, as ready to kill as to favor in case of opposition—but pushing, pushing, pushing—always toward that little door over there, from which there was no escape—no escape—just on and on—until at last they would push him through it never to return! (866)

The image here reverberates with the perception of the fatality of lynching in "Nigger Jeff": "It was like some axiomatic, mathematic law—hard, but custom. The silent company, an articulated mechanical and therefore terrible thing, moved on. It also was axiomatic, mathematic" (103).

Even if he is neither an African American like John Buckner or Jeff Ingalls, nor a Jew like Leo Frank or Isadore Berchansky, Clyde in death row hears "some religious chant into which [his fellow inmate, a young Jew] fell when his mental tortures would no longer endure silence" (849). The Jew deplores interminably: "I have been evil. I have been unkind. I have lied. Oh! Oh! Oh! I have been unfaithful. My heart has been wicked. I have joined with those who have done evil things" (849) and so on. Clyde, "on his cot, his thoughts responding rhythmically to the chant of the Jew—and joining with him silently—" (849), being so inarticulate, only listens to this fellow inmate's lamentation, as if he cannot otherwise give words to his own remorse for himself. Clyde's coalescence with a racially oppressed man at the last moment before his execution suggests his status as a victim of lynching in Dreiser's literary imagination. *An American Tragedy* proves to be a novel about lynching of a young man who barely escapes from an extralegal execution as an offender of a sex crime by a lynch mob, but eventually is to be executed through a legal lynching.

The abominable practice of lynching, whether extralegal or legal, remained continuing even after World War II, as is known by the legal lynching cases entailing allegations of rape such as the executions of Martinsville Seven and Willie Mcgee. This is stressed in Dayo F. Gore's "A Black Woman Speaks" (68), as well as the outright lynching cases such as the murder of Emmett Till. Those incidents evince the long-range historical relevancy that Dreiser's endeavor to write literary works on the subject matter of lynching as an American tragedy bears.

WORKS CITED

Apel, Dora. *Imagery of Lynching: Black Men, White Women, and the Mob*. New Brunswick: Rutgers UP, 2004.

Barrineau. Nancy Warner, ed. *Theodore Dreiser's* E'vry Month. Athens: The University of Georgia Press, 1996.

Dreiser, Theodore. *An American Tragedy*. Cleveland: The World Publishing Company, 1948.

____. *A Book About Myself*. Greenwich, CT: Fawcett Publications, 1965.

____. *The Bulwark*. Garden City, NY: Doubleday, 1946.

____. *The Hand of the Potter: A Tragedy in Four Acts. The Collected Plays of Theodore Dreiser*. 188–282

____. *Hey Rub-A-Dub-Dub: A Book of the Mystery and Wonder and Terror of Life*. New York: Boni and Liveright, 1920.

____. *A Hoosier Holiday*. Westport, CT: Greenwood Press, 1974.

____. "I find the Real American Tragedy." Jack Salzman. "I find the Real American Tragedy by Theodore Dreiser." *Resources for American Literary Study*, Vol. II, No. 1, Spring 1972: 3–74.

____. *Journalism: Volume One, Newspaper Writings, 1892–1895*. Ed. T. D. Nostwich. Philadelphia: University of Pennsylvania Press, 1988.

____. "Nigger Jeff," *Free and Other Stories*. St. Clair Shore, MI: Scholarly Press, 1971.

Franklin, John Hope. *From Slavery to Freedom: A History of Negro Americans, Fourth Edition*. New York: Alfred A. Knopf, 1974.

Goldsby, Jacqueline. *A Spectacular Secret: Lynching in American Life and Literature*. Chicago: University of Chicago Press, 2006.

Gore, Dayo F. "A Black Woman Speaks: Beah Richards's Life of Protest and Poetry." *Lineages of the Literary Left: Essays in Honor of Alan Wald*. Ed. Howard Brick, Robbie Lieberman, and Paula Rabinowitz. N.p.: Michigan Publishing, 2015.

Hill, Rebecca N. *Men, Mobs, and Law: Anti-Lynching and Labor Defense in U.S. Radical History*. Durham: Duke University Press, 2008.

Kaufman-Osborn, Timothy V. "Capital Punishment as Legal Lynching?" *From Lynch Mobs to the Killing State: Race and the Death Penalty in America.* Ed. Charles J. Ogletree and Austin Sarat. 21–54.

Lingeman, Richard. *Theodore Dreiser: An American Journey 1908–1945.* New York: G. P. Putnam's Sons, 1990.

Markovitz, Jonathan. *Legacies of Lynching: Racial Violence and Memory.* Minneapolis: University of Minnesota Press, 2004.

Newlin, Keith and Frederic E. Rusch, eds. *The Collected Plays of Theodore Dreiser.* Albany: Whitston Publishing Co., 2000.

Nostwish, T. D. "The Source of Dreiser's 'Nigger Jeff.'" *Resources for American Literary Study* VIII (Autumn 1978): 174–87.

Riggio, Thomas P., ed. *Dreiser-Mencken Letters: The Correspondence of Theodore Dreiser and H. L. Mencken, 1907–1945*, 2 vols. Philadelphia: University of Pennsylvania Press, 1986.

Ogletree, Charles J. and Austin Sarat, eds. *From Lynch Mobs to the Killing State: Race and the Death Penalty in America.* New York: New York University Press, 2006.

Rusch, Frederic E. *"The Hand of the Potter."* *A Theodore Dreiser Encyclopedia.* Ed. Keith Newlin. Westport, CT: Greenwood Press, 2003. 177–79.

Whitfield, Stephen J. *A Death in the Delta: The Story of Emmett Till.* Baltimore: The Johns Hopkins UP, 1992.

Williams, Raymond. *Modern Tragedy.* Stanford: Stanford University Press, 1977.

Wright, George C. "By the Book: The Legal Executions of Kentucky Blacks." *Under Sentence of Death: Lynching in the South.* Ed. W. Fitzhugh Brundage. Chapel Hill: University of North Carolina Press, 1997. 250–70.

Chapter Five

Faulkner on Lynching

Neil R. McMillen and Noel Polk

In *The Lynching Files* compiled by the Tuskegee Institute is a previously unknown letter William Faulkner published in the Memphis *Commercial Appeal* on February 15, 1931. It's an astonishing document for the biographical context in which it occurs and for the fact that it is signed "WILLIAM FALKNER," thus making it the only document we know of that Faulkner signed with the old family name since he had abandoned it more than a decade before. Mostly, however, it is astonishing for the baldness of the racial attitudes it expresses, its virtual defense of lynching as an instrument of justice.

Faulkner wrote in response to a letter by Mr. W.H. James, of Starkville, Mississippi, that had appeared in the same newspaper on February 2:

> From the Memphis "Commercial Appeal"
> February 2, 1931
> Letters to the Editor
> THEY CAN STOP LYNCHING
>
> To The Commercial Appeal:
> Now that the good women of Mississippi have organized themselves in a body to eradicate or fight the evils of lynching, we as colored people should feel more hopeful than ever. I am sure that they will have the prayers of all of my people, who seem to suffer most from this inhuman crime, which as they say is striking at the very foundations of our most sacred institutions.
> How strange it seems that history never gave a record of a single lynching until after the days of reconstruction. We are today for the most part as humble and submissive as we were then. The good women felt that something needed to be done. I have list(e)ned long for them and now they are here and with the backing of some of our good men I am sure they will succeed, because when

they are determined they know no defeat. I believe that the good lady, Mrs. J. Morgan Spencer, who heads this organization, would be an ideal one for governor. I do not feel embarrassed to say this, for I feel that we have some friends who will protect us against the crime which has been perpetrated against so many of us without even a possible chance to prove our innocence or guilt. But through the efforts of these good ladies, when we flee for protection to the strong arm of the law, we won't be met with the rope and torch.

W.H. James
Starkville, Miss.

Memphis Commercial Appeal
Sunday, February 15, 1931
Caption: Mob Sometimes Right

To The Commercial Appeal:

In the matter of W.H. James' letter on lynching in The Commercial Appeal Feb. 2.

History gives no record of lynching prior to reconstruction days for several reasons.

The slave-holders and slaves of the pre-Civil War time, out of whose relations lynchings did, or could, take place, were not representative of either people, any more than the Sicilian expatriates and shopping women in Chicago stores, out of whose accidental coinciding the murder of innocent bystanders (or fleers) occurs, are representative of European emigrants or American women and children, or of the General Cooks and the George Rogers Clarks who made Chicago possible.

Secondly, there was no need for lynching until after reconstruction days.

Thirdly, the people of the black race who get lynched are not representative of the black race, just as the people who lynch them are not representative of the white race.

No balanced man can, I believe, hold any moral brief for lynching. Yet we in America have seen, ever since we set up to guide our own integral destiny, miscarriage of elementary justice on all hands. Like all new lands, not yet aware of our own strength, we have been the prey of opportunist and demagogues; of men whose sole claim to rule us was that they had not a clean shirt to their backs. So is it strange that at times we take violently back into our own hands that justice which we watched go astray in the blundering hands of those into which we put it voluntarily? I don't say that we do not blunder with our 'home-made' justice. We do. But he who was victim of our blundering, also blundered. I have yet to hear, outside of a novel or a story, of a man of any color and with a record beyond reproach, suffering violence at the hands of men who knew him.

It will be said that the standard for a black man is stricter than that for a white man. This is obvious. To make an issue of it is to challenge and condemn the natural human desire which is in any man, black or white, to take advantage of what circumstance, not himself, has done for him. The strong (mentally or physically) black man takes advantage of the weak one; he is not only not censured, he is protected by law, since (and the white man the same) the law has found out that the many elemental material factors which compose a commonwealth are of value only when they are in the charge of some one, regardless of color and size and religion, who can protect them.

It requires a certain amount of sentimentality, an escaping from the monotonous facts of day by day, to make a lynching. Note the crimes in compensation of which lynching occurs. Sacredness of womanhood, we call it. Not a thing, but a reaction: something so violent and so nebulous that even all the law words can not pin it down, since the law words were all invented in lands and by people who had had time to outgrow (or who could not afford) our American susceptibility to vocal resonance.

Lynching is an American trait, characteristic. It is the black man's misfortune that he suffers it, just as it is his misfortune that he suffers the following instances of white folks' sentimentality.

Let James go to his county tax collector, who will tall him (his county being fairly representative of Mississippi hill country as distinct from the del.) that there is more white-owned land sold up for taxes than colored-owned, though the delinquent list be the same. There may be reason for this[,] white man's reason: as, for instance, it will be proved that the colored man had never had title to the land at all, having used, as they do, two or even three separate names in making trades or borrowing money from the government loan associations, and so having used the land tax-free for a year and made a cop and moved on. Thus: Joe Johnson arranges with a white man and a bank to buy a piece of land. He is about to make a good crop, he is a hard worker; maybe he runs the neighborhood blacksmith shop; he is getting ahead. Then one day the cashier of the bank and the Farm Loan secretary compare notes and they find that a certain John Jones has borrowed $700 on land identical in description with that in the temporary possession of one Joe Johnson. There's nothing to do. Joe Johnson, or Jo. Jones, tricked two white men. "Oh, well," the white men, the cashier and the secretary say, "he's a good man. He may make out." And he not only may and will, but he perhaps does make a good crop by hard work. But he has first committed one felony in person and a second one by pro, in permitting to compound it one of that unwitting race which holds with the Bible that justice is a matter of violent and immediate retribution on the person of the sinner: a sentimentalist.

There is a colored man, a friend who has helped me in my need and whom I have helped in his, who has eaten of my bread and between whom and myself the crass material balance of labor and recompense has long since faded from our ken, to be perhaps totted and receipted for in some better place, he hopes, who tells me now and then of his brother. They are sons of a slave. The brother went to Detroit years ago, where, he writes back, "he has not done a lick of work in 15 years, because the white folks up there give him food. All he has to do is, fall in a line at a designated place on a designated day, and receive the food or its equivalent in a printed form, which he sells to wop and bohunk immigrants who have not yet learned to talk enough English to save the middleman's profit."

In Europe they don't lynch people. But think of a man living for 15 years and doing nothing at all, in France say, or Italy. It cannot be done anywhere under the sun except in America.

James speaks of "as humble and submissive as. . . . " Let him think about this. Humility and submissiveness is usually the part of a weak person waiting to take his advantage, without regard to color. Humility and submissiveness are as false a part of a Hack man's social equipment as of a white man's. He does not need them. And the black man who is a valuable integer in the social fabric (property owner, merchant; any one who does a fair day's labor and receives a fair day's wage and applies it toward the comfort of his present life and the security of his old age) has no reason to assume humility. And he does not do it. In fact, there is a certain class of colored people who trade in humility just as there is a certain class of people who trade in man's other weaknesses and vices; it just happens that the colored man is better fitted to trade in humility, as the Irishman is for politics.

James reminds us that history records no lynchings prior to reconstruction days. Neither does history record any peculiar and noticeable removal to, and sojourn in, the south of Yankees until that period. Particularly New Englanders, who had some time since begun to practice the custom of hanging people of whose conduct they did not approve. I have lived in Mississippi all my 30 years, yet most of the lynching[s] with which I am acquainted have occurred in outland newspapers; vide three I read of in French newspapers in Paris during a period of nine weeks, one of which happened at Oregon, D.C., Washington, the second at Hair., Alabama, D.C., America, and the third at a place called NveZique. They had photographs, flames and all, and the men there, looking at the camera. Most of them wore smock coats, and one man near the front had on wooden shoes.

I hold no brief for lynching. No balanced man will deny that mob violence serves nothing, just as he will not deny that a lot of our natural and logical jurisprudence serves nothing either. It just happens that we—mobber and mobbee—live in this age. We will muddle through, and die in our beds, the deserving and the fortunate among us. Of course, with the population what it is, there are some of us that won't. Some will die rich, and some will die on cross-ties soaked with gasoline, to make a holiday. But there is one curious thing about mobs. Like our juries, they have a way of being right.

William Faulkner.
Oxford, Miss.

We are hard pressed to understand Faulkner's letter, since it stands so completely in accord with contemporary racial attitudes in white Mississippi and the South generally and runs so completely counter to the sensibility and the sympathies that write so profoundly about racial problems in his fiction. There is nothing like it in the Faulkner canon, we believe, except his claim, in his 1955 interview with Russell Howe, that "if it came to fighting, I'd fight for

Mississippi against the United States even if it meant going out into the street and shooting Negroes" (*LG* 261)—a statement which he later did not exactly repudiate but claimed "no sober man would make, nor . . . any sane man believe" (*LG* 265). According to Joseph Blotner, Faulkner remained throughout his life capable of overtly racist remarks and of a paternalistic attitude in correspondence and in private conversation; yet in print he was remarkably sympathetic to the problems of being black in the South and specifically to the outrageousness of lynching. Indeed, one of the more curious features of this letter is that it must have been written within days of the publication of one of his most enduring and powerful stories, "Dry September," a story directly concerned with the injustice of lynching, the unfairness of mob rule.

The most striking aspects of "Falkner's" letter are its exculpatory tone and its conventional, myth-ridden white assumptions, so blatantly articulated as to challenge Faulkner's reputation as a clear-eyed observer of the Southern racial scene and as a relative moderate in a time and place of dark tribal impulses. The juxtaposition of this letter to the publication of "Dry September" is so bizarre that it is tempting to see the letter as a forgery, to assume—hope—that not Faulkner but someone else wrote it and attributed it to him for reasons unknown. But in fact, we think the letter can be reasonably attributed to Faulkner himself. It seems hardly likely that anyone would have written such a letter to parody or to embarrass Faulkner this early in his career, since he had not yet begun to speak publicly against the racial status quo; when he did so in the mid-fifties, he ignited a firestorm of protest against him from all over the state, including public criticism from his brother John and other members of his family. He had not, in early February of 1931, reached any of the dubious celebrity, the local infamy, that was to befall him in a matter of days: indeed, *Sanctuary* was to be published on February 9, and the reviews, national and local, would begin very soon to establish him, fully blown, in the notoriety as a purveyor of Southern moral degradation that was to follow him all of his career. In any case, given the large readership in Oxford of the *Commercial Appeal*, the letter could not have escaped Faulkner's notice; surely Phil Stone or Mac Reed or any number of other Oxonians would have called it to his attention. If the letter is bogus, why were there no repercussions, no ripple effects? Surely the author of "Dry September" would have moved immediately to distance himself from such outrageous sentiments if they were not his own.

With its authenticity not easily denied, we are left with the problem of what to make of such a troubling document. Near the beginning and close to the ending, Faulkner tries to distance himself from the howling mob, professing to "hold no brief for lynching." But what he offers in between is pretty standard stuff, the routine exculpatory fare of those white supremacists who accepted the "inevitability" of lynching even as they wrung their hands at its unseemliness. If his soul is troubled by any one of the 304 lynchings recorded in Mississippi since 1897,[1] the year of his birth, he does not say as much here. Though he lived and wrote within the very buckle on the great Southern lynching belt—the state with the most total lynchings, the most multiple lynchings, the most per capita, the most female victims, the most victims taken from police custody, the most lynchings without arrest or conviction of mob leaders, the most public support for vigilantism (McMillen 228–33)—he would have his readers believe that summary executions were essentially a media creation, and mostly of unsympathetic "outland newspapers" at that. Surely, he meant to say that most lynchings known to him occurred and were reported elsewhere, *by* foreign or Yankee newspapers, *in* such never-never places as NveZique or in two such as yet uncharted neighborhoods of the District of Columbia as "Oregon, D.C., Washington" and "Halma, Alabama, D.C., America." The geography of the "outland" is unclear, and it is quite possible that these location names resulted from some kind of garbling in the *Commercial Appeal* typesetting of Faulkner's original letter. But though Faulkner's lynchers more smock coats and wooden shoes, even as they glared through leaping flames at French cameras, one should not assume that they were from the Netherlands or Luxembourg, because, as he later claims, "In Europe they don't lynch people."

The "good women" to whom W.H. James refers are the leaders and members of the Association of Southern Women for the Prevention of Lynching (ASWPL), a single-issue reform movement that traced its origins to white Southern women's missionary societies and, more directly, to the Atlanta-based Commission on Interracial Cooperation. Organized regionwide in 1930, the ASWPL formed a Mississippi council early in 1931. Led by Ethel Featherston Stevens of Jackson (i.e., Mrs. J. Morgan Stevens, not Mrs. J. Morgan Spencer) and Bessie C. Alford of McComb, the Mississippi ASWPL quickly became the model state council, the most active in the South. Targeting middle-and upper-class white women, the Mississippi organization endeavored to create an anti-lynching consensus in the most pro-lynching state. The "good women" of the Mississippi council spoke to service clubs and ladies' church, bridge, and literary societies, pressed the law-and-order cause on law enforcement personnel and elected officials, quietly investigated lynchings, and focused the glare of unfavorable publicity on lawlessness. On several occasions, it even confronted mobs of prospective lynchers (Hall, passim; McMillen 246–49).

As the tone of Faulkner's letter suggests, the organization did not enjoy immediate success in Mississippi. When Stevens, Alford, and their associates sought the support of fellow church women they were attacked in the press, often opposed by the men of their denominations, and sometimes criticized by their own husbands and by other women who thought them afflicted with a "Negro Complex." In 1933, for example, their efforts to win the endorsement of the Mississippi Baptist Convention, official body of the state's largest and most conservative denomination, were defeated from the floor. Not one conferee was willing to take the ASWPL's pledge of opposition to mob justice. Not until 1936, after five years of heavy lobbying, did the Mississippi Conference of the Southern Methodist Church adopt its first explicit anti-lynching resolution. With the pious, decent people of the state's mainstream white churches so reluctant to enlist, is there any wonder that the ASWPL's crusade made so little headway for so long? Very likely lynchings would have been less common in Mississippi had those who professed themselves the most God-fearing been less afraid to take a moral stand on the explosive issue of social justice.

Faulkner is mired in a mythological swamp when he accepts James's false assertion that history records no "home-made justice" until after Reconstruction, when he suggests that Southern mobs may have learned their lawless ways from New Englanders who had long practiced "the custom of hanging people of whose conduct they did not approve," and that otherwise decent people take the law into their own hands only after the "blundering hands" of "opportunist[s] and demagogues" somehow bobble the great ball of due process. More preposterous—if more tediously conventional—is his insistence that the "cause" of white vigilantism is black rape of white women, that the victims of lynching must themselves assume the blame because, having violated "the sacredness of [white] womanhood," the mobbee can expect nothing less "in this age" than to die "on cross-ties soaked with gasoline." If, in such instances, blacks are held to a stricter standard than are whites, Faulkner insists that they can nevertheless be comforted by the fact that the truly reproachless are never dispatched by mobbers who know them, and by the fact that softhearted white creditors all too indulgently forgive felonious black borrowing practices. For good or ill, at least in Oktibbeha County where James lived, blacks could quite literally go to the bank on "white sentimentality." Then, just as we hope we've heard it all, Faulkner tells as that, unfortunate as their deeds may be, lynchers—rather like jurors!—"have a way of being right." That closing judgment is the more astounding because immediately before it the writer seems to say that vigilantism serves no legitimate purpose; that is, this is what he said if we have accurately divined the meaning of an unbalanced sentence running deep with negatives: "No balanced man will deny that mob violence serves nothing."

In sum, according to Faulkner, lynchings happen most typically somewhere else, not in Europe and not in the South, but up North and elsewhere in the dimly defined regions of the "outland." When these unfortunate but inevitable breaches happen—particularly, it would appear, when they happen in Mississippi—they may be unnecessary and they could more properly be left to the state, but they are caused by black lawlessness. Best of all, only the defilers of white womanhood need worry because, rough as they are, the dispensers of "home-made justice" are about as discriminating as the courts, and rather more expeditious.

All moral questions aside, there are so many errors here that one scarcely knows where to begin. Of course, Faulkner's lynching letter must be understood in the context of his time and his place. He lived in a moment of radically different social sensibilities from our own, and he cannot be expected to know what we have learned about the tragedy of lynching in the sixty-three years since he wrote this fascinating letter. Clearly, he knew very little of the history and even less of the sociology of lynching upon which we may now draw. Yet one could surely assume that he would have been at least as conversant with the problem of mob violence[2] as were the plantation and business interests of the Deep South that had already, early in the interwar period, recognized that justice by torch light was an anachronism radically inconsistent with the needs of a modernizing society. Any one of W.H. James's "good women" could have provided him with enough statistics to explode nearly every myth that drives his letter.

Bessie Alford and Ethel Stevens would have disabused him of his notions as to the "cause" of lynching. Leaders in a Southern women's "revolt against chivalry" (Hall), the women of the ASWPL devoted much of their time to countering the patriarchal notion that only the fierce gallantry of Southern white men stood between the bestial lust of black males and the sacred honor of white females. Anti-lynching crusaders for several decades had noted that lynching victims were most frequently alleged to have committed the crime of murder, that many "mobbees" died for the most trivial reasons—for unpaid debts, for sassy talk and uppity ways, for reasons of mistaken identity. Nationwide, rape was alleged in only 19 percent of all lynchings; in Mississippi the figure was lower still, 12.7 percent. Even these figures are grossly exaggerated: the operative word is *alleged*. In an age when racial etiquette required that every black male eye be averted in a white woman's presence, when white men were all but universally afflicted with what Wilbur Cash called the "rape complex," even the most innocent encounter between a black male and a white female could be misconstrued. Of that relatively small fraction of "mobbees" charged with rape, most were in fact guilty of lesser affronts, ranging from as little as a misunderstanding or an inadvertent jostle to outright physical assault. Faulkner was also wrong when he suggested that lynching really served no purpose. Reformers knew, if he did not, that lynching was always an effective instrument of white control, the instrument in reserve, a last white resort when other means of fixing the Negroes' "place" seemed unavailing (Wells-Barnett, passim; Brundage 62–63; McMillen 235–37).

Nor was lynching unknown until after Reconstruction. In fact, the word itself comes from the Revolutionary era, when patriot mobs sometimes summarily dealt with British loyalists. In the antebellum period, it is true, the self-interest of Southern slaveholders was the best deterrent to lawless depredations against valuable human chattel. But when servile insurrection, real or imagined, threatened the peace and dignity of the Old South, summary justice often preempted the formal law of slave control. On the other hand, if by *lynching* both James and Faulkner mean *racial lynching*, as clearly they do, they are generally right. Before 1860, interracial conflict did not routinely figure in Southern vigilantism and the victims of mob violence were probably more likely to be white than black (we use the word *probably* here because no one was counting, and the record allows little more than conjecture). During the Confederate period, however, white terror was increasingly visited on blacks. By Civil War's end, Negro lynchings were commonplace in Mississippi and throughout the cotton belt. During the waning days of Reconstruction and the early years of reestablished white rule, mob executions were so frequent as to excite comment only in the black community (Williamson 183–85; Brundage 3–7; McMillen 228; Mounger, passim).

Such figures are well-known to be underestimates—revealing, as every student of the problem would agree, only the tip of the lynching iceberg. What is clear, however, is that Faulkner's assertions notwithstanding, lynching in his time was a problem peculiar to the Southern region, not to the American nation. Of approximately 4,700 total American lynchings recorded for the years from 1880 to 1930, nearly 4,000 of them occurred in the South. During the 1880s, 82 percent of all American lynchings occurred in the South; by the 1920s the figure had risen to 95 percent. If, as Faulkner seems to argue, white Southern mobs learned their vile habits from New Englanders, those same New Englanders had radically changed their ways by the time halfway reliable statistics became available. During the half century after 1880, vigilantes in the Northeast accounted for only nine "mobbees," two whites and seven blacks (Brundage 8).

More troubling than the false particulars of Faulkner's letter is its tone and its guiding assumptions: that James, the "good women" of the ASWPL, and other critics of white lawlessness are unduly alarmist; that the locus of the problem actually lies elsewhere; that the enormity of mob crimes were mitigated by the simple fact that vigilantes usually get the right man and by the regrettable but understandable impatience of good men when legal institutions are corrupted by blundering governmental officials. If much else in the letter is so poorly crafted, so full of nonsequiturs, so opaque as to defy clear understanding, this much seems to be beyond doubt.

The most charitable reading might require one to dismiss this document as unrepresentative, as the product of ill-considered haste, or momentary distemper, occasioned perhaps by a Jeffersonian localist's deep dismay over periodic efforts by organizations as disparate as the NAACP and the Communist Party-USA to win congressional enactment of an intrusive federal anti-lynching law. But there were numerous other factors at work in Faulkner's life at the time he wrote this letter. Indeed, severe complications in Faulkner's personal and professional lives may provide some context for understanding this document. The two months preceding the writing of the letter were extremely difficult ones for Faulkner. Much of November he had spent in the hasty but complete—and expensive—revision of *Sanctuary*; he returned the revisions to Hal Smith in early December and Smith published it on February 9, probably during the week that Faulkner wrote this letter. He was exhausted from the effort of revisioning and revising the novel and, as usual, went on a bender to escape his demons (Blotner 268–77).

The central event of the period, however, was the birth of his and Estelle's daughter Alabama on January 11, her death on January 20, and her burial soon thereafter, following a procession to the cemetery during which Faulkner held her coffin on his knees. Faulkner was so upset with the doctor who had attended Estelle and Alabama that he told friends he had shot him—a claim that started rumors flying around Oxford, rumors some believed; his actual response to his grief was to buy an incubator and donate it to the Oxford hospital. He was devastated by the loss and though he had been drinking heavily, swore, at graveside, that he was not going to escape into drinking.

After the funeral he set about to pay his bills by writing stories to sell to magazines. In the several days following Alabama's death, he wrote or revised "A Death-Drag," "Indians Built a Fence," "The Hound," "Aria Con Amore," and "The Brooch," the latter a version of an earlier story, that incorporates into the revision a painfully autobiographical fictionalized account of the effects of an infant's death on its parents. And there is no reason to think that Faulkner remained entirely true to his vow of sobriety: indeed, the quality of the writing in the letter might suggest that he was not fully in control as he wrote, except that the stories of the period, though not all normally considered among his best, don't bear any of the letter's marks of haste or carelessness, and we should not forget that some have accused him of drinking too much when writing *Absalom, Absalom!*.

Perhaps, however, the biographical context raises a more disturbing question than any it answers, as regards his comments on lynching. Simply put, if he were so desperate to make money, if he were so grief-stricken, so preoccupied with such important personal matters, why would he have taken the time to write such a letter, at such length, on such a topic, responding so hastily, so zealously, and—need we say it?—so mean-spiritedly, to the gentle gratitude of W.H. James? Clearly, James's letter must have intersected with some deep currents in Faulkner's life, touched some supersensitive nerve, that we do not have ready access to. Perhaps what set him off could be nothing more than the fact that his one racial lynching story, "Dry September," which he had written nearly a year earlier, was finally published in that self-same January of Alabama's brief life, so that James's letter and "Dry September" might have appeared in print almost simultaneously. But, as noted earlier, this juxtaposition is all the more curious in that the attitudes struck in "Dry September" are diametrically opposed to those expressed in the letter. Perhaps the best we can do is admit that Faulkner, for all his genius, was in all kinds of ways as much a citizen of Mississippi as his white neighbors, and necessarily shared, in his personal, communal life, many of his community's values. That he managed to transcend these values in his fiction, or at least to demonstrate how problematic they are, does not necessarily mean that he was able to do so in his private life. There's plenty of evidence, including the Russell Howe interview, that he did not. He had written strikingly sympathetic portraits of black characters in his fiction prior to this point. In August of that year, he would begin writing *Light in August*, the novel *par excellence* about the pathology of lynching. Over the rest of his career, he would, of course, write brilliantly and movingly about race relations in both fiction and nonfiction, and in the fifties he would engage himself openly in debates with and attacks on the culture that had nourished him. If there were, in the fifties, occasional, highly revelatory, slips, such as the Howe interview, his was still, for his time, a life exemplary of courage in a highly volatile world. And we might best take this 1931 letter, his first known nonfiction meditation on the subject of lynching, as a record of how far his personal sympathies had to come in order to get where he was in the 1950s, not to say in *Light in August*, *Absalom, Absalom!*, *Go Down, Moses*, and *Intruder in the Dust*.

Few people, certainly not William Faulkner, are so uncomplicated as to be of a single mind on the most explosive issues of their time. The great issues of law and social justice may now, at the most abstract level, be generally agreed upon by people of humane instincts. Tragically, in the Mississippi of 1931, such issues were anything but settled.

WORKS CITED

Blotner, Joseph. *Faulkner: A Biography*. New York: Random House, 1984.
Brundage, W. Fitzhugh, *Lynching in the New South: Georgia and Virginia*, 1880–1930. Urbana: U of Illinois P, 1993.
Daily Clarion Ledger (Jackson, MS), 10 September 1908.
Hall, Jacquelyn Dowd. *Revolt Against Chivalry: Jessie Daniel Ames and the Women's Campaign Against Lynching*. New York: Columbia UP, 1979.

McMillen, Neil R. *Dark Journey: Black Mississippians in the Age of Jim Crow.* Urbana: U of Illinois P, 1989.
Meriwether, James B, and Michael Millgate, eds. *Lion in the Garden: Interviews with William Faulkner 1926–1962.* New York: Random House, 1968.
Mounger, Dwyn M. "Lynching in Mississippi, 1830–1930." Master's Thesis, Mississippi State U, 1961.
National Association for the Advancement of Colored People, Thirty Years of Lynching in United States 1889–1918, (1919); reprint New York: Arno P, 1969.
———. Annual Reports. New York: NAACP, 1919–1930.
Tuskegee Institute Newsclipping File, microfilm reel 226, frame 0747.
Wells-Barrett, Ida. *On Lynchings: Southern Horrors; A Red Recorded; Mob Rule in New Orleans* (1892, 1895, 1900). New York: Amo, 1969.
Williamson, Joel. T. *Crucible of Race: Black White Relations in the American South Since Emancipation.* New York: Oxford UP, 1984.
We are grateful to Robert T. Zangrando, of The University of Akron, and James Hollandsworth, of the University of Southern Mississippi, for reading and commenting on this essay.
*Reprinted from *Faulkner Journal*, Vol. 8, No. 1 (Fall 1992), 3–14, by permission of the journal.

NOTES

1. Although there are no satisfactory lynching data, most scholarly analyses of the problem begin with the annual compilations of the Tuskegee Institute and the National Association for the Advancement of Colored People (NAACP).

2. Of the three lynchings then recorded by the NAACP for Faulkner's home county of Lafayette, two occurred in Oxford, one of them since his birth. A fourth Lafayette County lynching occurred in 1936, when a black defendant on trial for murder was taken from an Oxford jail and summarily executed. There is also evidence of at least one other lynching, this one occurring in 1885, too early to appear on the victim lists of either Tuskegee or the NAACP. On September 8, 1908, when Faulkner was eleven years old, Nelse Patton was lynched in Oxford. Among the leaders of the Patton mob was a former U.S. senator (*Daily Clarion Ledger*; NAACP; Blotner 32–33).

Chapter Six

Lynching in Richard Wright's "Big Boy Leaves Home"

Toru Kiuchi

The origin of the word "lynching" has several meanings. The most common account has is derived from Charles Lynch, a justice in Virginia, who excessively punished Loyalists during the Revolutionary War. Thus, extreme punishment became known as "Lynch Law." The early definition of lynching refers to frontier vigilantism. In June 1916 eight-year-old Richard Wright began to live with his maternal grandparents at Lynch Street, Jackson, Mississippi (Fabre 17). The name of the street was given in the honor of John R. Lynch, an African-American politician. Wright was familiar to the word "lynch" since his boyhood.

After the Civil War and Reconstruction, lynching took on a new, racial implication and was primarily carried out by whites against African Americans. This racial violence gave white southerners a way to express their white supremacy. According to the Tuskegee Institute archive, compiled in February 1979,[1] 4,743 people were lynched between 1882 and 1968 in the United States, including 3,446 African Americans and 1,297 whites. More than seventy-three percent of the lynchings in the post-Civil War period occurred in the southern states. The peak of lynching occurred in 1882, after Southern white Democrats had regained control of state legislators. In the South, an estimated two or three blacks were lynched each week in the late nineteenth and early twentieth centuries. Mississippi had the highest lynching rate from 1882 to 1963 among other states with 581 lynchings (42 whites, 539 blacks).[2]

The first two lynchings by mob violence in the history of the United States broke out along the Mississippi River in 1835 to suppress a massive slave revolt prepared to murder all the white men in the area (Dray 22–23). Since

Wright was born in 1908 near Natchez, a riverbank town of the Mississippi River, Wright's life began with fear of potential lynching. By the year 1908, lynching had come almost exclusively to mean "the summary execution of Southern black men" (Dray 18). The year 1908 is furthermore one of the turning points in the history of lynching because the race issue of lynching became a national problem, although it was only locally limited to the South until then.[3] In 1908 when a major race riot took place in Springfield, Illinois, one of the most "Northern" towns and the final resting place of Abraham Lincoln, the cause for the riot was "white anxiety over an influx of Southern blacks" into the city. The black residential areas were all leveled down by a mob with many black people lynched. Northerners noticed that it was time to "fight back, not against the South, but against race hatred itself" (Dray 169).

The now national concern led to the founding of National Association for the Advancement of Colored People (NAACP) next year in 1909, chiefly to launch out on an anti-lynching campaign across the United States (Dray 168–70). The long anti-lynch campaign of NAACP was undertaken by *The Crisis*, the official magazine founded in 1910 by W.E.B. Du Bois as an editor. Wright was in many ways connected to the NAACP in his life as an avid reader of the official magazine which often featured anti-lynch articles (Wright to Ellison, 21 May 1940, Library of Congress). He was awarded the Spingarn Medal for *Native Son* on 27 June 1941, a medal given annually by the association for outstanding achievements by an African American. Even during his childhood Wright was constantly exposed to articles and photographs about lynching published in the magazine because the circulation of the magazine reached 100,000 by 1918 and it became an integral part of black cultural life.

As Wright confronted the terror of lynching as a boy, 50 to 100 lynchings occurred annually across the South in most years from 1889 to 1923 according to Dray (x). Wright felt as if he were a lynching victim even though he was not in the immediate danger of being lynched as he confessed in his autobiography: "I had never in my life been abused by whites . . . but I had already become as conditioned to their existence as though I had been the victim of a thousand lynchings" (*BB* [*AH*] 87).[4] Congressman John Lewis (1940–2020) also confesses the identical memory with Wright: "As a young child, growing up very poor in rural Alabama, I heard stories about lynchings and about the nightriders coming through, intimidating and harassing black people. At the time it all seemed nightmarish, unreal US even unbelievable" (7).

The lynching scene at the end of Wright's short story, "Big Boy Leaves Home," is therefore a usually political representation of his fear for lynching based on his indirect experiences since his youth until he turned about the mid-thirties. In Wright's story, four black boys just appear naked before a white woman, but her scream develops into lynching. Big Boy knows that he, not Bobo, killed a white man but sees his totally innocent friend Bobo, who did not even touch the white woman, captured, hanged, and burned alive on a tree by vicious white vigilantes. He witnesses the deep-rooted racial prejudice against the sexual relationship between a black man and a white woman, namely "the myth of the black rapist," the complexities of lynching and rape, which was "encoded in the general critical discourse" (Schwenk 312). This chapter will examine how Wright deals with lynching in "Big Boy Leaves Home" and will discuss how lynching in Wright's story closely reflects real historical occurrences and how such retribution causes unbearable pain and traumatizes black people.

Lynching, "both in its literal form and as an abstract, brooding threat," is a motif in almost all of Wright's woks (Dray 367). At the age of three Wright unintentionally sets the house afire and partially destroys it in Natchez, Mississippi in winter 1911. His mother beats him severely, and he was kept to his bed with fever for several days. The severe beating overlaps with his image of lynching, amassed in his mind as he grows up, and never leaves his mind as he writes in the earliest draft of *Black Boy* tentatively entitled "Black Confession": "The terrible beating I receive is now dim in my memory and painful even to this day; perhaps I've never succeeded in veiling it with anything within me, or hiding it so deeply that it cannot come welling up in memory" (7). His grandmother's Seventh-Day Adventist's image of the hell is also influential as Butler interprets: "His grandmother's frighteningly severe view of the world is later ominously paralleled when Wright as a teenager hears about a black man being lynched, ritualistically hung, and burned when he is alleged to have violated the South's racial codes" (61).

After Wright's family moves to Memphis, Tennessee in fall 1911, his father orders his son to kill the noisy kitten when it disturbs his sleep. Knowing that his father does not mean it, Wright deliberately kills it:

> I found a piece of rope, made a noose, slipped it about the kitten's neck, pulled it over a nail, then jerked the animal clear of the ground. It gasped, slobbered, spun, doubled, clawed the air frantically; finally its mouth gaped and its pink-white tongue shot out stiffly. (*BB* [*AH*] 12)

His mother tells Wright to bury the cat in the ground at night to his frightening: "Shuddering, I fumbled at the rope and the kitten dropped to the pavement with a thud that echoed in my mind for many days and nights" (*BB* [*AH*] 15). The burning of the house, his mother's beating, and the hanging of the kitten at the beginning of his life are all similar to a lynching ritual and portends Wright's life as dominated by his fear for lynching.

As the beginning of the autobiography constructs Wright's image of lynching, the opening scenes in Wright's other novels and short stories more often than not reinforce his fears. In the opening scene in "Big Boy Leaves Home," other three boys insist going to swim in a white man's creek but only Big Boy disagrees with the idea saying "N git *lynched?* Hell naw!" (20).[5] But he finally witnesses the lynching of one of his friends Bobo.

When Wright's mother Ella brings her family to Elaine, Arkansas in 1916, lynching is not real terror but only a rumor to eight-year-old Wright. However, the reality of lynching becomes clear when Uncle Hoskins, a prosperous saloon owner,[6] with whom Wright lives for a while, ignores the threats from the whites and is killed. The Wrights immediately have to move to West Elaine, Arkansas, facing the lynching terror when his uncle Hoskins[7] "had simply been plucked from our midst and we, figuratively, had fallen on our faces to avoid looking into that white-hot face of terror that we knew loomed somewhere above us" (*BB* [*AH*] 64). In Wright's real life, the fear of lynching was always tangible for him with his boyhood experiences of "white terror at close hand" (Rowley 12).

Just back in Jackson in fall 1919 eleven-year-old Wright hears the news that the armed white mob and five hundred state militiamen killed several dozen African Americans of Elaine (Fabre 25) but he was safe because it happened just after the Wrights left there for Jackson. Jackson was also thrown into a commotion because the concerned whites formed a mob, many of whom came to Elaine from the surrounding states as far away as Mississippi and Tennessee. The mass lynching of black sharecroppers occurred not only in Elaine but also across the United States in 1919. There were twenty-eight public lynchings in the first half of the year and a series of twenty riots all over the United States. The following summer and fall came to be known as "The Red Summer" of 1919.

Three years later in 1922, when fourteen-year-old Wright starts to sell a Chicago newspaper in Jackson only to be ashamed to know that the paper is pro-Ku Klux Klan literature. A man to whom Wright tries to sell the paper notifies him about the shocking fact and "read aloud a long article in which lynching was passionately advocated as a solution for the problem of the Negro" (*BB* [*AH*] 154).[8] The national and local newspapers in 1922 printed many articles about lynching, further terrorizing Wright.

Two years later in summer 1924 Ray "Chunky" Robinson, a bellboy at Edwards Hotel, a large hotel in Jackson, was arrested for relationship with a white woman and tortured to death in the woods on the outskirts of the city. Wright was in Jackson and himself sexually mature at the age of sixteen, so he was horrified to know about this because Ray was the older brother of his classmate Carl T. Robinson (Fabre 51). Deeply shocked, he wrote in his autobiography: "What I had heard altered the look of the world, . . . creating a sense of distance between me and the world in which I lived" (*BB* [*AH*] 203). The feeling will lead to the poem of becoming a virtual lynching victim, "Between the World and Me," eleven years later published in the July–August

1935 issue of *Partisan Review*, which stressed: "And sooty details of the scene rose, thrusting themselves between the world and me" (246).

After Wright's arrival in Memphis, articles on lynching appear in the *Memphis Commercial Appeal*. In October 1925, five black men were accused of robbing and mortally wounding Grover Nicholas in Coahoma County, Mississippi. The five defendants included Lindsey Coleman, acquitted at the trial but abducted outside the courthouse and hanged on 19 December 1925. Numerous accounts concerning Coleman's trial and lynching continued to appear in *Memphis Commercial Appeal*.[9] H. L. Mencken's article "Police Near Solution of Headless Murder" in *Memphis Commercial Appeal* (25 January 1926) reports that "the body of a murdered young woman was found in the remains of a fire" and articles are published in *The Crisis* which deplored the increased number of lynching.[10]

In April 1927 floods in the Mississippi Valley caused property loss of $300 million. Memphis and western Tennessee were under water; so were Mississippi, Louisiana, and southwest Illinois. Wright later writes short stories, "Silt," "Fire and Cloud," "Down by the Riverside," and "The Man Who Saw the Flood," based on the Great Flood. The Great Flood brought on more violence than usual in the unusually violent South. Nearing his nineteenth birthday in late November 1927, Wright was exposed to more news about lynchings caused by white people's irritation with the flood in the South. As Wright laments that "News of lynchings were frequent" (*BB* [*AH*] 298), the *Memphis Commercial Appeal* (22 April 1927) reported that 400 black men were abandoned on top of the levee along with more lynching news.[11]

After he finally crossed the boundary line of the Black Belt from Memphis to Chicago in late 1927, Wright got a job at the post office in Chicago in summer 1928 following some menial work. Wright read the leftist literary magazine *Anvil*, which stimulates his decision to become a writer. In early 1929 Wright lost a job at the post office and returned to his dishwashing job at a cafeteria. The boss lady is amazed to find Wright reading a copy of the *American Mercury* (*BB* [*AH*] 322), in which Walter White, an anti-lynching NAACP activist, wrote "I Investigate Lynchings," an article on the number of lynchings: "Of the forty-one lynchings and eight race riots I have investigated for the National Association for the Advancement of Colored People during the past ten years, all of the lynchings and seven of the riots occurred in rural or semi-rural communities" (81). As White proves later in the article, the number of lynchings across the United States decreased throughout the 1920s but the number amounted to "twenty-two in just the first eight months of 1930" (81). The beginning of the Great Depression made things even worse for southern black people. White wrote James Weldon Johnson regarding the increase of lynching deaths: "I am inclined to believe that the unemployment and the financial depression play a part—lynchings usually go up in number when the price of cotton goes down" (22 August 1930, Yale University).

Depending on public welfare for bread during the early 1930s, Wright in abject poverty began to devote himself to the John Reed Club. Since the campaign to defend the Scottsboro Boys begins in spring 1931, Wright was always conscious of the development reported in black weekly newspapers such as *Chicago Defenders*.[12] As James Miller argues, Wright encounters Scottsboro "through the deeply embedded structures of thought, feeling, and memory that had been shaped by his experiences as a black man who had come of age in the Jim Crow South during the 1920s" (*Remembering Scottsboro* 144). However, Wright reorganized the importance of literature, learning much from Langston Hughes's *Scottsboro Limited: Four Poems and a Play in Verse* (1932) and other writers' works. Wright mentions the case in his works for this reason: "The Reds sure scared them white folks down South when they put up that fight for the Scottsboro boys" (*Lawd Today!* 152). Jan Erlone in *Native Son* asks Bigger Thomas: "You've read about the Scottsboro boys?" (*Native Son* 75).

Keenly interested in the development of the Scottsboro case, Wright went to Detroit in May 1934 to hear Allan Taub (1902–1995), one of the attorneys in the Scottsboro case, who almost got lynched himself, speak on behalf of the Scottsboro Boys. Wright is introduced to Taub who gave him a lift to Chicago. On the ride back to Chicago, "between bites of hamburgers, they found a great common interest—the Negro people" (*New York Age*, 24 May 1941).

The NAACP announcement in the December 1934 issue of *The Crisis* draws Wright's attention, declaring the war against lynching. The issue contained many stories about lynching written by members of the Writers' League against Lynching. Special messages were from Senators Edward P. Costigan and Robert F. Wagner, coauthors of the federal anti-lynching bill to be reintroduced in the next Congress in 1935 (351). The issue also revealed that over 5000 lynchings from 1882 to1934.

Wright starts his literary career as a leftist poet by publishing leftist poems in leftist magazines from 1934 to 1936. His early poems seemingly appeal to the workers of the world to unite. However, a small part of them is an outcry for anti-lynching action: "And the black hands waved and beat fearfully at the tall flames that cooked and charred the black flesh" ("I Have Seen Black Hands" 16); "*DEATH TO LYNCHERS!*" ("I Am a Red Slogan" 35); "Swinging Southward Plunging the radiator into the lynch-mob" ("Transcontinental" 54); and "Lynch Negro Who Wouldn't Say 'Mister'" ("Hearst Headline Blues" 14).

"Obsession," a poem published in the No. 2, February 1935 issue of *Midland Left*, has lynching itself as a theme: "Yet again I must speak of it.

... Of fire cooking human flesh" (14). In "Two Million Black Voices," a report of the first National Negro Congress in Chicago on 14–16 February 1936, Wright states that in "*Time*: an era of lynching, Jim Crowism" black America is a victim of oppression "Because Negroes are black, they are hated, lynched and murdered" (15).

Howard Nutt, a poet from Peoria, Illinois, and a friend from the Chicago John Reed Club, sees a call for submission to *The New Caravan* in the September 1935 issue of *The New Republic* and suggests Wright to submit a short story to it. Five years later Wright wrote an introduction to Nutt's collection of poems, *Special Laughter*, published in 1940: "Of all the poems in this volume, I like *Mother Goose* best. It is our poem, an American poem, as American as strawberry shortcake or lynching!" (xi). Lynching is, to Wright and Nutt, a contemporary significant subject because some of Nutt's poems in *Special Laughter*, such as "Decadent Finale" with lynching as a topic, were already published in the August 1936 issue of Harriet Monroe's *Poetry*. At the suggestion of Nutt, Wright sent the manuscript of "Big Boy Leaves Home" in late December 1935 to Paul Rosenfeld (1890–1946), one of the editors of *The New Caravan* to be published from W.W. Norton (Rosenfeld to Wright, 2 January 1936, Yale University).

Alfred Kreymborg (1883–1966), Lewis Mumford (1895–1990), and Rosenfeld were editors for *The New Caravan*. Kreymborg, a progressive poet himself, already published the first epoch-making anthology of imagism, *Des Imagistes*, in his little magazine *The Glebe* (February 1914). The anthology, later that year published as a book by Charles and Albert Boni in New York, and Harold Monro's Poetry Bookshop in London, launched the new poetry movement known as Imagism. Kreymborg was so responsive to a new literary trend that it was not difficult for him to discern the unprecedented originality of the lynching scene in "Big Boy Leaves Home." The short story is thus unanimously accepted for the anthology on 3 March 1936 with the editor's opinion that "Of all the *Caravan* stories I have so far read, yours is the one which moves me most" (Rosenfeld to Wright, Yale University). One of the editors Kreymborg is moved to read "Big Boy Leaves Home" and write a poem "The Old South: For Richard Wright," ironically warning white people not to let a black man learn how to read and write: "Or he will arouse the human race / to overthrow the Night!" (*The Crisis* [January 1941]: 29). Wright was lucky enough to be understood by Kreymborg and other editors in terms of a literary breakthrough achieved in the short story.

The story marks for the first time that that Wright has been noticed by the non-Communist white press, published in a book, and paid for his writing (Fabre 133). Wright wrote a short autobiographical notice "Richard Wright" for *The New Caravan*:

I am a Negro and was born in 1909 in the state of Mississippi, twenty-five miles from the nearest railroad. While still in grammar school my parents dragged me through the following towns: Natchez, Mississippi; Jackson, Mississippi; Greenwood, Mississippi; Carters, Mississippi; Elaine, Arkansas; Helena Arkansas; West Helena, Arkansas, and Memphis, Tennessee. At fifteen, on finishing grammar school, I ran away from home. To make a living I washed dishes, swept streets, dug ditches, portered, waited on tables, bus-boyed, bell-boyed, carried messages, off-barred in brickyards, sold insurance, and clerked in the United States Post Office. I've published in the *New Masses*, *International Literature*, *Partisan Review*, and the *Anvil*. At present I'm busy with a novel. (663)

In this autobiographical sketch, Wright deliberately distorts facts probably at the suggestion of editors. Wright was born in 1908, not in 1909. He does not specify Roxie, Mississippi for his birthplace. Roxie still had a Y. & M. V. Railroad station in 1908, so it is not "twenty-five miles from the nearest railroad." It is only his mother, not his parents, who dragged him through the states. At fifteen in 1923, Wright did not yet finish his grammar school, Smith-Robertson Public School in Jackson, but graduated from the school two years later on 29 May 1925. He did not run away from home yet after the graduation but entered Lanier High School in Jackson in September 1925. He ran away from home on 10 October 1925 when he was seventeen (*BB [AH]*, 244). He pretends to be an uneducated author, putting verbs to an improper use with the intention of showing that he is a writer coming from a poverty background.

The reason for all the intentional alteration in writing is that Wright does not want readers to identify him. The lynching scene at the end of "Big Boy Leaves Home" is so graphic, shocking, and disturbing in comparison with other contemporary fiction that Wright does not want his readers to track him down and find out who the author is. It was still quite courageous for a black writer to write a provocative lynching scene in 1936. Two following facts prove Wright's carefulness. The cover of the April 1935 issue of *The Crisis* features the picture of three black men, Ed Brown, Yank Ellington, and Henry Shields of Kemper County, Mississippi, who "Escapes Noose; Near Death from Torture." On 1 May 1935 the anti-lynching Wagner-Costigan bill, declaring that "National problems demand national remedies," fell through at the Congress due to the filibuster by Senators from Southern states even though 53.7 million Americans supported it (Dray 356).

When he was fourteen years old in Jackson, Mississippi in summer 1922, Wright was the head of a group of the most active and self-reliant children of the neighborhood. The group included Dick Jordan, Perry Booker, and Joe Brown (Fabre 43). Bobo,[13] Lester, Buck, and Big Boy in "Big Boy Leaves

Home" are the corresponding characters who are old and strong enough to jump onto Jim Harvey's back, "striking the man in the mouth with the barrel" of the rifle (29). In Wright's poem, "Spread Your Sunrise!," a line of "Go on, Big Boy, go on!" (26), a desperate call to "a bushy-haired giant-child," might be evidence for the original idea of the name for the protagonist in the short story.

The short story begins with an Edenic setting where the four boys enjoy themselves in nature seemingly in the American South, namely Jackson, singing the dozens "*Yo mama.*" Margaret Walker answers the interviewer about the source of the song: "You open Richard Wright and read, 'Your mama don't wear no drawers.' Where did he get it? He got it from Zora" (Graham 181). Wright's review of *Their Eyes Were Watching God* by Hurston was published in 1937 and Walker sent Wright some African-American folk tales for his information (Walker to Wright, 1 July 1937, Yale University). Muck-Boy, one of the characters reminiscent of Big Boy, begins to chant the dozens toward the end of Hurston's novel:

Yo' mama don't wear no *Draws*
    Ah seen her when she took 'em *Off* (232–33)

Similarly, "Big Boy Leaves Home" begins with the dozens four black boys singing:

Yo mama don wear no drawers . . .
    Ah seena when she pulled em off (17)

Wright borrowed the dozens from Hurston but tried to show, by putting the folk song of African-American vernacular tradition at the very beginning of the short story, that he could present a truer picture of black life because in his review of Hurston's novel he criticizes that Hurston's characters "swing like a pendulum eternally in that safe and narrow orbit in which America likes to see the Negro live: between laughter and tears" ("Laughter and Tears" 25).

"Big Boy Leaves Home" has three more kinds of songs in total, each placed at the pivotal point. The second is "*Dis train bound fo Glory*" (19), traditional gospel song popular during the 1920s, with which four black boys are "thinking of a train bound for Glory" (19). Because the story's setting of time and place is supposedly the early 1920s and Jackson, four kinds of trains on the "Illinoy Central" (43) are running in the story. According to the Illinois Central Railroad timetable, published on 12 May 1929, number four is the *Panama Limited* northbound when one of the boys calls out, "There goes number fo!" (19). Number seven is the *Panama Limited* southbound when one of the boys hears from Harvey's swimming pool, "There goes number seven" (26). Number nine is the *Seminole* southbound when Big Boy hides in the hole, waiting for Bobo, imagining that he is Casey Jones[14] on the Southern Pacific[15] (42) and says to himself: "He heard number nine, far away and mournful" (42). Number twelve, the *Hawkeye Limited* northbound, is heard when the white mob catches Bobo: "Then he heard number twelve, its bell tolling and whistle crying as it slid along the rails" (47).

The third song is *"Bye n bye / Ah wanna piece of pie"* (22), kid's hand-clapping song, with which they "climbed over a barbed-wire fence" (22) and enter another white world. And the fourth song is *"We'll hang ever nigger t a sour apple tree"* (47), a deliberate mockery of the famous marching song "John Brown's Body" during the Civil War, sung to the tune of "The Battle Hymn of the Republic," whose lyrics are changed from "hang Jeff Davis on" to *"hang ever nigger t."* While the first three songs are sung by four black boys, the fourth song alone is sung by a lynch mob, who deteriorate African-American vernacular tradition at the beginning of lynching. Here the environment changes suddenly as Bobo is caught by the white mob: "WE GOT IM! WE GOT IM!" (47). The warm sun takes the place of the chill of the cold water and "The sky sagged low, heavy with clouds. Wind was rising" (48).

Not only the black writers but also white writers tried their hand at a lynching scene before "Big Boy Leaves Home."[16] However, as far as the representation of a lynching scene is concerned, no other writers than Wright are successful in transforming of "white-on-black lynching from a symbol of black death to a symbol of black disempowerment" (Hill 102). As James Miller notes that "no African American writer before him had captured more effectively the devastating social and psychological terror unleashed on black men" (*Remembering Scottsboro* 144), Big Boy's imagination of fighting with white people in spite of Bobo's being lynched at the end is an unprecedented portrayal of a black boy's violent if imaginative counterattack murder of a white man.

For example, a lynching scene in Paul Laurence Dunbar's short story "The Lynching of Jube Benson" (1904)[17] is indirectly narrated as Doctor Melville unemotionally relates to Gordon Fairfax and Handon Gay, to which the reader listens: "Well, that part was the least of it, save that Hiram Daly stepped aside to let me be the first to pull upon the rope. It was lax at first. Then it tightened, and I felt the quivering soft weight resist my muscles. Other hands joined and Jube swung off his feet" (7). The narrative structure is the same as Wright's first short story "Superstition" (1931), in which the reader indirectly listens to Fently Burrow narrate "a strange incident" to Matt Brocson and Bert Meadows. Wright finds the narrative structure in "Superstition" unsuccessful, deciding not to use his middle name Nathaniel ever for his works. "Big Boy

Leaves Home" is narrated in the third person directly to the reader because, after reading Henry James's *The Art of the Novel: Critical Prefaces*, which he regarded as the literary Bible momentarily, Wright rewrote the short story (Fabre 110), changing from the first person narrative to the third person at the suggestion of James who observed: "Suffice it, to be brief, that the first person, in the long piece, is a form foredoomed to looseness, and that looseness, never much my affair, had never been so little so as on this particular occasion" (364).

For another lynching scene at the end of *Holiday* (1923), Waldo Frank ends with the novel, providing an ordinary murder scene: "The men work fast. Day glooms. Day dies. The Square sinks into a well of night. A rope whips taut. A body dangles in air. A body dangles in flame" (232). In Erskine Caldwell's short story "Kneel to the Rising Sun" (1935), a black sharecropper Clem's defiance instigates brutal landlord Gunnard to lynch Clem. Wright was first "enthusiastic about *Kneel to the Rising Sun*" after the reading (Washington *Star*, 11 November 1945) (*Books & Writers* 23) but not much to his satisfaction because Caldwell's presentation sounds like an ordinary murder scene: "The crumpled body was tossed time after time, like a sackful of kittens being killed with an automatic shotgun, as charges of lead were fired into it from all sides" (295–96).

The lynching depicted in "Big Boy Leaves Home" is partially based upon Wright's real experiences in Jackson in summer 1922. When he was fourteen years old, Wright swam in the Rock Bottom Creek, southwest of the city, but was alarmed by Mr. Barrett (Fabre 43). Wright recalls the incident in "Black Confession":

> One Sunday spring morning a group of us boys met on the church grounds. It seemed inhuman to go inside and sit still for hours on such a glorious day. Somebody remarked that the creek in Barret's Pasture was full, just right for swimming. And the sun was shining, growing hotter each moment. We began to edge away from the church, and finally we were out of sight of the church steeple and its white cross and we felt better. Ditching church for good, we hiked toward the woods. It had rained recently and the green earth had a strong wet sweet smell. We soon saw other boys who, too, had felt as we had felt and who were on their way to swim, and sang songs, joked, wrestled, argued, dared each other, and filled the woods with wild laughter. (231)

The autobiographical fact is quite similar to the beginning of four boys' escape from school in "Big Boy Leaves Home" although the episode was left out from *Black Boy* when the book was published. Hereafter, however, the story goes in a different direction. Robert Ellis, one of the four boys, dived in the water of the creek but the current was so strong that he did not come up and was drowned. Wright recollects the result after the incident in "Black Confession":

> They found Robert Ellis's body the next week, some two hundred yards from where he had dived. We talked about it at school—feeling safely away from the creek—with the air of boys who knew. Those of us who had seen him dive took on a new dignity and growupness in the eyes of the others and we related our versions of how it happened with lurid detail, yet within still trembling a little from our fright. We still played hooky from Sunday School, but we did not go swimming. (234)

Wright got the idea of the first half of "Big Boy Leaves Home" from this accident of his friend Robert Ellis. On the other hand, the last half comes from an episode related in the interview with David Poindexter (Dex), who worked as a stevedore on the Mississippi River and later settled in Chicago, making friends with Wright as an active comember of the Communist Party. Wright took a keen interest in Poindexter's life and conducted many interviews with him. Wright began to spend many evenings at his friend Poindexter's apartment in December 1934 to write an African-American's biographical sketch (Fabre 106). He finished a two-page draft of "Biography of a Bolshevik, Notes on David Poindexter" based upon the conversation with him. But the Communist Party advises him not to see "Dex" at all since "Dex" opposes the Party's Popular Front (Fabre 107), forcing Wright to give up the sketch but the incident happens to initiate the writing of "Big Boy Leaves Home":

> I gave up the idea of the biographical sketches and settled finally upon writing a series of short stories, using the material I had got from Ross [Poindexter] and his friends, building upon it, inventing. I wove a tale of a group of black boys trespassing upon the property of a white man and the lynching that followed. The story was published in an anthology under the title of *Big Boy Leaves Home*, but its appearance came too late to influence the Communists who were questioning the use to which I was putting their lives. (*BB [AH]* 399–400)

Poindexter relates an episode to Wright in the interview:

> I remember during the midst of the war two friends of mine went to a nearby creek to fish. This creek was near the estate of a big white planter and landlord, a deputy sheriff, one of the rulers of that region. This planter had a son about the age of my two friends, Chester Hogan and Clyde Boyd. While fishing there the son of this landlord came by and asked the boys: Well, niggers, what have you caught? And, as boys will, they answered: We done caught a cold. With that the planter's son left wordlessly. A little later, unknown to the boys, he returned with a loaded, double-barrel shot-gun. Laying the barrel of the gun upon the fence, he called to my two friends and said: Niggers, what did you say you had caught?

When they turned around to see who or what was speaking to them, the planter's son fired, killing Hogan instantly. (4).

The episode continues with the counterattack of Boyd, who shot and instantly killed the planter's son, just out of prison on bail, with a double-barrel shot-gun, just as Big Boy who takes back a rifle from a white man and shoots him dead in "Big Boy Leaves Home." This boy Clyde, according to the interview with Poindexter, had three uncles who lived on the outskirts of the city who sheltered Clyde and who stated that they were willing to fight for him with their own lives. These three uncles are reminiscent of three uncles, Brother Sanders, Brother Jenkins, and Elder Peters, whom Big Boy's father calls immediately after he knew what happens to Big Boy.

"Big Boy Leaves Home" is accordingly the creative combination of the author's own experiences and the episode in the interview with Poindexter. The lynching scene, however, is Wright's total imagination starting from the scene where Big Boy hides in the kiln to escape the lynch mob. Big Boy gets ready for the coming lynch mob:

> But ain no use in thinkin erbout tha; wait till trouble come fo yuh start fightin it. But if tha mob came one by one hed wipe em all out. Clean up the whole bunch. He caught one by the neck and choked him long and hard, choked him till his tongue and eyes popped out. Then he jumped upon his chest and stomped him like he had stomped that snake. When he had finished with one, another came. He choked him too. Choked till he sank slowly to the ground, gasping . . .
> "Hoalo!"
> Big Boy snatched his fingers from the white man's neck and looked over the fields. (44–45)

The paragraph is narrated in a special way. The subjunctive mood is employed in the sentence: "But if tha mob came one by one hed wipe em all out." However, the tense is changed to the past in the sentence: "He caught one by the neck and choked him long and hard, choked him till his tongue and eyes popped out." The choking of white men is done in Big Boy's daydream. Big Boy is then awakened from the daydream by the real lynch mob's cry "Hoalo!" Followed is the combination of the first half in the subjunctive mood and the latter half in the past tense: "Big Boy snatched his fingers from the white man's neck and looked over the fields." This style gives ambience to Wright's reading of the lynching scene.

In January 1935 Wright read a longer version of "Big Boy Leaves Home" to his friend Jane Newton's to substantiate the story's effect, but did not know how to continue the narrative, so he condensed it into a short story (Fabre 113). In May Wright was invited to give a reading at the Literary Society at the University of Illinois, Chicago by William Attaway, his friend and a writer, who heard him there and was impressed with it. After the first paragraph, half the audience fled and nobody except Attaway and Wright were in the room at the end of the reading (*Daily Worker*, 26 June 1939). Frank Marshall Davis, one of the comembers of the Chicago's South Side Writers Club, paints a picture of Wright at one meeting:

> When he finished, nobody spoke for several minutes. We were too much moved by his power. Then there was a flood of praise. Frankly I was overwhelmed. We realized this was a major talent, but none of us dreamed how great he would become. (240)

In late May the short story was completed, but Wright continued to revise it, on the advice of his friends Bill Jordan, and James Farrell. He then read the manuscript at Northwestern University at Evanston in June. Professor Lawrence Martin there was so enthusiastic at Wright's reading that he recommended Wright for fellowships (Fabre 134; 547n19). Wright gave another reading at the Literary Society at the University of Illinois, Chicago in late June (Kiuchi and Hakutani 47–48).

Wright performed another reading at the Roosevelt Road Cultural Center under the aegis of the South Side Writers' Group, arranged by Abraham Chapman in mid-April 1936 (Chapman to Wright, 8 April 1936, Yale University). Margaret Walker recalls Wright's powerful reading at the center: "I heard a man expounding on the sad state of Negro writing at that point in the thirties and he was punctuating his remarks with pungent epithets. I drew back in Sunday-school horror, totally shocked by his strong speech, but I steeled myself to hear him out" (Ray and Farnsworth 50).

In the narrative method Big Boy is thus represented to fight an imaginary but realistic battle with a lynch mob and then to see his innocent friend Bobo captured, hanged, and burned alive on a tree by vicious white vigilantes. Wright puts a question on himself in his autobiography: "The short story, *Big Boy Leaves Home*, had posed a question: What quality of will must a Negro possess to live and die with dignity in a country that denied his humanity?" (*BB* [*AH*] 402). Big Boy's imaginary battle with white men and the lynching of Bobo provides Wright's answer. Although Bobo is powerless to prevent his lynching, "he refuses to divulge Big Boy's hiding place. By doing so, Wright suggests that Bobo chose to die on his own terms rather than those of the lynchers" (Hill 97).

The next morning after the lynching Big Boy becomes aware of a still moment when he sees light against dark, the transcendental beauty of nature against the ugly aspect of human nature. Dawn breaks with a peaceful morning coming for the truck to deliver Big Boy to Chicago. Wright created social fiction not so much with the artistry the author can put into it as with a sense of urgency the subject demands. In this story the urgency does not come from the collective will of black people but from the conscience of humanity, the collective will of decent individuals living anywhere.

WORKS CITED

Austen, Jane. *Pride and Prejudice*. Ed. Joseph Pearce. 1898. San Francisco: Ignatius Press, 2008.

Butler, Robert J. "Seeking Salvation in a Naturalistic Universe: Richard Wright's Use of His Southern Religious Background in *Black Boy (American Hunger)*." *Richard Wright: New Readings in the 21st Century*. Ed. Alice Mikal Craven and William E. Dow. New York: Palgrave Macmillan, 2011. 55–68.

Caldwell, Erskine. "Kneel to the Rising Sun." *The Oxford Book of the American South: Testimony, Memory, and Fiction*. Ed. Edward L. Ayers and Bradely C. Mittendorf. Oxford: Oxford UP, 1997. 277–96.

Davis, Frank Marshall. *Livin' the Blues: Memoirs of a Black Journalist and Poet*. Madison: U of Wisconsin P, 1992.

Dray, Philip. *At the Hands of Persons Unknown: The Lynching of Black America*. New York: Random House, 2002.

Dunbar, Paul Laurence. "The Lynching of Jube Benson." *Black American Short Stories: A Century [One Hundred Years] of the Best*. Ed. John Henrik Clarke. New York: Hill and Wang, 1993. 1–8.

Fabre, Michel. *The Unfinished Quest of Richard Wright*. Urbana: U of Illinois P, 1993.

Frank, Waldo. *Holiday*. 1923. Urbana: U of Illinois P, 2003.

Graham, Maryemma, ed. *Conversations with Margaret Walker*. Jackson: UP of Mississippi, 2002.

Hill, Karlos K. *Beyond the Rope: The Impact of Lynching on Black Culture and Memory*. New York: Cambridge UP, 2016.

Hurston, Zora Neale. *Their Eyes Were Watching God*. 1937. Urbana: U of Illinois P, 1978.

James, Henry. *The Art of Novel: Critical Prefaces*. New York: Charles Scribner's Sons, 1934.

Johnson, James Weldon. *Along This Way*. 1933. New York: Penguin, 1990.

Kiuchi, Toru, and Yoshinobu Hakutani. *Richard Wright: A Documented Chronology, 1908–1960*. Jefferson, NC: McFarland, 2014.

Lancaster, Guy. *Arkansas in Ink: Gunslingers, Ghosts, and Other Graphic Tales*. Little Rock, Arkansas: Butler Center Books, 2014.

Lewis, John. "Foreword." *Without Sanctuary: Lynching Photography in America*. Ed. James Allen et al. Santa Fe, NM: Twin Palms, 2000.

Miller, James A. *Remembering Scottsboro: The Legacy of an Infamous Trial*. Princeton: Princeton UP, 2009.

Miller, W. Jason. *Langston Hughes and American Lynching Culture*. Gainesville: UP of Florida, 2010.

Ray, David, and Robert M. Farnsworth, eds. *Richard Wright: Impressions and Perspectives*. Ann Arbor: U of Michigan P, 1973.

Rowley, Hazel. *Richard Wright: The Life and Times*. New York: A John Macrae Book, 2001.

Schwenk, Katrin. "Lynching and Rape: Border Cases in African American History and Fiction." *The Black Columbiad: Defining Moments in African American Literature and Culture*. Ed. Werner Sollors and Maria Diedrich. Cambridge: Harvard UP, 1994. 312–24.

White, Walter. "I Investigate Lynchings." *American Mercury* (1 January 1929): 81.

Wright, Ellen, and Michel Fabre, eds. *Richard Wright Reader*. New York: Harper & Row, 1978.

Wright, Richard. "Between the World and Me." E. Wright and Fabre, 246–47.

———. *Black Boy (American Hunger)*. New York: Harper Perennial, 1993.

———. "Black Confession [Earlier Draft of *Black Boy*]." Box 9, folder 202, JWJ Collection, Yale University.

———. "Blueprint for Negro Writing." E. Wright and Fabre, 36–49.

———. "Biography of a Bolshevik, Notes on David Poindexter." Box 6, folder 112, JWJ Collection, Yale University.

———. "Hearst Headline Blues." *New Masses* 19 (7) (12 May 1936): 14.

———. "I Am a Red Slogan." *International Literature* 4 (April 1935): 35.

———. "I Have Seen Black Hands." *New Masses* 11 (13) (26 June 1934): 16.

———. "Introduction." *Special Laughter*. Howard Nutt. Prairie City, Illinois: the James A. Decker Press, 1940. ix–xii.

———. "Laughter and Tears." *New Masses* 25 (2) (5 October 1937): 22–23.

———. *Lawd Today!* New York: Walker, 1963.

———. *Native Son*. New York: Harper & Row, 1940.

———. "Obsession." *Midland Left* 2 (February 1935): 14.

———. "Spread Your Sunrise!" *New Masses* 16 (1) (2 July 1935): 26.

———. "Superstition." *Abbott's Monthly Magazine* 2 (April 1931): 45–47, 64–66, 72–73.

———. "Transcontinental." *International Literature* 5 (January 1936): 52–57.

———. *Uncle Tom's Children*. New York: Harper & Row, 1940.

NOTES

1. http://archive.tuskegee.edu/archive/handle/123456789/511 (accessed on 7 May 2019).

2. This is the number of lynchings by state in "Lynching, Whites and Negroes, 1882–1968," according to the record in the Tuskegee University archive (http://archive.tuskegee.edu/archive/).

3. The year 1908 sees lynchings of 8 whites and of 89 blacks according to the record in the Tuskegee University archive (http://archive.tuskegee.edu/archive/).

4. Richard Wright, *Black Boy (American Hunger)* (New York: Harper Perrennial, 1993); all the subsequent references are cited by page in the text as the abbreviation of *BB (AH)*.

5. Richard Wright, "Big Boy Leaves Home," *Uncle Tom's Children* (New York: Harper & Row, 1940): 17–53; all the subsequent references are cited by page in the text.

6. Wright explains that the reason why Uncle Hoskins was killed is that he was envied "by whites who had long coveted his flourishing liquor business" (*BB [AH]* 63), but Prohibition in Arkansas, the strictest dry state among others, is also most likely to be behind the lynching of Hoskins: "In 1915, the General Assembly passed the Newberry Act, effectively banning the manufacture and sale of alcohol in the state. In addition, the act failed to exempt the sale of alcohol for medicinal purposes. In 1916, 'wets,' or those who favored loosening alcohol restrictions, managed to campaign successfully for a referendum on the issue, but efforts to repeal the Newberry Act—and restore liquor sales—failed by a two-to-one margin. The following year, the legislature made Arkansas one of the first states to pass complete prohibition by outlawing the importation of alcohol" (Lancaster 96).

7. According to the 1910 U.S. Census, Silas Hoskins was born in 1882 in Natchez (Ward 4), Mississippi and 34 years old in 1916. According to the 1880 U.S. Census, Margaret Hoskins was born in 1879 in Leflore (Beat 3), Mississippi, and was 37 when her husband Silas was killed in 1916.

8. At the time Chicago had three weekly newspapers published by the Ku Klux Klan: *Dawn: The Herald of a New and Better Day*, published from 21 October 1922 to 9 February 1924; *The Illinois Kourier*, published from 1924–1925; and *Illinois Fiery Cross*, published from 1924–1925. Because Wright starts to sell it in October 1922, it is *Dawn* that is the weekly newspaper which Wright tried to sell.

9. The paper reports more on 18 October 1925; 23, 31 December 1925; 2, 7, 8 January 1926; and 21 March 1926.

10. *The Crisis* reports on the number of lynchings: 33 (3) (Jan. 1927): 131; 33 (4) (Feb. 1927): 180–81.

11. More news about lynchings follow in *Memphis Commercial Appeal*: "Troops Patrol Little Rock after Lynching" (5 May 1927): 1; "Mississippi Mob Lynches Another One" (9 July 1927): 1; "Mississippi Mob Burns Two at the Stake" (18 June 1927): 1; and "Mississippi Mob Stages Lynching Bee" (28 May 1927): 2.

12. *Chicago Defenders* carries numerous articles: "Help Scottsboro Victims" (6 May 1933): 1; "Alabama to Burn 9 in Chair" (6 January 1934): 1, 2, 11; "Is This the Voice of the South? Dixie's Sentiment on Race Problem is Aired in Nation" (6 January 1934); "Ask Reversal in Scottsboro Case" (13 January 1934): 1; "Scottsboro Hearing Postponed to February 24" (3 February 1934): 4; "Scottsboro Case Stirs Cubans" (10 February 1934): 1; "French Citizens Appeal for Scottsboro Boys" (17 February 1934): 16; "Scottsboro Boys Are Mistreated" (14 April 1934): 13; "Uncover More Details of Scottsboro Boys Torture" (28 April 1934): 13; "Scottsboro Mothers Honored" (12 May 1934): 4; "President Refuses to See Mothers of Scottsboro Boys" (26 May 1934); "Indians Aid Fight for Scottsboro Boys" (18 August 1934): 2; and "High Court Rules Scottsboro Boys Must Die" (13 October 1934): 24.

13. The name might have been taken from "a person who enjoys the trappings of success but nevertheless espouses countercultural values," from "*b*ourgeois *b*ohemian," but surely too close to a clown's name to be coincidence (*The New Partridge Dictionary of Slang and Unconventional English*, ed. Tom Dalzell and Terry Victor. New York: Routledge, 2013, p. 237). By contrast, the name of Big Boy alone is conspicuous, consisting of two words in comparison with one-word name: Bobo, Buck, and Lester.

14. Casey Jones is a railroad engineer who died in 1900, when he collided with another train. He was immortalized as an American folk hero with the song "The Ballad of Casey Jones."

15. The Southern Pacific is an American railroad network that existed from 1865 to 1998 operating in the Western United States.

16. For example, James Weldon Johnson's novel *The Autobiography of an Ex-Colored Man* (1912), Theodore Dreiser's short story "Nigger Jeff" (1918), Carl Sandburg's reportage *The Chicago Race Riots, July 1919* (1919), Mary Powell Burill's play *Aftermath* (1919), Claude McKay's poem "If We Must Die" (1919), Angelina Weld Grimké's short story based upon 1918 lynching in Georgia of Mary Turner, "Goldie" (1920), Countee Cullen's poem "Christ Recrucified" (1922), Langston Hughes's short story "Father and Son" (1926), Jean Toomer's novel *Cane* (1923), Floyd J. Calvin's article "The Present South" of lynching of a young black man in Hope, Arkansas (1923), Robert Bagnal's short story "The Unquenchable Fire" (1924), Sterling Brown's "He Was a Man," a ballad of the lynching of Mack Williams on 4 December 1931 in Salisbury, Maryland (1932), Langston Hughes's poem "Christ in Alabama" (1932), and Esther Popel's poem on the lynching of George Armwood in Princess Anne, Maryland on 18 October 1933, "Flag Salute" (1934).

17. Originally included in *The Heart of Happy Hollow*, a collection of short stories published by Dodd, Mead and Company, New York, pp. 1–8.

Chapter Seven

Lynching in Modern American Short Stories and Sexual Crime in Classic Myth

Yoshinobu Hakutani

Richard Wright's "Big Boy Leaves Home" (1940) and Theodore Dreiser's "Nigger Jeff" (1947) have been the best-known stories of lynching in American literature. Lynching in both stories result from the alleged sexual crimes African-American men committed. This form of punishment was caused by racial prejudice and was extremely cruel, inhumane, and unjust. Lynching was and is entirely antithetical to American democracy and national character. It has been regarded as a national shame and the ugliest event in American life. Compared to the form of punishment for sexual crime in an ancient myth, in which there was no racial prejudice, lynching in these modern stories is glaringly different and appalling.

"Big Boy Leaves Home," the first story in the 1938 and 1940 editions of *Uncle Tom's Children*, features a young black boy's escape from his violent southern community.[1] Four innocent, happy-go-lucky black boys are discovered naked by a white woman while they are swimming in a pond and later drying their bodies on a white man's premises. When she screams, her male companion without warning begins shooting and kills two of the boys. Big Boy manages to overcome the white man and accidentally kills him. Now the two surviving boys must take flight: Bobo gets captured, but Big Boy reaches home and is told by black church leaders to hide in a kiln until dawn, when a truck will come by to take him to Chicago. While hiding, he poignantly watches Bobo be lynched and burned. Witnessing such an event gives Big Boy not only a feeling of isolation, terror, and hatred but also a sense of self-awareness and maturity. Although the events take place in less than twenty-four hours as in classical drama, the story is divided into five parts, like the acts of a play, that correspond to the crucial stages in his development from innocence, through violence, suffering, and terror, to freedom.

As the plot unfolds, it becomes apparent that the central theme of the story is the problem of miscegenation in America. The southern white community ever since the days of slavery has regarded miscegenation as prohibited if the relationship is between a white woman and a black man, but as condoned if it is between a white man and a black woman. Wright underscores these unjust sexual mores by having an angry white mob exclaim while lynching and burning Bobo: "Ah tell yuh they still here, somewhere." "But we looked all over!" "What t hell! Wouldnt do t let em git erway!" "Naw. Ef they git erway notta woman in this town would be safe" (*UTC*, 46). Big Boy, the protagonist of the story, hiding in a kiln, hears this exchange and experiences the greatest fear he has ever known in his life. Not only does his friend Bobo become a scapegoat for the white people's terror, but what happens to him is also given as a lesson for the black men who dare to transgress the taboo.

Margaret Walker, a fellow black writer and friend of Wright's, considers "Big Boy Leaves Home" "a lynching story dealing with southern racism," but observes that the story has little to do with black boys' sexuality. Other critics, however, regard the story as closely related to black boys' sexual initiation. Hal Blythe and Charlie Sweet, for instance, maintain: "As a result, the Big Boys of black America are forced to retreat into the womb, never realizing their full sexual maturation. Through its sexual symbolism, then, 'Big Boy Leaves Home,' like Ralph Ellison's 'Battle Royal,' anatomizes the white racist dream of halting what it seems to fear most, the black man's sexuality."[2] By creating such a scene, Wright enables the reader to condemn the white men for the physical cruelty they perpetrate upon the innocent black boys, as well as for the psychological wound such violence inflicts upon Big Boy. Even though Big Boy can escape this ordeal and does leave home, he has not learned how to relate to the white world, let alone how to associate with white women.

The genesis of "Big Boy Leaves Home" is found in several of the episodes Wright sketches in "The Ethics of Living Jim Crow." In one episode, the young Wright felt humiliated when he saw a white man freely slap a black maid on her buttocks. Afterward she told Wright, "Don't be a fool! Yuh couldn't help it!" (*UTC*, 13). In another episode, when a black woman shoplifted at a clothing store, she was kicked in the stomach and brutalized by the white owner of the store and his son so that she was found bleeding. The black porter who witnessed the white men's brutality told Wright: "Shucks! Man, she's a lucky bitch! . . . Hell, it's a wonder they didn't lay her when they got through" (*UTC*, 9). Such an episode reveals not only that black men often acquiesce to the brutality white men perpetrate on black people, but also that white men are expected to exploit black women sexually.

It is a cultural reality that a black man's sexual relationship with a white woman was taboo in the South as late as the 1930s. At one time the young Wright, a bellboy, was called up to a hotel room where a white man and a white prostitute were in bed naked. Asking Wright to buy some liquor, the woman got up and walked nude across the floor to get money from a dresser drawer. Naturally Wright watched her, but the white man was offended and said: "'Nigger, what in hell you looking at?' . . . 'Nothing,' I answered, looking miles deep into the blank wall of the room. 'Keep your eyes where they belong, if you want to be healthy!' he said" (*UTC*, 11). In another episode, "one of the bell-boys was caught in bed with a white prostitute. He was castrated and run out of town." Immediately after this incident all the hall-boys and bell-boys were warned by the hotel management that the next time it "would not be responsible for the lives of 'trouble-makin' niggers" (*UTC*, 12).

Black mothers were expected to warn their sons about the problem of miscegenation in the Deep South during the 1920s. As *Black Boy* reveals, however, Wright's mother was seldom concerned with sexual matters, let alone with miscegenation. In a way "Big Boy Leaves Home" serves as a criticism of the black mother. When Big Boy reaches home, the first person he sees is his mother, who does not console him but asks God to help him. When Big Boy tells her what happened, she exclaims: "*White* woman? . . . Lawd have mercy! Ah knowed yuh boys wus gonna keep on till yuh got into somethin like this!" (*UTC*, 32–33). An episode in "The Ethics of Living Jim Crow" is also critical of Wright's mother. Wright was involved in a fight between black and white boys in his neighborhood. While the black boys attacked the white boys with cinders that gave them only bruises, the white boys retaliated by throwing broken bottles. Wright was once injured in such a battle, sustaining a deep cut on the neck. His mother, he recalls, "came from the white folks' kitchen. I raced down the street to meet her. I could just feel in my bones that she would understand. I knew she would tell me exactly what to do next time. . . . She examined my wound, then slapped me. . . . She grabbed a barrel stave, dragged me home, stripped me naked, and beat me till I had a fever of one hundred and two. She would smack my rump with the stave, and, while the skin was still smarting, impart to me gems of Jim Crow" (*UTC*, 4).

In his later fiction as well, Wright portrays the black mother who fails to instruct her son about racism and to help him attain sexual maturity. In *Native Son*, fanatic religion is what obsesses Bigger's mother. All she can do after Bigger's capture is beg Mrs. Dalton to spare her son's life as though a slave asked his master for mercy. Even though Mrs. Thomas's willingness to plead for Bigger's safety out of her motherly love may be considered admirable, her unwillingness to fight for her daughter's safety earlier in the novel betrays her deeply ingrained prejudice against women and her inferiority complex about black women. In *The Outsider*, Cross Damon repudiates his mother not only because she taught him only subservient ethics but also because she was an epitome of sexual repression. This pious mother, Wright emphasizes, "had evoked in his pliable boy's body an aching sense of pleasure by admonishing him to shun pleasure as the tempting doorway opening blackly onto hell. . . . And this constituted his sense of dread."³

Not only is "Big Boy Leaves Home" based upon Wright's personal experience, but the sexual taboo that precipitates this tragedy originates from a fact both black and white people in the South knew so well. In "How 'Bigger' Was Born," Wright reminds the reader of this fact:

> In the main, this delicately balanced state of affairs has not greatly altered since the Civil War, save in those parts of the South which have been industrialized or urbanized. So volatile and tense are these relations that if a Negro rebels against rule and taboo, he is lynched and the reason for the lynching is usually called "rape," that catchword which has garnered such vile connotations that it can raise a mob anywhere in the South pretty quickly, even today. (*NS*, xii)

The white woman who suddenly appears near the swimming hole, as the story unfolds, is closely guarded and protected by the white world. "In that world," as Blyden Jackson has noted, "at least when 'Big Boy Leaves Home' was written, all Negro males, even young and with their clothes on, were potential rapists. And so this woman screams, and screams again, for someone named Jim, and Jim himself, a white man from her world, comes apace, with a rifle in his hands."⁴

Instead of being compared to the facts of racism in America, "Big Boy Leaves Home" has been compared to an ancient myth. In Ovid's *Metamorphoses*, the myth of Actaeon and Diana is told this way:

> Actaeon and his companions are out hunting at midday when Actaeon calls an end to the chase since "Our nets and spears / Dip with the blood of our successful hunting." Nearby, in a grotto pool nestled in a valley, the goddess Diana, herself tired from hunting, disrobed and disarmed, bathes with her maidens. Quite by accident, Actaeon, now alone, comes upon the idyllic scene. Finding no weapon nearby, Diana flings a handful of the pond's water on the hapless hunter, taunting, "Tell people you have seen me, / Diana, naked! Tell them if you can!" He flees from the scene, by stages transformed into a stag, a metamorphosis he does not comprehend (though he marvels at his own speed) until he pauses to drink. Then he "finally sees, reflected, / his features in a quiet pool 'Alas!' / He tries to say, but has no words." Stunned he hears his hounds approach. "The whole pack, with the lust of blood upon them / Come baying. . . . Actaeon, once pursuer / Over this very ground, is now pursued. . . . He would cry / 'I am

Actaeon. . . . ' / But the words fail." The hounds set upon him "And all together nip and slash and fasten? Till there is no more room for wounds." Meanwhile, his companions arrive, call for him, and rue that he is missing the good show. "And so he died, and so Diana's anger / Was satisfied at last."[5]

The parallels between Wright's story and this classical myth are indeed striking. Both tales begin with idyllic scenes before the plot focuses on an initial encounter between the opposite sexes. Big Boy, the leader of the group, and three friends, who are supposed to be at school, walk through the woods, laughing, beating vines and bushes as if they are hunting anything that interests them. In the prologue, Wright refers to the legendary southern pastoral in the form of a popular song:

> Is it true what they say about Dixie?
> Does the sun really shine all the time?
> Do sweet magnolias blossom at everybody's door,
> Do folks keep eating 'possum, till they can't eat no more?
> Is it true what they say about Swanee?
> Is a dream by that stream the sublime?
> Do they laugh, do they love, like they say in ev'ry song? . . .
> If it's true that's where I belong.

As Big Boy, accompanied by his sidekicks, is pursuing his avocation in a most enjoyable environment, Actaeon, too, with his companions, is hunting in good weather. Before the unexpected appearance of a woman, both Actaeon and Big Boy are at rest, Actaeon tired with hunting and Big Boy warming his body after swimming in the cold pond. Another point of similarity is the hero's fleeing of the scene. Before seeing Diana, Actaeon is alone after his companions have retired from hunting; upon seeing her, he flees the scene. Similarly, Big Boy flees the scene alone since two of his friends are killed and Bobo takes a separate route and eventually gets captured. Finally, both protagonists sustain serious wounds during their flight. It is, furthermore, significant that the wounding of the hero occurs in two stages. Actaeon suffers what Michael Atkinson calls "the transformative sprinkling with pondwater, which removes his humanity, and the obliterative tearing by the dogs' teeth, which destroys the last form and vestige of life."[6] In Wright's tale, Big Boy first suffers the loss of Buck and Lester, whose blood is sprinkled over him; then he suffers from watching Bobo's body be mutilated.

But the points of difference between the tales are equally striking and significant. While in the Roman myth the male protagonist alone encounters a goddess, in Wright's story a group of young boys see an adult woman. However accidental it might be, it is Actaeon who comes upon the scene where Diana is already bathing with her maidens in a secluded pond. The circumstances under which Wright's story begins are reversed: it is the lady who comes upon the scene where Big Boy is already swimming with his friends. The initial setting Wright constructs in "Big Boy Leaves Home" thus poses the serious question of whether underage boys should be judged morally wrong when they are seen naked, while swimming, by an adult woman. In the Actaeon myth, given the tradition of privacy behind it, Actaeon is clearly guilty of watching a naked goddess surrounded by her maids. If Big Boy were in the position of Actaeon, he would be arrested as a Peeping Tom in any modern society. Even if Big Boy were Peeping Tom, Big Boy's punishment would be only blindness as legend tells that Peeping Tom looked at Lady Godiva riding naked through Coventry and was struck blind. But blindness, the price Peeping Tom paid for his offense, is a far cry from the psychological wounds Big Boy and all other black boys in America indeed suffered: the shooting death of Buck and Lester caused by an army officer on leave and the lynching of Bobo perpetrated by a white mob.

It is also significant that, unlike Actaeon, none of the black boys in Wright's story is alone when a member of the opposite sex appears on the scene. The woman in question, moreover, is fully protected by an adult male companion with a shotgun that could legally be used should she be molested and raped by the unarmed black boys. In the myth, however, the goddess is protected neither by anyone who can overcome a potential seducer nor by any weapon save for her flinging of a few drops of magical pond water. In terms of crime and punishment, those who are guilty in Wright's story, the lynch mob and the woman who screams, go unpunished, whereas those who are innocent, the four black boys, are physically or psychologically destroyed. In the myth, Actaeon, the only one who is guilty, meets his death while all the innocent—Diana, her maids, and Actaeon's companions—survive the ordeal. If the Actaeon myth and the legend of Peeping Tom tell us anything significant about an ancient system of justice that meted out punishment for humankind, then the system of justice Wright condemns in "Big Boy Leaves Home" is not only unjust but fundamentally corrupt.

While "Big Boy Leaves Home" and the classical myth of Actaeon and Diana are thematically different, Wright's treatment of the sexual theme in this story has a closer resemblance to Theodore Dreiser's "Nigger Jeff." According to Donald Pizer, the germ of Dreiser's story is found in his unpublished manuscript entitled "A Victim of Justice" at the University of Virginia Library. "Nigger Jeff" as published in Dreiser's *Free and Other Stories* is slightly revised from its first published version in a magazine."[7] In *Black Boy* Wright acknowledges that he was profoundly influenced by realist and naturalist writers such as Dreiser. It is quite likely that before writing "Big Boy Leaves Home" Wright read "Nigger Jeff." Dreiser's story, in which a white mob lynches a black youth, deals with the same problems of race and miscegenation in America as does Wright's story. In "Nigger Jeff," one day a white cub reporter named Elmer Davies is sent out by the city editor to cover the lynching of an alleged black rapist, Jeff Ingalls. Jeff is first captured by a sheriff to await trial but later taken away by a mob of white men led by the brother and father of the supposed rape victim and finally hanged from a bridge over a stream. After learning about the circumstances of the rape, Jeff's behavior, his family's grief, and above all the transcending beauty and serenity of nature in contrast with the brutality and criminality of the mob, Davies realizes that his sympathies have shifted.

At the outset of each story, the author stresses the peace and tranquility of the setting where people, black and white, are meant to enjoy their lives in harmony with nature. In Wright's story, the four innocent, happy black youths, as mentioned earlier, roam about the woods and pasture, laughing, chanting, smelling sweet flowers. "A quartet of voices," Wright describes, "blending in harmony, floated high above the tree tops" (*UTC*, 17). In Dreiser's story, a young impressionable man comes upon the beautiful setting on a lovely spring day in the countryside of Pleasant Valley. Just as Big Boy and his friends are happy not only with themselves but also with the world, Davies, as Dreiser describes, "was dressed in a new spring suit, a new hat and new shoes. In the lapel of his coat was a small bunch of violets . . . he was feeling exceedingly well and good-natured—quite fit, indeed. The world was going unusually well with him. It seemed worth singing about" (*F*, 76). Under such circumstances no one would expect violence to occur and destroy peace and harmony.

Both stories are told through the protagonist's point of view. In the beginning both Big Boy and Elmer Davies are young and naive, but the violence and injustice they witness make them grow up overnight. In the end, Big Boy, though stunned and speechless, is determined to tell the world what he has learned. As *Black Boy*, Wright's autobiography, suggests, Big Boy was modeled after the young Richard Wright himself growing up in the twenties. Dreiser's *A Book about Myself*, like *Black Boy* one of the finest autobiographies in American literature, also suggests that Elmer Davies was indeed the young Theodore Dreiser himself when the future novelist was a newspaper reporter in St. Louis in the early 1890s. As Wright fled the South for Chicago to write his early short stories, Dreiser left the Midwest for New York to write his.

In both stories, the plot, which does not hinge upon a conflict of social forces, thrives on a progression of vision. Each story opens with pastoral idylls, moves through visions of violence and injustice, and shows the hero's losing his relative state of innocence. Both writers take pains to demonstrate that the protagonist—rather than society, the antagonist—is capable of vision. The climactic scene in Wright's story, where the victim is hanged and mutilated, is presented with bright firelight. The mob is situated so close to the scene of violence that its members cannot see what is transpiring. Big Boy, hiding in the dark in a kiln, can see it far better than the mob. "Big Boy," Wright says, "shrank when he saw the first flame light the hillside. Would they see im here? Then he remembered you could not see into the dark if you were standing in the light" (*UTC*, 48). Dreiser, too, presents the climax for Elmer Davies to see rather than for the mob to see: "The silent company, an articulated, mechanical and therefore terrible thing, moved on. . . . He was breathing heavily and groaning. . . . His eyes were fixed and staring, his face and hands bleeding as if they had been scratched or trampled upon. . . . But Davies could stand it no longer now. He fell back, sick at heart, content to see no more. It seemed a ghastly, murderous thing to do" (*F*, 103–4). Seeing an asinine murder makes Davies feel as though he has become a murderer himself and seems to retard the progression of the story, but the pace of the revelation increases as Dreiser continues:

> Still the company moved on and he followed, past fields lit white by the moon, under dark, silent groups of trees, through which the moonlight fell in patches, up low hills and down into valleys. . . . In the weak moonlight it seemed as if the body were struggling. . . . Then after a time he heard the company making ready to depart, and finally it did so, leaving him quite indifferently to himself and his thoughts. Only the black mass swaying in the pale light over the glimmering water seemed human and alive, his sole companion. (*F*, 104–5)

In Wright's story, too, Big Boy remains in the kiln through the night after the mob departs and becomes the victim's sole companion. Just as morning comes for the truck to deliver Big Boy to Chicago, dawn breaks for Davies to return to his office. After the crowd departs, Davies thinks of hurrying to a nearby post office to file a partial report. But he decides against it since he is the only reporter present, just as Big Boy is, and because "he could write a fuller, sadder, more colorful story on the morrow" (*F*, 105), just as Big Boy could have when he left for Chicago in the morning. This momentary delay in Davies's action gives his revelation a heightened effect.

Moreover, Dreiser's description of dawn in "Nigger Jeff," as of the opening scene, is tinged with a transcendental vision:

> As he still sat there the light of morning broke, a tender lavender and gray in the east. Then came the roseate hues of dawn, all the wondrous coloring of celestial halls, to which the waters of the stream responded. The white pebbles shone pinkily at the bottom, the grass and sedges first black now gleamed a translucent green. Still the body hung there black and limp against the sky, and now a light breeze sprang up and stirred it visibly. At last he arose, mounted his horse and

made his way back to Pleasant Valley, too full of the late tragedy to be much interested in anything else. . . . Then he left, to walk and think again. (*F*, 105–6)

Throughout Dreiser's description of the lynching, Davies sees the signs of evil indicated by the struggling body, the black mass, and the black body hanging limp. The images of the dark are intermingled in his mind with those of the light that suggest hope: "the weak moonlight," "the pale light," "the glimmering water," "the light of morning," "a tender lavender and gray in the east," "the roseate hues of dawn," "the white pebbles [shining] pinkily at the bottom." As the story progresses, the images of hope increasingly dominate those of despair.

The same pattern of imagery is also created toward the end of Wright's story. During the night Big Boy has to protect himself from cold wind and rain as well as a persistent dog. Even though morning arrives with the warm sunlight and brightened air, he is still reminded of "a puddle of rainwater" and "the stiff body" of the dog lying nearby. "His knees," Wright describes, "were stiff and a thousand needlelike pains shot from the bottom of his feet to the calves of his legs. . . . Through brackish *light* he saw *Will's truck* standing some twenty-five yards away, *the engine running*. . . . On hands and knees he looked around in the *semi-darkness*. . . . *Through two long cracks* fell *thin blades of daylight*. . . . Once he heard *the crow of a rooster*. It made him think of *home*, of *ma* and *pa*" (*UTC*, 51–52; emphasis added). In the final scene the nightmare that has tormented Big Boy throughout the night is chased out of his mind and destroyed by the blades of the sun: "The truck swerved. He blinked his eyes. The blades of daylight had turned brightly golden. The sun had risen. The truck sped over the asphalt miles, sped northward, jolting him, shaking out of his bosom the crumbs of corn bread, making them dance with the splinters and sawdust in the golden blades of sunshine. He turned on his side and slept" (*UTC*, 53).

In the ending of "Nigger Jeff" as well, Dreiser makes the hero's consciousness move back and forth between hope and despair as if the images of light and dark were at war. When Davies visits the room where the body is laid and sees the victim's sister sobbing over it, he becomes keenly aware that all "corners of the room were quite dark. Only its middle was brightened by splotches of silvery light." For Davies, another climactic experience takes place when he dares to lift the shirt covering the body. He can now see exactly where the rope tightened around the neck. The delineation of the light against the dark is, once more, focused on the dead body: "A bar of cool moonlight lay just across the face and breast" (*F*, 109–10). Such deliberate contrasts between light and dark, good and evil, suggest that human beings have failed to see "transcending beauty" and "unity of nature," which are merely illusions to them, and that they have imitated only the cruel and the indifferent that nature appears to symbolize.

At the end of the story, Davies is overwhelmed not only by the remorse he feels for the victim, as Big Boy is, but also by his compassion for the victim's bereft mother, whom he finds in the dark corner of the room:

> Davies began to understand. . . . The night, the tragedy, the grief, he saw it all. But also with the cruel instinct of the budding artist that he already was, he was beginning to meditate on the character of story it would make—the color, the pathos. The knowledge now that it was not always exact justice that was meted out to all and that it was not so much the business of the writer to indict as to interpret was borne in on him with distinctness by the cruel sorrow of the mother, whose blame, if any, was infinitesimal. (*F*, 110–11)

The importance of such fiction is not the process of the young man's becoming an artist-Big Boy or the young Richard Wright is surely not trying to become merely an artist. It is the sense of urgency in which the protagonist living in American society is compelled to act as a reformer. With his final proclamation, "I'll get it all in" (*F*, 111), Davies's revelation culminates in a feeling of triumph. Although, to Dreiser as well as to Wright, human beings appear necessarily limited by their natural environment and by their racial prejudice, both writers in their respective stories are asserting that human beings are still capable of reforming society.

In sum, protest fiction, the category to which critics have assigned "Big Boy Leaves Home," becomes successful literature only if it is endowed with a universal sense of justice, as exemplified by "Big Boy Leaves Home" and "Nigger Jeff." Such discourse, moreover, must address an actual and pressing social issue, whether it is a lynching Dreiser, a white writer, witnessed in a border state in the 1890s, as he reported in a newspaper, or a problem of race and miscegenation a black writer like Wright encountered in the Deep South of the 1920s. As both stories show, great social fiction can be created not so much with the artistry the author can put into it—much of which is taken for granted in these stories—as with a sense of urgency the subject matter demands. In "Big Boy Leaves Home," this urgency does not come from the intensity and quality of Big Boy's will, nor is it anything to do with the collective will of black people. Rather, it comes from the conscience of humanity, the collective will of decent individuals living anywhere. It is a revelation given to Big Boy, as it is given to Elmer Davies. And through the protagonist and the skill of a gifted writer, it is disseminated to the world at large.

NOTES

1. "Big Boy Leaves Home" first appeared in an anthology, *The New Caravan*, ed. Alfred Kreymborg et al. Page references to Wright's stories are to the 1940 edition of *Uncle Tom's Children*. Subsequent references to this volume will appear parenthetically in the text as *UTC*.

2. Walker, *Richard Wright: Daemonic Genius*, 82; Blythe and Sweet, "'Yo Mama Don Wear No Drawers': Suspended Sexuality in 'Big Boy Leaves Home.'"

3. Richard Wright, *The Outsider*, 18. Subsequent references will appear parenthetically in the text as *O*.

4. "Richard Wright in a Moment of Truth," 172.

5. See Michael Atkinson, "Richard Wright's 'Big Boy Leaves Home' and a Tale from Ovid: A Metamorphosis Transformed," 251–52.

6. Ibid., 257.

7. For a discussion of Dreiser's revision in this story, see Donald Pizer's "Theodore Dreiser's 'Nigger Jeff': The Development of an Aesthetic." References to this story are to the *Free* edition and will appear parenthetically in the text as *F*.

Chapter Eight

The Southern Ritual of Lynching in Faulkner's *Light in August* and Ellison's *Three Days before the Shooting*

Robert Butler

Ralph Ellison on several occasions made an important distinction between what he called his literary "relatives" and his literary "ancestors." In an essay in which he tried to minimize the influence of Richard Wright on his work he observed:

> But perhaps you will understand when I say he did not influence me if I point out that, while one can do nothing about choosing one's relatives, one can, as an artist, choose one's "ancestors." Wright was, in a sense, a "relative"; Hemingway, an "ancestor." . . . Eliot, whom I was to meet only many years later, and Malraux and Dostoievsky and Faulkner, were "ancestors." (*Shadow*, 145)

"Relatives," therefore, are writers with whom he shares a common cultural background but who may have little or no effect on his writing, while "ancestors" are writers who deeply influenced his work, both in technique and vision.

Throughout his career, Ellison would express admiration for Faulkner as a "very literary artist" (Rampersad, 248) who was able to explore profoundly America's racial problems as well as develop black characters who were both realistic and examined in great depth. Ellison's regard for Faulkner was so great that he considered him "the supreme American novelist since the Civil War" (Rampersad, 314).[1]

Anyone studying *Invisible Man* immediately senses parallels between its richly poetic style and Faulkner's complex, sometimes Shakespearean prose. The two writers also shared a fascination for myth and ritual as well as an abiding interest in the tragic dimensions of southern culture and history. Faulkner's preoccupation for how the past and present interplay with each other also strongly influenced Ellison's complex treatment of time in his major fiction.

The most Faulknerian of all Ellison's work is *Three Days before the Shooting*, a novel Ellison worked on for forty years and was never able to complete. This immense project, which was published posthumously in 2010, closely resembles Faulkner's Yoknapatawpha fiction in both style, vision, and scope, attempting to understand America's racial problems by delving into the intricacies of southern history and culture and using a wide variety of stylistic techniques to probe the psychological depths of its main characters.

The Faulkner novel which *Three Days* most closely resembles is clearly *Light in August*. Its central character, Bliss, is modelled after Joe Christmas. Both have racially ambiguous origins that are never resolved, and both undergo painful, lifelong identity problems as they try to discover their true selves and how they fit into a racially divided culture. And both are the victims of terrible violence.

Lynching is central to both novels and becomes for Ellison and Faulkner a terrifyingly perverse expression of the darkest expressions of southern myth and ritual. Faulkner, who focused on lynching in several of his fictions and made it a central epiphany in *Light in August*, said very little about lynching in the majority of his published essays or interviews. But Ellison, who in one of his earliest stories, "A Party Down at the Square," describes a lynching in graphic detail, wrote perceptively about lynching as a cultural phenomenon in several of his essays. For example, in "An Extravagance of Laughter," included in *Going to the Territory*, he describes lynching in the following way:

> For the lynch mob, blackness is a sign of satanic evil given human form. It is the dark consubstantial shadow which symbolizes all that its opponents reject in social change and democracy. Thus, it does not matter if its sacrificial victim is guilty or innocent, because the lynch mob's object is to propitiate its insatiable god of whiteness, the myth-figure worshipped as the true source of all things bright and beautiful, by destroying the human attributes of its god's antagonist which they perceive as the power of blackness. In action, racial discrimination is as non-discriminating as a car bomb detonated in a public square because the car bomb and the lynch rope are savagely efficient ways of destroying distinctions between members of a hated group while rendering quite meaningless any moral questioning that might arise regarding the method used. The ultimate goal

of the lynchers is that of destroying the lynchers' identification with the basic *humanity* of their victims. (*CERE*, 641)

This explains exactly how lynching functions in "The Party Down at the Square" and *Three Days*, fictions that serve as book ends for Ellison's entire career. The story, written almost fifty years earlier than the essay, is narrated from the point of view of a young boy from Cincinnati, who observes a grim initiation ritual introducing him to southern life. Set in a public square and overlooked by the statue of a Confederate general who seems to look on approvingly, the lynching's main purpose is to keep black people in their "place" (*Flying*, 11) by reminding them of the steep price they will pay for violating the strictures of southern society. The anonymous victim is never named and is repeatedly referred to only as "the nigger" (3, 4, 5, 9, 11). We are never told about his alleged "crime" or whether or not he is guilty of it. For the white townspeople who have organized this ghastly ritual, it does not matter as they work out what Ellison describes in "An Extravagance of Laughter" a "ritual of purification" to appease their "god of whiteness." What emerges from the story is a Dantean vision of "hell" (15) as white people gather in a "circle" (4) on a bitterly cold night to watch their victim expire in "a ring of fire" (5).

In *Three Days*, the lynching is not described directly but it acquires a central importance in the novel as a frightening revelation of the darkest, most pathological aspects of southern life. Hickman's brother Robert is lynched when an unmarried white woman becomes pregnant and attempts to defend her "virtue" by falsely claiming that she has been raped by a black man. Robert thus is victimized on "the old disgusting sacrificial altar" (462) of southern justice. When Hickman asks the woman "why Bob?" (469), a man she barely knew, she answers "I didn't want to hurt him. . . . He just didn't exist for me. He was just a name" (465). In her attempt to "protect" (465) herself, she considers it was her "fate" (465) to scapegoat an anonymous Negro. Like the white southerners in "A Party Down at the Square," she participates willingly in "a ritual of purification" to appease "the god of whiteness" (*CERE*, 641).

Faulkner's portrayal of the lynching of Joe Christmas is presented in a very similar way. It too is described as a cultural ritual designed to preserve caste and racial lines and is presided over by a representative of the community, Percy Grimm. The town who regard this pathetic figure with "awe," "respect," and "faith" (456–57) give him the authority to act on their behalf. He organizes a vigilante committee to assist him and these people give him "blind and untroubled faith in the infallibility of his actions" (459). The townspeople also blindly submit to his will, seeing him as someone who can reassert "order" (451) in the community. Once set in motion, the lynching is acted out in a mechanical way as part of a "Fate" (460) imposed on Joe, treating him as a "pawn" (422) in a kind of cultural chess game. They go along with this "emotional barbecue" and actually enjoy it as a "Roman holiday" (289) because it enables them to exorcise their racial fears and put black people back in their "place."

The purpose of this ritual is not only to provide a kind of group anonymity to the nameless individuals attending to the lynching but also to depersonalize Joe as a "nigger" (353) rather than a human being. When the sheriff is told of Joanna's murder he instinctively blurts out "Get me a nigger" (290). Just as the woman in *Three Days* claims that the victim of her accusation "didn't exist for me" (465) Joe becomes a nearly anonymous figure sacrificed on the altar of white racism. He never is referred to by his full name and most often is identified only as "the nigger" (353). This ritual of dehumanization is completed when Grimm literally strips Joe of his manhood by castrating him, a ghastly procedure often performed at the conclusion of a lynching of a black man.

It is possible to see Joe's entire life as a kind of extended lynching. He is repeatedly labelled as a "nigger" when characteristics such as the dietician, Bobbi, and Lucas Burch scapegoat him to deflect attention from their own questionable behavior and free themselves from taking responsibility for their actions. The "paved street" of Joe's life is finally revealed as a deterministic "circle" (339) of dehumanizing experiences which have stripped him of individuality and personhood. Joe's behavior at the end of the novel indicates his acceptance of the role society has imposed on him. After killing Joanna, he realizes that he is headed inevitably for a lynching and returns to Mottstown where he knows his executioners await him. He does not hide his identity, makes no serious attempts to escape and refuses to use his gun to defend himself. His death is described as a kind of "passive suicide" (453) and he looks up at his killer with "peaceful" (463) eyes.

Light in August and *Three Days before the Shooting* however, are not fundamentally pessimistic works because both balance the grimly deterministic narratives centered in lynchings with powerful counternarratives providing substantial affirmations. Joe's tragic story is juxtaposed against Lena's positive story which culminates in the birth of her child and her being restored to the healing worlds of nature and community. In a very comparable way, *Three Days* contrasts Bliss Sunraider's failed life culminating in his assassination with Reverend Alonzo Hickman's heroic life as a minister, father, and leader.

From the outset of *Light in August* Lena and Joe are seen as inhabiting racially different worlds even though they actually live in some of the same geographical spaces and share the same segregated southern culture. Like Joe, Lena is initially described as a "stranger" (9) but the road she travels is diametrically opposed to the "bleak street" which Joe is forced to travel.

Lena's road is lyrically presented as a warm, sunny, "dreamlike" (11) place where she is welcomed by strangers like Mr. Armstid who offers her a ride and Mrs. Armstid who gives her food and egg money. Even at the novel's conclusion when she is unlikely to ever find the man who impregnated her and she is liable to be scorned by a Calvinistic society which takes a harsh view of mothers out of wedlock, she is presented as being delighted with her three-week-old baby and happy to be on the road again, "just travelling" (493) and fascinated with the new things she is discovering along the way. She is part not only of a vibrant natural world which is constantly renewing itself but also a welcoming social world. The travelling sewing machine salesman, Ratlitt, offers her a ride on his wagon at the end of the book just as Mr. Armstid gave her a lift at the onset of the novel. And Byron Bunch continues to care for her and her baby as he renews his quest of marrying her.

Joe's story begins and ends in precisely the opposite way. When he arrives in Jefferson he is characterized as a "rootless" man who looks as though "no town or city was his, no walk, no square of earth his home" (31). Whereas Lena gratefully accepts and is nourished by food, Christmas rejects Byron's offer to share his lunch with him, angrily snapping "keep your muck" (35). Indeed, he seems not to need food, even though he has not eaten in three days and seems to have "lived on cigarettes" (35). Lena's physical robustness contrasts dramatically with Joe's "gaunt, ghostly pallor," his flesh "a dead parchment color" (34). This opening scene telescopes Joe's isolation as orphan, his estrangement as an adopted child, and his existential aloneness as an adult. The "thousand savage and lonely streets" (330) which comprise his life lead inevitably to his being brutally lynched by southern racists, some of whom like Mr. Armstid and Ratlitt, have extended such generosity and kindness to Lena. (It's quite revealing that the same Ratlitt who speaks so lovingly about Lena in the novel's final chapter coldly refers to Joe as the "nigger" (497) who got lynched.)

How does Faulkner connect these two radically opposite narratives, integrating them into one coherent work of art? Cleanth Brooks many years ago asked the question of whether the novel's two contrasting stories would "rend the book in two" (Brooks, 55). But he found the novel to be united by a comic vision rooted in an affirmation of community. Others have faulted the book for failing to unify adequately its major plots while some critics have argued that the book carefully balances Joe's and Lena's stories in a complex tragicomic vision. But this much is clear—Faulkner did achieve a high degree of formal coherence not only by employing a unified setting but also by artfully connecting all of the novel's narratives through the agency of Byron Bunch who literally "bunches" together all of the novel's major characters. He is the only one in the novel to have firsthand knowledge Joe, Lena, and Hightower, showing empathy for Joe and Hightower and love for Lena. He literally brings them together in Hightower's house at the end of the novel. In a very real sense, he is the novel's moral center.

Ellison, perhaps signifying on *Light in August*, centers *Three Days* in two main characters:

1. Bliss, a child of racially indeterminate origins who eventually becomes a racist southern senator who is shot on the floor of the senate by the son he has abandoned at birth.
2. Reverend Alonzo Hickman, a heroic minister who undergoes a conversion experience when he delivers Bliss as a baby, adopts him, and raises him as a black person.

Bliss closely resembles Joe in many important ways. He too is never able to resolve his racial identity and his life is a restless, spatially undirected journey where he, like Joe, assumes a bewildering variety of jobs and roles which drain him of any core self. He is described at one point in the novel as "Mr. No Man from Nowhere" (748), a characterization that could just as easily apply to Joe.

Just as the birth of Lena's child is a critically important scene in *Light in August*, the birth of Bliss has a central importance in *Three Days*. Hickman, who is outraged because of the lynching of his brother, visits the white woman who has made the false accusations of rape and is intent on exacting revenge by murdering her and her unborn child. But at a critical point, he transforms into a character resembling Hightower and Byron when he delivers and commits himself to raising the child as his own son. He thus transcends all of the racial prohibitions of the segregated south, rejecting its dehumanizing rituals and myths. Ellison, like Faulkner, uses Christian motifs to endow the birth scene with mystic resonance. Just as Lena rests in the "assurance that the "Lord will see" to it that a "family ought to be together when a chap comes" (21) and that "Thy Lord will see what is right will be done" (25), Hickman hears the voice of the "Lord" who tells him "I am starting you out right here—with flesh and with Eden and Christmas squeezed together" (471). He feels "called" (471) to his new role as father in the same way as Lena's "inward lighted quality" (18) calls her to the role of mother.

But whereas Faulkner was able to fashion a coherently integrated novel out of his two opposed plots, Ellison never could aesthetically connect the two main narratives of *Three Days* and this played a major role in his failing to complete the novel. Ellison's initial concept for *Three Days*, as Adam Bradley has pointed out, was as a kind of "call-response" (Bradley 123) continuation or sequel to *Invisible Man*. The second novel would provide "the next phase" (*Invisible*, 576) of the central character's life where he would emerge from the underground and assume a "socially responsible role"

(*Invisible*, 581). Hickman, a robust, physically imposing man, was imagined by Ellison as a character who could fulfill Ellison's expectations for a modern hero by committing himself as minister, father, and leader to fighting racism and revitalizing American democracy. Bliss, his adopted son, would be the vehicle through which this transformation of American life would take place. As Hickman imagined Bliss's life, he was to be "set aside" to fulfill a Lincolnesque role of preserving the sacred principles of justice and equality as he became a charismatic leader who would bring about a new redeemed America freed from its racist past. He would thus affirm "the principle" (*Invisible*, 574) of American democracy upon which invisible man meditates at the end of the novel.

The Brown vs. Board of Education Supreme Court Decision of 1954, which eliminated the legal basis of segregation, reinforced Ellison's hope for America as he was engaged in the early phases of writing *Invisible Man*. He was further encouraged by Dr. Martin Luther King's great victories in Montgomery and Birmingham and perhaps might have even have seen Dr. King as a historical parallel to his fictional hero, Hickman. But as America developed in the latter part of the twentieth century, history undermined hopes for an affirmative novel centered in a belief in a redeemed America. The Viet Nam war, the assassinations of John Kennedy, Malcolm X, Martin Luther King and Robert Kennedy as well as the collapse of the Civil Rights Movement and the emergence of Black Nationalism revealed to Ellison that America was in a process of cultural decay and worsening racial relations. As M. Cooper Harris has observed, "History would not sit still for Ellison" (251) as the radical instability and fragmentation of late twentieth-century American culture eroded Ellison's initially affirmative plan for the novel. As a result, the narrative of Bliss Sunraider becomes increasingly more prominent in the novel. And his degeneration into a racist white politician who is likely to have been assassinated comes to symbolize the chaos of late twentieth-century culture, something which Hickman can observe and lament but do little to prevent.

Thus, caught between an affirmative narrative centered in a potentially heroic figure like Hickman and essentially antiheroic character such as Bliss Sunraider, Ellison's imagination was short-circuited, and he could not complete what promised to be his masterwork. "Three Days," like Melville's *Billy Budd*, Twain's *The Mysterious Stranger*, Gogol's *Dead Souls* and Kafka's *The Castle*, must remain for us a brilliant but unfinished work of great importance.

Faulkner's influence on Ellison has been the source of critical controversy as several scholars and writers have faulted him for being too closely by Faulkner's work and, as a result, either muted or lost his voice as a black writer. Arnold Rampersad, for example, has argued that Ellison "was perhaps in thrall to Faulkner" (359) and this weakened his own development as an African-American novelist. Toni Morrison, a writer who was also strongly influenced by Faulkner, nevertheless criticized Ellison for using the "tragic mulatto" theme he found in Faulkner which she considered obsolete, "dead" (Rampersad 359). Norman Podhoretz put the case most strongly when he argued that Faulkner's influence on Ellison was a kind of "literary enslavement" (56) which was responsible for Ellison's failure to complete *Three Days*.

Recently, however, Joseph Fruscione has argued convincingly that Faulkner exerted a very positive influence on Ellison's writing. For Fruscione, "Faulkner exercised an active and dynamic mode of influence on Ralph Ellison, both as a racially attuned novelist and as a publicly active critic" (133). He regards Faulkner as a "literary-racial touchstone" (138) who helped Ellison more fully understand the cultural dynamics of American racism and its roots in southern slavery and segregation.

But as this study has tried to demonstrate, Ellison benefited as an artist by being so strongly influenced by Faulkner's work, particularly *Light in August*. Far from being "enslaved" by Faulkner, he learned much from Faulkner as a stylist and interpreter of southern culture. And Faulkner's influence in *Three Days* was by no means monolithic. Ellison, whom Henry Louis Gates has called "the Great Signifier" (242), was deeply influenced by a number of great writers such as T. S. Eliot, F. Scott Fitzgerald, and James Joyce. *Three Days* owes much of its thematic and stylistic richness to the complex ways in which Ellison made creative use of these writers rather than slavishly imitating them.

WORKS CITED

Ellison, Ralph. *Invisible Man*. New York: Vintage Books, 1989.
———. *Shadow and Act*. New York: Signet Books, 1966.
———. *Flying Home and Other Stories*: Random House, 1996.
———. *The Collected Essays of Ralph Ellison*. New York: Modern Library, 1995.
———. *Three Days before the Shooting*. New York: Modern Library, 2010.
Faulkner, William. *Light in August*. New York: Vintage Books, 1990.
Fruscione, Joseph. "The President Has Asked Me: Faulkner, Ellison, and Public Intellectualism." In *Faulkner and the Black Literature of the Americas*. Jay Watson and James G. Thomas, Jr. Jackson: The University Press of Mississippi, 2016
Gates, Henry Louis. *Figures in Black: Words, Signs, and the Racial Self*. New York: Oxford University Press, 1987.
Harriss, M. Cooper. "Civil Rights and Civil Religion in Ralph Ellison's Second Novel." *African American Review*. Summer/Fall, 2014, p. 247–66.

McMillen, Neil R. and Noel Polk. "Faulkner on Lynching." *Faulkner Journal*. Vol. 8 No 1 (Fall 1992), 3–14.
Rampersad, Arnold. *Ralph Ellison: A Biography*. New York: Alfred Knopf, 2007.
Podhoretz, Norman. "What Happened to Ralph Ellison?" *Commentary*, July–August, 1999, p. 46–58.

NOTE

1. As Neil R. McMillen and Noel Polk have convincingly argued, however, Faulkner, using the family spelling of his name without a "u" wrote a letter on February 15, 1951 to the Memphis *Commercial Appeal* which contained a bizarre and irrational justification of lynching. While claiming "I hold no brief for lynching" and pointing out that "No balanced man will deny that lynching serves nothing," he also argued that lynching could be used to protect the "sacredness of womanhood" and that lynchers, like our juries have a way of being right" (McMillen and Polk, 4, 3, 4).

McMillen and Polk stress that such a brutal defense for lynching dramatically contradicts the way Faulkner portrays lynching in his fiction, most notably "Dry September" and *Light in August*, ironically two works he was composing when he wrote his letter to the Memphis newspaper. They conclude that, however Faulkner was "mired in a mythical swamp" (8) in the public postures he articulated as a white Mississippian of his times, he was able to transcend such racism in his fiction, denouncing lynching as a barbaric cultural ritual which reflected the South's most atavistic attitudes.

Chapter Nine

The Electric Execution of Bigger Thomas in Wright's *Native Son*

Yoshinobu Hakutani

The lynching of an African-American male for the alleged rape of a white woman occurred less frequently in America in the twentieth century. By the time Richard Wright wrote *Native Son* in the 1930s, the lynching of a black male had become a less viable theme in fiction. Instead, the electric execution of an innocent black man has replaced lynching. The electric execution of Bigger Thomas is the central theme of this novel. Based on a similar incident reported in the newspaper, *Native Son* became a novel with artistic and structural devices. Wright's portrayal of Bigger Thomas convinces the reader that a victim of racial prejudice, despite his death sentence, has become an existential hero.

Appraising the relation of *Native Son* to American culture, Irving Howe said: "No matter how much qualifying the book might later need, it made impossible a repetition of the old lies. In all its crudeness, melodrama and claustrophobia of vision, Richard Wright's novel brought out into the open, as no one ever had before, the hatred, fear and violence that have crippled and may yet destroy our culture."[1] Not only does Howe's statement address the problems of race, but also it reminds the reader that Wright was the first major writer to deal with sexual relationships between black and white people. Because of this racial discourse, miscegenation became no longer taboo. What happens to Bigger and Mary in *Native Son* reinforces the image central to the tragedy, an image of the forbidden sexual relationship between a black man and a white woman in particular. This sexual encounter, however spontaneous and natural, is suppressed and condemned as socially unacceptable. Since a black man and a white woman can only dream about such an experience, it has the status of myth in American culture.

In *The Long Dream*, Wright's last novel, Fishbelly Tucker gradually comes to the realization that he cannot call himself a human being until he has the freedom of sexual relationship with a woman regardless of her skin color. The problem of miscegenation thus underlies Fishbelly's battle in achieving manhood. How seriously Wright intended to deal with this problem in his work is suggested by what he says about it in *Black Boy*. It is true that *Black Boy* is not focused on the hero's sexual initiation. In *Black Boy*, sex, like religion, tends to victimize rather than develop an adolescent. The only woman to whom the young Wright is sexually attracted is a black woman depicted in grotesque and physical expressions instead of pleasant and spiritual images.[2] Such a description indeed debases his attitude toward human sexuality. Even though Wright is not concerned with the hero's sexual awakening in *Black Boy*, he defines the following subjects as taboo:

> American white women; the Ku Klux Klan; France, and how Negro soldiers fared while there; Frenchwomen; Jack Johnson; the entire northern part of the United States; the Civil War; Abraham Lincoln; U.S. Grant; General Sherman; Catholics; the Pope; Jews; the Republican Party; slavery; social equality; Communism; Socialism; the 13th, 14th, and 15th Amendments to the Constitution. (*BB*, 253)

Among the nineteen topics of taboo listed, the first four are directly related to miscegenation. It is beyond dispute that miscegenation occupied the mind of the young Wright as he came of age in the Deep South. While *Black Boy* merely intimates that white men do not mind black men's talking about sex as long as it is not interracial, most of Wright's novels powerfully demonstrate this fact. Wright tries to show that miscegenation is the reason white people have a preconceived notion of black people's place in America.

But another kind of miscegenation was regarded not as myth but as history. Slavery in America allowed the plantation owner to exploit black women for sex. The scene of miscegenation as presented in *Native Son*, however, is considered a myth, for neither Bigger nor Mary takes advantage of the other for materialistic gains. The slave owner, on the other hand, took advantage of the slave woman for sex in exchange for financial compensation or because he literally owned her and could do it for nothing. This situation is similar to the white man's sexual relationship with a black woman in the story "Long Black Song," in which a man and a woman exploit each other for their own emotional or physical needs. Such a relationship, moreover, has derived from an interracial mentality widely accepted and maintained in the system of slavery, as Silas, the wronged black husband, accuses white men of raping black women.

By contrast, Wright portrays the interracial sexual scene in *Native Son* with genuinely human sentiments rather than with social and economic motives. Without fear of social ostracism, as Wright depicts the scene, both Bigger and Mary are involved in a purely personal relationship. Wright's original description of the scene—which, as Keneth Kinnamon has pointed out, Wright deleted from the galleys in fear of censorship—bears out the reading that the sexual feelings expressed at the scene are mutual. As Arnold Rampersad has shown, the original passage included a more explicit description of Mary's sexual arousal: "He tightened his arms as his lips pressed tightly against hers and he felt her body moving strongly. The thought and conviction that Jan had had her a lot flashed through his mind. He kissed her again and felt the sharp bones of her hips move in a hard and veritable grind. Her mouth was open and her breath came slow and deep."[3]

Well before this climactic scene, Wright accounts for Bigger's sexual attraction to a white girl. Near the beginning of the novel Bigger and his friend Jack go to the movies and watch double features. *Trader Horn*, in which black men and women are dancing in a wild jungle, shows Bigger only life in a remote world. *The Gay Woman*, portraying love and intrigue in upper-class white society, quickly attracts his attention. This movie shows, "amid scenes of cocktail drinking, dancing, golfing, swimming, and spinning roulette wheels," a young white woman having an affair while her rich husband is too busy with his work. In contrast to the struggling young black woman Bigger is so familiar with, this young white woman appears carefree and glamorous. Jack, equally fascinated by her, tells Bigger: "Ah, man, them rich white women'll go to bed with anybody, from a poodle on up. Shucks, they even have their chauffeurs. Say, if you run into anything on that new job that's too much for you to handle, let me know" (*NS*, 33). For Bigger, then, the gay woman first seen in the movies and later realized in his own life becomes a symbol not only of success and affluence in white society but also of the fulfillment of his youthful dreams and desires. In the original manuscript, moreover, Wright included a scene in the movie theater where Bigger watches in the newsreel none other than Mary Dalton. Bigger and Mary's sexual encounter, which the members of jury deeply resent and fail to understand, can be defended on humanistic grounds. Neither Bigger nor Mary is motivated to exploit the other: they are simply infatuated with each other. In contrast, Bigger and Bessie are interested in each other for spurious reasons, motives that do not exist in the relationship of Bigger and Mary. While Wright has great sympathy for Bigger's infatuation with Mary, he feels contempt for Bigger's treatment of Bessie.

It seems as though Wright in *Native Son* idolizes Mary Dalton, a liberal white girl who rebels against her racially condescending father and sympathizes with a poor black boy like Bigger. This image of a white girl, moreover, is in stark contrast to "the purity of white womanhood" the Ku Klux Klansmen try to protect in the South.[4] At the same time Wright portrays black women as if they were morally and intellectually deficient. Bigger's sister Vera is a tired and fearful girl; alcohol is what sustains Bessie. Similarly, in *The Outsider*, an existentialist novel, Wright degrades black women. Cross Damon's relationship with his mother betrays not only their estrangement but also his hostility to her religious fanaticism (*O*, 23). The young Damon's desire to free himself from such a bondage is closely related to his inability to love any black woman, as shown by his relationship with Gladys, his estranged wife, or Dot, his pregnant mistress. The only woman he loves is the white woman Eva, the wife of his Communist friend.

Wright's idealization of white women like Mary in *Native Son* and Eva in *The Outsider*, however, does not mean that Wright was attracted to these women because they were white. "The Man Who Killed a Shadow," a short story Wright first published in French in 1949, features a white woman who tries to seduce a black man who in turn murders her.[5] The story, like *Native Son*, deals with a young black man who inadvertently kills a white woman. But the two white women are entirely different in character and circumstance. The woman in "The Man Who Killed a Shadow" is a middle-aged, sexually repressed librarian. As Saul, the black man, tries to get away, she starts screaming and he brutally strikes her to death in fear of being accused of rape. Unlike Bigger, Saul is used in the story as a symbol of sexual abandon. Ironically, Saul falls victim to a white woman's sexual exploitation of a black man.

The tragedy that befell Saul and the librarian would not have occurred if their relationship were not interracial. The scene of Mary's murder in *Native Son* also shows that Bigger is sexually aroused by Mary, and vice versa, and that he is terrified of being caught in her bedroom. In each case, racial prejudice gets in the way and prevents a man and a woman from consummating their union. Indeed, it was Richard Wright who first brought out into the open and viewed this sexual myth from a genuinely humanistic perspective.

When *Native Son* appeared in 1940, critics as well as readers hailed it a phenomenal success.[6] As a Book-of-the-Month Club selection it became at once a best-seller, earning a popularity accorded to no previous African-American novel. Sterling Brown, a distinguished black critic, was quick to recognize the revolutionary status the book achieved, asserting that if a single book could awaken the conscience of the whole nation, that book would be *Native Son*. Brown regarded as Wright's greatest achievement the creation of Bigger Thomas, not the revolutionary setting or the thrilling narrative. Brown saw Bigger's characterization as the first to exhibit "a psychological probing of the consciousness of the outcast, the disinherited, the generation lost in the slum jungles of American civilization."⁷ *Native Son* has captured, as no other book has, the powerful emotions and deep-seated frustrations of black people.

Some readers, however, have not considered *Native Son* a successful novel. James Baldwin, for example, considered Bigger Thomas a monster who does not reflect the complex truths of the black experience in America. To Baldwin, Wright fails to understand the true meaning of humanity and the genuine struggle of African-American life; Wright merely records "that fantasy Americans hold in their minds when they speak of the Negro." Bigger, Baldwin believed, is a misrepresentation of the black man because he "has no discernible relationship to himself, to his own life, to his own people, nor to any other people . . . and his force comes, not from his significance as a social (or antisocial) unit, but from his significance as the incarnation of a myth." The serious limitation Baldwin saw in Bigger's character is not in Wright's use of Bigger as a symbol, but in the absence of the social and human relations underlying that symbol. Baldwin would have treated Bigger's story differently: "To tell his story is to begin to liberate us from his image and it is, for the first time, to clothe this phantom with flesh and blood, to deepen, by our understanding of him and his relationship to us, our understanding of ourselves and of all men."⁸ Baldwin also disagreed with Wright in his method of portraying the ordeal of black people because Baldwin saw *Native Son* as rooted in the tradition of naturalistic protest fiction. The protest novel, Baldwin argued, is written out of sympathy for the oppressed but fails to transcend their trauma or the rage such a novel expresses.

Partly in response to the critical tendency to extol *Native Son*, recent critics have discussed Bigger's language in its relation to the narrator. Laura E. Tanner, for instance, makes an inquiry into what she calls the narrator's "miserable" failure in representing Bigger's voice. She attempts to account for "this textural rupture" between the narrative voice and Bigger's voice, between Wright's "sophisticated," "symbolic" language and Bigger's "unsophisticated," "awkward," "broken English." Attributing Wright's inability to fill the gap to the stylistic weakness of the novel, she concludes that "Bigger at last becomes author and narrator of his own text, driving from the novel the voices that would overwhelm his own" and that "*Native Son* is a novel about the insufficiency of novels, a story about the insufficiency of words."⁹ While Tanner's reading is a conscientious effort to apply Derridian theory of discourse to Wright's discourse in *Native Son*, it explains neither the source nor the effect of the power of the narrative. Despite an effort to discard the old cloak of the New Criticism, her reading smacks of the hegemonic literary judgment that has often characterized that mode of criticism. The problem with her analysis stems from her rigid judgment of Bigger's language. "Bigger's voice," she persists, "is marked by a form of halting expression that frequently deteriorates into stuttering repetition." Bigger's language, she repeatedly argues, is characteristic of "his awkward relationship with the master language."[10] Granted, Bigger is not a literate person, but neither is Huck Finn. However awkward and clumsy Bigger's voice may sound to an educated person in the story, it does not sound so to Bigger, nor does it to the reader. Billy Budd stutters, Bartleby prefers not to talk, and Clyde Griffiths and Joe Christmas are at times utterly incoherent speakers.

On the other hand, Joyce Ann Joyce tries to show the cohesiveness between Bigger's voice and the narrative voice, "the connection between Wright's characterization of Bigger and his unique use of sentence structure and figurative language." Whereas Tanner tries to divide the narrative structure into a binary opposition, a juxtaposition of two mutually exclusive strands of language, Joyce finds "a linguistically complex network of sentences and images that reflect the opposing or contradictory aspects of Bigger's psyche and thus synthesize the interrelationship between Wright's subject matter and his expression of it."[11] While Joyce recognizes that the power of the narrative is generated by the fierce battle Bigger wages against racist society, she cogently shows that the impact of the tragedy on the reader comes directly from Wright's complex narrative strategy. Instead of monolithically resonating the voice of Bigger as a victim of his racist environment, Wright, as Joyce argues, amply succeeds in portraying him in terms of dialectical images and ideas: sun and snow, black and white, hero and murderer, fear and blindness, humiliation and insensitivity.

Chiding Joyce for making "no distinction between 'Bigger's thoughts' and the thoughts attributed to him by the narrator," Tanner says that "Joyce fails to detect any tension generated by the placement of' contrasting ideas inside similar grammatical structures.'"[12] The issue, however, is not whether there is any tension between the protagonist's voice and the narrator's voice, since there is always some sort of narrative tension in great novels, like *Moby Dick*, *Crime and Punishment*, and *An American Tragedy*. The central question is how well the novelist uses that tension to his or her advantage to maximize the effect of the narrative. Bigger's spontaneous response and the narrator's thoughtful language do not necessarily collide because Wright creates other strands of narrative voice that mediate the two voices. But Tanner ignores the effects of such voices as the Daltons's language and the speech of Boris Max, the Marxist lawyer, let alone the effect of what is common between Bigger's voice and the narrator's. For example, the Daltons's language, larded with sociological jargon and racial condescension, sounds so far apart from both Bigger's and the narrator's voices as to create the effect of coalescing them. Tanner points out that the Daltons "utilize the master language" with ease[13]; not only do the words fall on deaf ears to Bigger, but to the reader they even sound far more awkward than Bigger's words and indeed ridiculous, thereby creating a superb parody. In Tanner's reading, just as the Daltons's language is equated with "the master language," so is Max's voice intermixed with the narrator's. Although there is some affinity between Max's language and the narrator's and some readers might regard Max as Wright's mouthpiece, their voices at crucial points in the story are poles apart: Max's is strengthened by mind and fact as Wright's is resonated by heart and metaphor.

Although it is often true that literature and sociology, as Baldwin cautioned, are not synonymous, it is also true that a successful protest novel is a work of art that transcends the limitations of didactic writing. One of Wright's techniques to transform this sociological book into a novel is the creation of Boris Max to defend Bigger. Malcolm Cowley, generally very positive about *Native Son*, deplored Max's courtroom plea for Bigger's life as thematically weakening. He argued that Max's speech, on behalf of the whole black population, would be quite meaningful but that Bigger must die to stand as an individual, not a symbol.[14] Bigger, of course, is the major character, but he is not Wright's deepest concern until the very end of the novel. Through Max, Wright speaks for and to the nation, thereby creating a narrative voice, a point of view that is indeed sympathetic to Bigger but entirely impersonal in developing a racial discourse.

Because Wright's mission in *Native Son* as racial discourse is to determine the cause of Bigger's murders, Wright places his emphasis in the third section of the book. As several critics have pointed out, book 3 is the best part of the novel. Edward Kearns, in "The 'Fate' Section of *Native Son*," argues that despite the abstractness of Bigger's speech, the third section of the novel enables Bigger to achieve his identity, a thematic strategy that serves Wright's aim. Paul N. Siegel, in "The Conclusion of Richard Wright's *Native Son*," regards Max's long speech in the courtroom as original and suggests that it does not follow a Marxist party line. Max, Siegel suggests, hands the case to a judge, thereby rejecting a trial by an all-white jury. On the strength of book 3, Wright is able to shift the burden of Bigger's guilt to society.[15] As Wright's development of the story clearly indicates, *Native Son* is built on the inevitable results of Bigger's unpremeditated murder of a white girl. However gruesome and unbelievable his actions may appear, Bigger finds no other way to defend himself but to burn her body and make false accusations. And he cannot help killing Bessie, lest she implicate him. It is inevitable as well that Bigger is captured by white police and brought to a trial by an all-white jury. Given a racist climate, all the scenes take place one after another as if planned. The denouement of the story is convincing not only because Wright adheres to Zola's deterministic philosophy but also because the plot is partly based on the actual murder of a white woman by a black man as reported in the *Chicago Tribune* in 1938. While writing the first draft of *Native Son*, Wright read in a long series of *Tribune* articles that the case of murder "involved Robert Nixon and Earl Hicks, two young Negroes with backgrounds similar to that of Bigger." One of the articles, on May 27, 1938, reported that one Florence Johnson "was beaten to death with a brick by a colored sex criminal . . . in her apartment." The two black men, as Keneth Kinnamon notes, "were arrested soon after and charged with the crime. Though no evidence of rape was adduced, the Tribune from the beginning called the murder a sex crime and exploited fully this apparently quite false accusation."[16]

Max's final speech in the court abounds in irony. While Max is aware of the racist tone of the press against Bigger, he deplores "the silence of the church." "What is the cause of all this high feeling and excitement?" he asks. "Is it the crime of Bigger Thomas? Were Negroes liked yesterday and hated today because of what he has done?" (*NS*, 356). Personally, as well, Max satirizes the landlord Dalton who refuses to rent apartments to black people anywhere but in the black belt. According to Max, then, it turns out that confining Bigger "in that forest" as a stranger had in fact made him an acquaintance of Mary, whom he murdered. (*NS*, 362). Through his killing of a white girl, Bigger is able to see himself as an individual. As James Nagel points out, this scene becomes "the pivotal point for not only the structure and theme but the imagery as well: it is a moment of 'recognition' in the classical sense."[17]

In creating literary discourse, Wright uses other stylistic and structural devices to transcend the limitations of sociological prose. The first scene, in which Bigger and his brother Buddy corner a big rat and Bigger smashes it with a skillet, suggests the plight of black people in white society. Such a violent scene implies the conditions and frustrations of black people in general, but its dramatic impact is not fully appreciated until book 3, where Max delivers the eloquent speeches at the inquest and at the trial.

The scenes of confinement and estrangement are also reflected in the language of the people involved. When Mrs. Dalton is introduced to Bigger by her husband at their residence, she speaks: "Don't you think it would be a wise procedure to inject him into his new environment at once, so he could get the feel of things? . . . I think it's important emotionally that he feels free to trust his environment. . . . Using the analysis contained in the case record the relief sent us, I think we should evoke an immediate feeling of confidence." Bigger tries to listen to their conversation, Wright says, "blinking and bewildered" (*NS*, 48). Not only does her language indicate how strange the white world appears to Bigger; it also allows Wright to satirize the condescension and esotericism of social workers.

Bigger's estrangement from the white world, on the other hand, is reflected in the language of his friends and in that of his enemies. When Bigger and his friend Jack go to see the movie *The Gay Woman*, they are both puzzled by certain words used in the dialogue:

"Say, Jack?"

"Hunh?"
"What's a Communist?"
"A Communist is a red, ain't he?"
"Yeah; but what's a red?"
"Damn if I know. It's a race of folks who live in Russia, ain't it?"
"They must be wild."
"Looks like it. That guy was trying to kill somebody." (*NS*, 34–35)

This dialogue, part of which is quoted here, is a replacement for the original manuscript version, which indicates that both Bigger and Jack are well acquainted with Communism and that Bigger identifies the man kissing Mary Dalton in the newsreel as a Communist. Wright's portrayal of Bigger and Jack in the original manuscript, therefore, makes them more knowledgeable about world affairs than they are in the published version.[18] Later Bigger meets Mary and her Communist friend Jan, and their talk about Communists, demonstrations, class struggle, and black liberation bewilders him. However sympathetic their demeanor may appear, Bigger finds it difficult to understand their language. Feeling alienated from his black friends and resentful toward Mary and Jan, he even resists going into Ernie's Kitchen Shack because he dreads his black friends' asking one another: "Who're them white folks Bigger's hanging around with?" (*NS*, 71). Jan tells Bigger that Communists like Jan and Mary have been fighting to "stop" the kind of killing in a riot in which Bigger's father was also a fatality, but Bigger fails to see the connection between the Communist and Civil Rights movements. Apparently to make Bigger as uninformed and innocent a youth as possible, Wright omitted in the Harper edition a dialogue in which Peggie, the maid at the Daltons, intimates to Bigger that Mary's "wild ways" vex her conservative parents.

Another significant omission in the Harper edition is a page-long passage of Max's speech that characterizes Mary as a compassionate woman. In this passage, Max reminds the court that despite the racial segregation rampant in the country, including the very court where Bigger is standing accused of murder, she genuinely had tried to have sympathy and understanding for Bigger. "It has been said," Max emphasizes, "that the proof of the corrupt and vile heart of this boy is that he slew a woman who was trying to be kind to him. In the face of that assertion, I ask the question: Is there any greater proof that his heart is not corrupt and vile than that he slew a woman who was trying to be kind?" (*EW*, 818). By deleting such a passage, Wright made *Native Son* less didactic and avoided a cumbersome recapitulation of the earlier scene. Leaving this passage, on the other hand, would have undermined Wright's attempt to portray a black youth like Bigger as estranged from Mary, a symbol of white society. The passage would also contradict Wright's assertion that the estrangement between Bigger and Mary rather than the emotional affinity between them is what caused Mary's death. Wright attempted to prove that racism, not their infatuation with each other, resulted in the whole tragedy.

Not only do Max's speeches as they are delivered in the published version awaken in Bigger a consciousness of freedom and autonomy of which he has not been aware before, but they also contrast sharply with the talk of Mr. and Mrs. Dalton, which is larded with sociological jargon. Moreover, Max's final speech at the trial, as Joyce Ann Joyce has noted, is comparable to the chorus in a Greek tragedy.[19] That is, Max's final speech is not a description of something, but, as Aristotle said of tragedy, an action. Wright approaches Aristotelianism in the way he structures Max's dialogue with Bigger in book 3, for Bigger's response to Max is not simply a description of Bigger's sensations at the end of his life but a dynamic development in Bigger's character.

Few critics question that *Native Son* is a superb discourse on race based upon the naturalistic tradition in American literature. Wright's work is often compared with one of the finest social novels written in that tradition, Theodore Dreiser's *An American Tragedy*. Dreiser is, among modern novelists, one of the most influential predecessors of Wright. In an episode from *Black Boy*, Wright tells of being inspired by Dreiser's fiction, which was to the fledgling writer "nothing less than a sense of life itself" (*BB*, 274). Such acknowledgment must have convinced critics that the primary source of his best-known work, *Native Son*, was *An American Tragedy*. In fact, several early reviewers of *Native Son* pointed out that the two novels share the same theme and technique. And both novels convince their readers that the crimes they dramatize are inevitable products of American society and that both protagonists are morally free from guilt. Clifton Fadiman, for instance, wrote, "*Native Son* does for the Negro what Theodore Dreiser in *An American Tragedy* did a decade and a half ago for the bewildered, inarticulate American white."[20]

Except for the obvious issues of race, Wright and Dreiser shared similar experiences before they became novelists. From their boyhoods both were economically hard-pressed; they were always ashamed that they had grown up on the wrong side of the tracks. As boys they witnessed struggling and suffering and felt excluded from society. They grew up hating the fanatic and stifling religion practiced at home. In both lives, the family suffered because of the father's inadequacies as a breadwinner; the son inevitably rebelled against such a father, and the family was somehow put together by the suffering mother. Under these circumstances, their dream of success was merely to survive; they tried to hang on to one menial job after another. As a result, both nurtured a brooding sensibility. At twelve, Wright held "a notion as to what life meant that no education could ever alter, a conviction that the meaning of living came only when one was struggling to wring a meaning out of meaningless suffering" (*BB*, 112). This statement indeed echoes what Dreiser recorded in his autobiography:

> In considering all I have written here, I suddenly become deeply aware of the fact that educationally speaking, where any sensitive and properly interpretive mind is concerned, experience is the only true teacher—that education, which is little more than a selective presentation of certain stored or canned phases of experience, is at best an elucidative, or at its poorest, a polishing process offered to experience which is always basic.[21]

But this close kinship between the lives of Wright and Dreiser need not necessarily have resulted in the similarities between *Native Son* and *An American Tragedy*. Although both novels are obviously concerned with the crime and guilt of a deprived American youth struggling to realize his dreams of success, the characterization of the hero fundamentally differs in the two novels. Clyde Griffiths in *An American Tragedy* is seen by Dreiser as a representative type, and the novel's psychological focus serves to delineate the frustrations of not only an individual but also a class. Bigger Thomas in *Native Son* is presented as a particular individual in Wright's imagination. Wright's essay "How 'Bigger' Was Born" suggests an extension of Bigger to include all those rebels the author had known in the South, and even white victims of the system who actively fought against it. Nevertheless, within the confines of the novel itself, we find no other character remotely like Bigger, once the murder triggers the creation of his personality, and no similar identification between character and author. It is significant in this regard that, as *Black Boy* demonstrates, Wright always considered himself unique, an outsider, not only from white persons but also from most of the black persons with whom he grew up.

It would seem that both authors, being literary naturalists, used authentic court records. Dreiser drew on the Gillette murder case in upstate New York; Wright on the Leopold and Loeb kidnapping-murder as well as the Robert Nixon murder trial and conviction in Chicago. The titles of both books strongly imply that Clyde and Bigger are the products of American society and that society, not the individuals involved in the crimes, is to blame. But doesn't a naturalistic novel *always* create tensions in the life of the hero, growing out of an environment over which he has no control and about which he understands very little and, therefore, by which he is *always* victimized? If so, *Native Son* does not appear to fit into this genre. Bigger's transcendence of the type of defeated, determined protagonist of which Clyde in *An American Tragedy* is a good example provides the clearest distinction between the two works. Despite the obvious parallels between *Native Son* and *An American*

Tragedy, the comparison is of limited value, and this reading is to show significant differences between the two books.

It is true that both novels employ crime as a thematic device. In *Native Son*, the murder of Bessie is the inevitable consequence of Mary Dalton's accidental death; in *An American Tragedy*, Clyde's fleeing of the scene of the accident that kills a child is what leads to his plotting of murder later in the story. Without the presence of crime in the plot neither author would have been able to make significant points about his protagonist. But the authors' focus is different in the two books. Wright's center of interest, unlike Dreiser's, is not crime but its consequences—its psychological effect on his hero. Before committing his crime Bigger is presented as an uneducated, uninformed youth; indeed he is portrayed as a victim of white society who grew up in the worst black ghetto of the nation. We are thus surprised to see him gain identity after the murder. The crime gives him some awareness of himself and of the world of which he has never been capable before. We are surprised to learn that after the murder Bigger is well versed in world affairs. "He liked to hear," Wright tells us, "of how Japan was conquering China; of how Hitler was running the Jews to the ground; of how Mussolini was invading Spain" (*NS*, 110). By this time, he has learned to think for himself. He is even proud of Japanese, Germans, and Italians, because they "could rule others, for in actions such as these he felt that there was a way to escape from this tight morass of fear and shame that sapped at the base of his life" (*NS*, 109–10).

Book 1 of *Native Son* is entitled "Fear," and ironically Wright's characterization of Bigger makes his stature deliberately smaller and less courageous than we might expect of a fighter against racial oppression. No wonder Mary Dalton's death is caused by Bigger's fear of white people and their world. His killing of Mary is an accidental homicide. In *An American Tragedy*, Clyde is placed in a situation so oppressive that only violence can provide the hope of dignity. But the oppression for Clyde has a corollary of hope, not fear, on his part. Clyde is an optimistic character, always seeking opportunities for success in life. While Bigger can only kill accidentally, Clyde in the same position can consciously plot murder. Even though the boat into which Clyde lures Roberta overturns when he has not planned it, and her actual death may legally prove to have been accidental, Clyde is not entirely innocent. On this ground alone the interpretation of the death of a girl as a central episode vastly differs between *Native Son* and *An American Tragedy*.

Throughout his story Dreiser implies that Clyde's aspirations to rise in the world are not matched by his abilities. Near the beginning Dreiser makes known that Clyde, overly impressed by every sign of success in his future, "lacked decidedly that mental clarity and inner directing application that in so many permits them to sort out from the facts and avenues of life the particular thing or things that make for their direct advancement."²² This is why whatever he does is so inept that he is easily caught after the crime. At the trial, Clyde after such a harrowing experience is called by the prosecutor "a loose, wayward and errant character" (*AT*, 525). Before execution Clyde remains "a mental and moral coward," as his defense attorneys have presented him. Not only has he become a puppet of his own lawyers for their political purposes, but he ends his life as an immature youth without a sense of remorse, let alone self-confidence.

By contrast, Bigger after committing two crimes has for the first time redeemed his manhood. Bigger tells Max: "But really I never wanted to hurt nobody. That's the truth, Mr. Max" (*NS*, 388). Bigger's earlier evasion of life has been converted to participation. The fact that he had killed a white girl, a symbol of beauty for white society, makes him "feel the equal of them" (*NS*, 155). Bessie's murder also marks a new development in Bigger's manhood. For the first time he desires to be at peace with himself. Bigger is no longer a slave but a free man who claims his right to "create." Bessie's murder results from a willful act, a clear departure from the accidental killing of Mary Dalton.

Finally, in both *Native Son* and *An American Tragedy* a preacher appears before the trial to console the accused. But in *Native Son* the black preacher is described in derogatory terms. Bigger immediately senses that the Reverend Hammond possesses only a whitewashed soul and functions merely as an advocate of white supremacy. Wright offers this explanation: "The preacher's face was black and sad and earnest" (*NS*, 264).

During his act of liberation, too, Bigger is consciously aware of his own undoing and creation. To survive, Bigger is forced to rebel, unlike Clyde, who remains a victim of the tensions between individual will and social determinism. In rebelling, Bigger moves from determinism to freedom. Bigger knows how to escape the confines of his environment and to gain an identity. Even before he acts, he knows exactly how Mary, and Bessie later, has forced him into a vulnerable position. No wonder he convinces himself not only that he has killed to protect himself but also that he has attacked the entire civilization. In *An American Tragedy*, Dreiser molds the tragedy of Clyde Griffiths by generating pity and sympathy for the underprivileged in American society. In *Native Son*, however, Wright departs from the principles of pity and sympathy that white people have for black citizens. In "How 'Bigger' Was Born," Wright admits that his earlier *Uncle Tom's Children* was "a book which even bankers' daughters could read and weep over and feel good about." In *Native Son*, however, Wright did not allow for such complacency. He warns readers that the book "would be so hard and deep that they would have to face it without the consolation of tears" (*NS*, xxvii).

The meaning of *Native Son* therefore derives not from crime but from its result. Dreiser's interest in *An American Tragedy*, on the other hand, lies not in the result of crime but in its cause. While Bigger at the end of his violent and bloody life can claim his victory, Clyde at the end of his life remains a failure. *Native Son* thus ends on an optimistic note; *An American Tragedy* as a whole stems from and ends on the dark side of American capitalism. F.O. Matthiessen is right in maintaining that the reason for Dreiser's use of the word *American* in his title "was the overwhelming lure of money—values in our society, more nakedly apparent than in older and more complex social structures."[23] Furthermore, Helen Dreiser seems to confirm Dreiser's central thought in interpreting materialism as the cause of Clyde's tragedy. On Dreiser's choice of the Chester Gillette murder case for fictionalization, she comments:

> This problem had been forced on his mind not only by the extreme American enthusiasm for wealth as contrasted with American poverty, but the determination of so many young Americans, boys and girls alike, to obtain wealth quickly by marriage. When he realized the nature of the American literature of that period and what was being offered and consumed by publishers and public, he also became aware of the fact that the most interesting American story of the day concerned not only the boy getting the girl, but more emphatically, the poor boy getting the rich girl. Also, he came to know that it was a natural outgrowth of the crude pioneering conditions of American life up to that time, based on the glorification of wealth which started with the early days of slavery and persisted throughout our history.[24]

Dreiser's fascination with this subject resulted in his treatment of Clyde as a victim of the American dream. Bigger, too, a product of the same society, cherishes a dream of his own. Like anyone else, he reads the newspapers and magazines, goes to the movies, strolls the crowded streets. Bigger is intensely aware of his dreams: "to merge himself with others and be a part of this world, to lose himself in it" (*NS*, 226). Unlike Dreiser, Wright must have clearly recognized his hero's sense of alienation from the rest of the world. It is an alienation that Wright himself, not Dreiser, often experienced as a boy and as a man. But it never occurs to Bigger that he can pursue such a dream. Indeed, throughout the text Wright amply documents the prevailing social mores, economic facts, and public sentiments to prove that Bigger's actions, attitudes, and feelings have already been determined by his place in American life. It is understandable for James Baldwin to say of *Native Son* that every black person has "his private Bigger Thomas living in the skull."[25] Given such a determined state of mind, Bigger would not be tempted to pursue his dreams. Ironically, the racial oppression and injustice in fact enhance his manhood. To Clyde Griffiths, however, the flame of temptation is brighter and more compelling. He is easily caught, and he thrashes about in a hopeless effort to escape the trap. Under these circumstances, "with his enormous urges and his pathetic equipment,"[26] as Dreiser once characterized the plight of such an individual in America, there is no way out for Clyde but to plot murder.

The central meaning of *An American Tragedy* thus comes from the economic and social forces that overpower Clyde and finally negate his aspirations. Where a Bigger Thomas before liberation must always remain an uninformed, immature youth, a Clyde Griffiths is one whose mind is already ingrained with that glorious pattern of success measured by money; one must climb the social ladder from lower to middle to upper class. At the beginning of the story Dreiser directly shows how the family's mission work in which Clyde is compelled to take part looks contrary to his dreams. Dreiser at once comments that "his parents looked foolish and less than normal—'cheap' was the word. . . . His life should not be like this. Other boys did not have to do as he did" (*AT*, 12). A basically sensitive and romantic boy, he cannot help noticing the "handsome automobiles that sped by, the loitering pedestrians moving off to what interests and comforts he could only surmise; the gay pairs of young people, laughing and jesting and the 'kids' staring, all troubled him with a sense of something different, better, more beautiful than his, or rather their life" (*AT*, 10). The function of this scene is in great contrast to that of a similar scene in *Native Son*. Near the beginning Bigger goes to the movies to see the double feature. The portrayal of upper-class white society in *The Gay Woman*, after quickly attracting his attention, quickly loses it, and *Trader Horn*, in which black men and women are dancing in a wild jungle, shows him only life in a remote world. Bigger is thus placed in no man's land; he is only vaguely aware that he is excluded from both worlds. Unlike Wright, Dreiser places his hero in *An American Tragedy* at the threshold of success and achievement.

Clyde is also a victim of sexual forces. Early in the story his family is confronted by his older sister Esta's elopement, pregnancy, and desertion. Although Clyde is aware that sex leads to exploitation and misery on the part of the girl, he does not blame the whole problem on the seducer. This ambivalence in his attitude toward sex foreshadows his own affair with Roberta. For Bigger, sex is merely a biological force that plays a minor role in his life. For Clyde, however, sex is not only viewed materialistically but weighed in the gradations of the economic and social scale. Clyde is first attracted to the incipient whore, Hortense Briggs, because her eyes remind him of an alcove in the hotel hung with black velvet. To her suggestion that "fellows with money would like to spend it" on her, Clyde boasts: "I could spend a lot more on you than they could" (*AT*, 79). To win her love he must buy her an expensive fur coat beyond his means. Sondra Finchley, his ultimate love, for whom he is forced to sacrifice his second girlfriend, Roberta, is called "the most adorable feminine *thing* he had seen in all his days" (*AT*, 219; emphasis added). Dreiser can make us feel what Clyde feels: "Indeed her effect on him was electric-thrilling-arousing in him a curiously stinging sense of what it was to want and not to have—to wish to win and yet to feel, almost agonizingly that he was destined not even to win a glance from her" (*AT*, 219–20). In short, sex becomes not a romantic force of love but the symbol and substance of material success in the American dream.

Thus, Clyde is presented as a helpless victim of society. Characterized by the defense attorneys as a man of weak character, he is not strong enough to oppose the system, nor is he well equipped to transcend his spurious dreams. On the contrary, Bigger in *Native Son* is represented to his disadvantage by the defense attorney. A more convincing argument in that courtroom would have been for the defense to plead insanity rather than to demonstrate that Bigger was a victim of society. In Clyde's defense in *An American Tragedy*, neither pleading insanity nor demonstrating societal victimization occurs. Jephson most faithfully equates Clyde's infatuation with Sondra with a "case of the Arabian Nights, of the ensorcelled and the ensorcellor. . . . A case of being bewitched, my poor boy—by beauty, love, wealth, by things that we sometimes think we want very, very much, and cannot ever have" (*AT*, 681). Dreiser's theme therefore becomes the baffling problem of justice. Jephson, Dreiser's mouthpiece during the trial, tells Clyde and the court: "Clyde—not that I am condemning you for anything that you cannot help. (After all, you didn't make yourself, did you?)" (*AT*, 675). This pronouncement is later echoed by Clyde's own reflections in the prison:

> Was it not also true (the teaching of the Rev. McMillan—influencing him to that extent at least) that if he had led a better life—had paid more attention to what his mother had said and taught—not gone into that house of prostitution in Kansas City—or pursued Hortense Briggs in the evil way that he had—or after her, Roberta—had been content to work and save, as no doubt most men were—would he not be better off than he now was? But then again, there was the fact or truth of those very strong impulses and desires within himself that were so very, very hard to overcome. (*AT*, 784)

Other naturalists who often show their characters being destroyed by overwhelming forces always remind us how small and helpless human efforts are. "Men were nothings," says Frank Norris toward the end of *The Octopus*, "mere animalcules, mere ephemerides that fluttered and fell and were forgotten between dawn and dusk."[27] Dreiser never does this because he is always seeking the possibility of magnitude and self—determination in human existence. No matter how small and weak a man like Clyde may prove to be,

Dreiser never gives up searching for his humanity and individual worth. In an interview in 1921 Dreiser flatly stated his predilection for little men that was to explain his treatment of Clyde Griffiths: "I never can and never want to bring myself to the place where I can ignore the sensitive and seeking individual in his pitiful struggle with nature."[28]

Both Wright and Dreiser are intensely concerned with the forces in society that one must battle for survival. Some naturalist writers see human beings easily destroyed by social forces, while others make their novels thrive upon such a battle. Wright's racial discourse shows that his hero stands at the opposite end of this human struggle, for Bigger, unlike Clyde, is victorious in his battle against the social forces. True, Bigger is condemned to die as a murderer, but this defeat is really a triumph for Bigger, who has rejected society's rules and values and established his own. Dreiser, on the other hand, stands between defeat and triumph. If naturalism faces the tension between will and determinism, Dreiser is content to keep the tension unresolved. Despite Clyde's destruction in the end, Dreiser refuses to indict life. Instead, he tenaciously seeks its beauty and exaltation until the end.

The two novelists' divergent attitudes toward the problem of guilt are reflected in the style and structure of their books. *Native Son* is swift in pace and dramatic in tone and displays considerable subjectivity, involving the reader in experiences of emotional intensity. The thirties were hard times for both white and black people, and it was not possible to take a calm and objective view of the situation. Wright himself was a victim of the hard times, and he could speak from his heart. Moreover, Bigger Thomas is a conscious composite portrait of numerous black individuals Wright had known. As indicated in "How 'Bigger' Was Born," all of them defied the Jim Crow order, and all of them suffered for their insurgency (*NS*, xii). As in the novel, Wright lived in a cramped and dirty flat, and he visited many such dwellings as an insurance agent. In Chicago, while working at the South Side Boys' Club, he saw other prototypes of Bigger Thomas—fearful, frustrated, and violent youths who struggled for survival in the worst slum conditions.[29]

The twenties, the background of Dreiser's novel, had not of course erupted into the kind of social strife witnessed a decade later. Unlike the hostile racial conflicts dramatized in *Native Son*, what is portrayed in *An American Tragedy* is Clyde Griffiths's mind, which is deeply affected by the hopes and failures of the American dream. A later reviewer of *An American Tragedy* accused Dreiser of scanting, "as all the naturalists do, the element of moral conflict without which no great fiction can be written, for he fobbed the whole wretched business off on that scapegoat of our time, society."[30] But the depiction of such a conflict was not Dreiser's intention for the novel in the first place. Rather, the poignancy of Clyde's tragedy comes from his helpless attraction and attachment to the dream society had created. Dreiser defines this essential American psyche in an essay:

> Our most outstanding phases, of course, are youth, optimism and illusion. These run through everything we do, affect our judgments and passions, our theories of life. As children we should all have had our fill of these, and yet even at this late date and after the late war, which should have taught us much, it is difficult for any of us to overcome them. Still, no one can refuse to admire the youth and optimism of America, however much they may resent its illusion. There is always something so naive about its method of procedure, so human and tolerant at times; so loutish, stubborn and ignorantly insistent at others, as when carpetbag government was forced on the South after the Civil War and Jefferson Davis detained in prison for years after the war was over.[31]

In contrast to Bigger's violent life, Clyde's mind can be conveyed only by a leisurely pace and undramatic tone. Dreiser's approach is basically psychological, and this allows us to sympathize with the character whose principal weakness is ignorance and naïveté. Consequently, we become deeply involved with Clyde's fate. Above all, the relative calmness and objectivity with which Clyde's experience is traced stem from a mature vision of the tribulations shared by any of us who have ever dreamed.

The lack of dramatic tone in *An American Tragedy* is also due to the novel's changes of setting. Dreiser's restless protagonist begins his journey in Kansas City, flees to Chicago, and finally reaches his destination in upstate New York. In contrast, Wright achieves greater dramatic intensity by observing a strict unity of setting. All of the action in *Native Son* takes place in Chicago, a frightening symbol of disparity and oppression in American life. Wright heightens the conflict and sharpens the division between the two worlds early in the novel. In the beginning, the Thomases's apartment is described as the most abject place imaginable, while the Dalton mansion suggests the white power structure that ravages black people and destroys their heritage. The conflict is obvious throughout, and the descriptions of the two households present ironic contrasts. Whereas everything at the Thomases's is loud and turbulent, at the Daltons's it is quiet and subdued. But the true nature of the racial oppressor is later revealed: Mr. Dalton, real estate broker and philanthropist, tries to keep black residents locked in the ghetto and refuses to lower the rents. During the trial, the prosecutor, the press, and the public equally betray the most vocal racial prejudice and hatred, as mentioned earlier. Thus, the central action of book 3 is for the defense to confront and demolish this wall of injustice if Bigger is to be spared his life.

The narrative pattern in *An American Tragedy* is entirely different. Although the novel is divided into three parts, as is *Native Son*, Dreiser's division is based upon changes of time and characters. Each part has its own complete narrative, and one part follows another with the same character dominating the central scene. Each unit is joined to the other not only by the principal character but by the turn of events that underlies the theme of the novel. Book 1 begins with Clyde's dreams of success but ends in an accident that forebodes a disaster. This narrative pattern is repeated in book 2, beginning with a portrayal of the luxurious home of Samuel Griffiths in Lycurgus and ending with the murder. Book 3 opens with a depiction of Cataraqui County, where Clyde is to be tried and executed. Clyde's defense, resting upon the most sympathetic interpretation of his character as a moral and mental coward, clearly indicates the possibility of hope but nonetheless ends on a note of despair. The death of a child caused by an automobile accident at the end of book 1 does not make Clyde legally guilty, but his fleeing the scene of the accident makes him morally culpable. This pattern is also repeated at the end of book 2, where he willfully ignores Roberta's screams for help, an act of transgression for which he is tried and punished. Such a narrative pattern is not given to the death of Mary and Bessie in *Native Son*, since one murder is necessarily caused by the other. Despite the fact that Bessie's death is caused by a premeditated murder, Bigger's crime does not raise the same moral issue as does Clyde's.

There are also many other parallels that thread the three parts together in *An American Tragedy*. Esta's seduction and abandonment by a traveling actor early in the story foreshadow what happens to Roberta. Clyde's attraction to Hortense Briggs has a great deal in common with his helpless enticement to Sondra Finchley with her beauty and wealth. Roberta and Clyde, in fact, come from similar backgrounds, both trying to extricate themselves from the past in order to realize their dreams of social and economic success. Furthermore, the entire book is enclosed, in the beginning and in the end, by almost identical vignettes. The novel opens with Clyde and his family preaching on a street of Kansas City at dusk of a summer night and closes with an almost identical scene in San Francisco, with Russell, Clyde's nephew, now taking his place. Dreiser's implication is unmistakable: given the same temperament and circumstance, Russell will grow up to be another Clyde Griffiths and encounter another American tragedy.

Such parallels and ironies not only dominate Dreiser's narrative structure but also constitute the naturalistic detail that characterizes a Zolaesque experimentation. A literary naturalist, as does a scientist experimenting in a laboratory, minutely observes how a given character acts in accordance with his or her milieu. In *An American Tragedy*, unlike his earlier novels such as *Sister Carrie*, Dreiser conducts his experiment with the characters not once but twice to prove the process of a natural phenomenon. What underlies the plot development in this novel is Dreiser's constant reminder for readers to refer to their own flashbacks and reflections.

In *Native Son*, Wright allows readers as little interruption of the action as possible. Unlike *An American Tragedy*, Wright's discourse has no chapter divisions and only an occasional pause to indicate a transition or change of scene. Before Mary's murder, for example, Wright gives readers only three brief glimpses of Bigger's life: his relations with his family, his gang, and his girlfriend. Before Roberta's murder, on the other hand, which occurs at the end of book 2, Dreiser provides a comprehensive background of Clyde's life: his relationships with his family including Esta, with all his friends and associates, and with all the girls with whom he has attempted to make friends. Whereas Dreiser's presentation is complete and direct, Wright's is selective and metaphorical.

Wright thus differs from the traditional naturalist who piles detail upon detail to gain verisimilitude. He is more akin to his contemporaries like Faulkner and Steinbeck in using the devices of the symbolic novel. He writes with great economy, compressing detail in small space and time; readers must supply the rest. But his ideas are scarcely misinterpreted, because *Native Son*, as James Baldwin aptly pointed out, is a protest novel with the author's voice dominating the discourse. Baldwin argues that although this authorial voice records black anger as no African American before him had done, that is also, unhappily, the overwhelming limitation of *Native Son*. What is sacrificed, according to Baldwin, is a necessary dimension to the novel: "the relationship that Negroes bear to one another, that depth of involvement and unspoken recognition of shared experience which creates a way of life . . . it is this climate, common to most Negro protest novels, which has led us all to believe that in Negro life there exists no tradition, no field of manners, no possibility of ritual or intercourse, such as may, for example, sustain the Jew even after he has left his father's house."[32] Bigger is therefore meant to be not so much a character as a symbol, though some critics consider this a confusion in the book. Edward Margolies, for instance, observes an inconsistency of tone in book 3, "where the reader feels that Wright, although intellectually committed to Max's views, is more emotionally akin to Bigger's." What Margolies regards as inconsistent might more profitably be interpreted as a thematic juxtaposition of points of view, the personal (Bigger's) and the ideological (Max's), with both of which Wright is sympathetic.[33]

In *An American Tragedy*, the author's voice is relatively absent. In *Sister Carrie*, for example, Dreiser is noted for a lengthy philosophical commentary inserted at every significant turn of event, as well as for a strong tendency to identify with his characters, especially his heroine. But in *An American Tragedy* Dreiser's comments are not only few but short. Despite Clyde's resolution to work hard and steadily once he has reached the luxurious world of the Green-Davidson, Dreiser's comment is devastatingly swift: "The truth was that in this crisis he was as interesting an illustration of the enormous handicaps imposed by ignorance, youth, poverty and fear as one could have found" (*AT*, 384).

In contrast to *Native Son*, Dreiser in *An American Tragedy* also reduces the author's omniscience by relying upon indirect discourse. When Clyde is helplessly trapped between his loyalty to Roberta and his desire for Sondra, the insoluble dilemma is rendered through his dreams involving a savage black dog, snakes, and reptiles. About the possibility of Roberta's accidental murder, Dreiser depicts Clyde trying to dismiss the evil thought but at the same time being enticed to it. Clyde's actual plot to murder, suggested by the newspaper article, now thrusts itself forward, as the narrator says, "psychogenetically, born of his own turbulent, eager and disappointed seeking" (*AT*, 463). This crucial point in Clyde's life is explained in terms of a well-known myth:

> there had now suddenly appeared, as the genie at the accidental rubbing of Aladdin's lamp—as the efrit emerging as smoke from the mystic jar in the net of the fisherman—the very substance of some leering and diabolic wish or wisdom concealed in his own nature, and that now abhorrent and yet compelling, leering and yet intriguing, friendly and yet cruel, offered him a choice between an evil which threatened to destroy him (and against his deepest opposition) and a second evil which, however it might disgust or sear or terrify, still provided for freedom and success and love. (*AT*, 463–64)

The immediate effect of such a passage for the reader is to create compassion for the character whose mind is torn between the two forces with which he is incapable of coping. Given Clyde's weaknesses, then, the reader is more likely to sympathize with than despise such a soul.

On the contrary, Bigger's manhood—which is as crucial a point in his life as Clyde's dilemma is in his—is rendered through direct discourse. It is not the narrator's voice but the character's that expresses his inner life—the newly won freedom. His murder of a white girl makes him bold, ridding him of the fear that has hitherto imprisoned him. In the midst of describing Bigger's intoxication over his personal power and pleasure, Wright shifts the tone of the narrative to let Bigger provide a lofty voice of his own. While preparing a ransom note, Bigger utters: "Now, about the money. How much? Yes; make it ten thousand. *Get ten thousand in 5 and 10 bills and put it in a shoe box....* That's good.... He wrote: *Blink your headlights some. When you see a light in a window blink three times throw the box in the snow and drive off Do what this letter say*" (*NS*, 167). Even more remarkable is Bigger's final statement to Max:

"What I killed for must've been good!" Bigger's voice was full of frenzied anguish. "It must have been good! When a man kills, it's for something.... I didn't know I was really alive in this world until I felt things hard enough to kill for 'em.... It's the truth, Mr. Max. I can say it now, 'cause I'm going to die. I know what I'm saying real good and I know how it sounds. But I'm all right. I feel all right when I look at it that way." (*NS*, 392)

Bigger's utterance, in fact, startles the condescending lawyer. At this climactic moment Max, awestruck, "groped for his hat like a blind man" (*NS*, 392). Interestingly enough, Dreiser's presentation of Clyde in the same predicament is given through indirect discourse:

> He walked along the silent street—only to be compelled to pause and lean against a tree—leafless in the winter—so bare and bleak. Clyde's eyes! That look as he sank limply into that terrible chair, his eyes fixed nervously and, as he thought, appealingly and dazedly upon him and the group surrounding him.
>
> Had he done right? Had his decision before Governor Waltham been truly sound, fair or merciful? Should he have said to him—that perhaps—perhaps—there had been those other influences playing upon him? ... Was he never to have mental peace again, perhaps? (*AT*, 811)

In contrast to this portrait of Clyde, who is largely unaware of his guilt and his manhood, the final scene of *Native Son* gives the ending its dramatic impact. Despite his crimes and their judgment by white society, Bigger's final utterance elicits from readers nothing but understanding and respect for the emerging hero.

The sense of ambiguity created by Dreiser's use of portraits, dreams, and ironies in *An American Tragedy* is thus suited to the muddled mind of Clyde Griffiths. Bigger Thomas, however, can hardly be explained in ambivalent terms, for he has opted for the identity of a murderer. Clyde is presented as a victim of the forces over which he has no control, and Dreiser carefully shows that Roberta's murder—the climax of the book—has inevitably resulted from these forces. The principal interest of the novel, centering upon this crime, lies in Clyde's life before the murder and its effect on him. In book 3, Clyde is depicted not merely as a victim of society but more importantly as a victim of his own illusions about life. In the end, then, he remains an unregenerate character as Dreiser has predicted earlier in the story.

Like Clyde, Bigger in *Native Son* is presented in the beginning as a naive character, and his life is largely controlled by fear and hatred. He kills Mary Dalton because he fears his own kindness will be misunderstood. He hates in turn what he fears, and his violence is an expression of this hatred. But unlike Clyde, he has learned through his murders how to exercise his will and determination. Each of the three sections of *Native Son* is built on its own climax, and book 3, "Fate," is structured to draw together all the noble achievements of Bigger's life. Significantly, each of the changes in Bigger's development is also measured by his own language. With artistic and structural devices, Wright has converted a similar incident in journalism to a novel. This novel convinces the reader that Bigger Thomas is solely a victim of racial prejudice unlike Clyde Griffiths, who is a victim of the materialistic American dream.

NOTES

1. *A World More Attractive*, 98–110.
2. Richard Wright, *Black Boy: A Record of Childhood and Youth*, 125. Subsequent references will appear parenthetically in the text as *BB*.
3. Kinnamon, "Introduction," in *New Essays on Native Son*, 14. Wright, *Early Works*, ed. Arnold Rampersad, 524. Subsequent references to this edition of *Native Son* are given in the text as *EW*.
4. Richard Wright, *Pagan Spain*, 237. Subsequent references will appear parenthetically in the text as *PS*.
5. "The Man Who Killed a Shadow," in *Eight Men*, 193–209.
6. See the reviews of *Native Son* collected in John M. Reilly, ed., *Richard Wright: The Critical Reception*, 39–99. Subsequent references to these reviews are cited as *Reilly*; the bibliography provides information on their initial publication.
7. See Brown's review in *Reilly*, 95–98.
8. "Many Thousands Gone," 672, 673, 679.
9. "Uncovering the Magical Disguise of Language: The Narrative Presence in Richard Wright's *Native Son*," 134–37, 145.
10. Ibid., 134.
11. "The Figurative Web of *Native Son*," 171. Joyce's essay, originally entitled "Technique: The Figurative Web," is reprinted from her *Richard Wright's Art of Tragedy*.
12. "Uncovering the Magical Disguise of Language," 138.
13. Ibid., 136.
14. See Cowley's review in Reilly, 67–68.
15. See Phyllis R. Klotman, "Moral Distancing as a Rhetorical Technique in *Native Son*: A Note on 'Fate.'"
16. "*Native Son*: The Personal, Social, and Political Background," 68.
17. "Images of 'Vision,'" 113.
18. See *EW*, 472–75.
19. *Richard Wright's Art of Tragedy*, 48.
20. "A Black 'American Tragedy'"; see also Peter Jacks, "A Tragic Novel of Negro Life in America—Richard Wright's Powerful 'Native Son' Brings to Mind Theodore Dreiser's 'American Tragedy.'"
21. Theodore Dreiser, *Dawn*, 586.

22. Theodore Dreiser, *An American Tragedy*, 169. Subsequent references will appear parenthetically in the text as *AT*.

23. *Dreiser*, 203.

24. *My Life with Dreiser*, 71–72.

25. "Many Thousands Gone," in *Notes of a Native Son*, 33.

26. Quoted by Matthiessen in *Dreiser*, 189.

27. *The Octopus*, 343.

28. Matthiessen, *Dreiser*, 189.

29. See Richard Wright, "The Man Who Went to Chicago," in *Eight Men*, 210–50; and Keneth Kinnamon, *The Emergence of Richard Wright*, 120.

30. J. Donald Adams, "Speaking of Books."

31. "Some Aspects of Our National Character," 24.

32. *Notes of a Native Son*, 27–28.

33. *Art of Richard Wright*, 113.

Chapter Ten

Lynching as Surrealism
Leon Forrest's "The Vision"

Keith Byerman

In his first novel, *There Is a Tree More Ancient Than Eden* (1973), Leon Forrest established his distinctive style—surreal, fast-paced, and highly allusive. He defined himself as the American James Joyce ("Angularity"), though he was less interested in invention at the level of the word than he was in bringing together a wide range of discourses. The body of his fictional works engages matters of race, religion, history, gender, politics, social class, family, identity, region, and violence not as distinct themes but as a matrix of interdependent American concerns. In the "Vision" section of *There Is a Tree*, he uses these elements to depict a lynching/crucifixion.

It is useful to begin by recalling the tradition of literary lynchings in American writing. The slave narratives included various acts of physical violence against the enslaved, but no matter how gruesome the images, these were usually private acts against those who were considered property. It was only after Emancipation, when blacks had gained citizenship, that lynching, in the sense of extra-legal killings, with or without claims of wrongdoing, can be said to occur. In the late nineteenth and early twentieth century, as writers such as Ida B. Wells and W.E.B. Du Bois began exposing the practice, it became a topic for literary work. Theodore Dreiser, William Faulkner, James Weldon Johnson, and Jean Toomer, among others, created scenes or entire stories in which black men (even though women were also killed in reality) died at the hands of mobs. The best-known piece is Richard Wright's "Big Boy Leaves Home." The traditional pattern has largely been to create graphic violence that challenges white reader assumptions about black humanity and white civilization.[1]

The value of this brief survey is to establish the different representation that Forrest offers in "Vision." Like Toomer, he takes an approach that draws attention to its own literariness. Ralph Ellison, in a posthumously published story,[2] creates his own surreal narrative. Finally, Alice Walker's story "The Flowers" does not depict the violence at all, but instead a girl's discovery of a corpse and a noose. But where Toomer is impressionistic in his depiction, Ellison focuses on twists in the action, and Walker is highly allusive, Forrest blends discourses that produce a surreal effect that he obviously considers more in keeping with the nature of lynching. One of the first points to note is that this version of the event is much longer than usual. It runs for over thirty pages, whereas the usual practice is to keep the scene relatively brief. One reason for this abbreviation is that the focus of the lynching itself tends to be on the victim; once he is dead, the writer has little more to say about what has just happened. Other parts of these narratives discuss the preparation and aftermath of the killing.

Forrest, in contrast, takes a more complex approach in his dream-narrative. He brings together a wide range of actors in what he implies is a form of American passion play. There are the crowds who come to see the spectacle, their leaders, soldiers, various tangential figures, animals, and angels. The scapegoat receives relatively little attention and is not particularly individualized. In other words, Forrest presents this as a societal (even national) ritual with extensive political, racial, religious, and historical implications. The lynching is highly symbolic, even allegorical, in Forrest's rendering. He pushes the boundaries of language and representation in suggesting what racial violence means.

"The Vision" is a key chapter in *There Is a Tree More Ancient than Eden* (1973). The book as a whole narrates a day in the life of Nathaniel Turner Witherspoon, a young black man who has just lost his mother. It thus fits the pattern of the author's use of the trope of orphanhood to represent the black American experience. The sections of the book include "The Nightmare," "The Dream," "The Vision," and "Wakefulness," representing different stages of consciousness.[3] Stylistically, the narrative is primarily stream of consciousness, employing the discourses of the Bible, folklore, African American history, mythology, black music, and classical and modernist literature.

"The Vision" is both longer and more fantastical than any of these. It opens with immediate cross-references: "The lance rises and falls in the hands of a soldier, who seems to be practicing and testing its weightiness, and the crowds are moving down into the floor of the valley, with bloodhounds chained to their wrists" (115). This brief paragraph opens with an image from the crucifixion story, with the lance that will penetrate the body of Christ; Forrest shows the soldier preparing himself and his instrument for his role in the ritual. At the same time, the "practicing" has an erotic element, since the action can be read as sublimated masturbation, which reinforces the sexual elements implicit in the act of lynching. Linked to this individual image syntactically is the movement of the anonymous crowds, distinguished only by the bloodhounds they bring with them. By using the plural "crowds," the author implies a mass of people, perhaps the nation itself. The bloodhounds are present as a signifier, since their work is already done; the man to be killed is mentioned in the next paragraph. The dogs inform us that we have shifted to a lynching narrative from the crucifixion story.

Within these opening lines, then, we are given the rhythm of the narrative between two different tales of execution, the movement from individual focal points to more general views, and some suggestion of the ways violence interacts with the erotic. Having established this framework, Forrest then introduces the key players in this drama. From the "upper regions" of the valley, emerges a "golden-suited leader," carrying a very large tree. From the "lower end" walks a man led by another leader. The man is "taunted and cursed" by the mass of people. But still he is moving with a muted dignity (his head a bit to the right, not quite cocked) even though his tunic was fouled and muddied and the tears were streaming down his face, as men and women kept kicking at him although they could see he was wearing a long chain welded to a brace about his left ankle. . . . And he dragged it just a little as he moved. . . . Yet there was a majesty in his gait. . . . And the chain mournfully clanged, against smoking rocks and swollen earth. (116)

While the chain and the response of the crowd recall both written and visual images of lynching, other elements suggest the designation Man of Sorrows used to refer to Christ.[4] In addition, the earth itself seems to be repudiating the actions of the mob in its smoking and swelling. Finally, despite the effort at humiliation, the man retains a superiority to those attacking him. Not only is there the majesty of his gait, but also the almost-cock of the head, which suggests an attitude of greater knowledge of what is happening and a distance from it all.

The two sides meet next to the river ("Down by the Riverside"), which itself has confusing qualities: it is only three feet deep and three feet across, so barely a river at all. Moreover, it flows "east west, yes and to north and to south/crisscross" (116). Thus, if we read this as an American reference, it is both the Mississippi and Ohio Rivers, but it also, as the narrative develops, becomes the Jordan River, the River Styx, and the Nile. The river is then all rivers, seen as geographical elements with historical and even spiritual meaning.

Next to this natural setting for the ritual, Forrest literally sets up a human construction. The tree mentioned earlier becomes a cross-like structure, though not the emblematic biblical cross. He goes into detail about how it is pieced together with supports on three sides and a cross bar at the top. This description suggests careful planning and coordination, even if the emotion of the scene implies spontaneity. In this sense, Forrest depicts the duality of a lynching. On the one hand, it is necessary to bring the mob to a fever pitch, often through accusations of an assault on a white woman and to link this to the racism of the white community, in order to justify extra-legal violence. On the other hand, the event must be publicized and arranged, so as to maximize the size of the crowd and provide a record of the experience. Special trains were often hired, advertising was sent out, and photographers were encouraged to be present and even, in some cases to sell their work as postcards.[5] By detailing the lynching structure and having the leaders bring their communities together, Forrest undermines the notion that these executions were spontaneous expressions of righteous indignation; rather they are deliberate acts of murder motivated by racial hostility.

As the ritual develops, Forrest constructs a rhythm, drawn from a Biblical phrase: "And as these things were being accomplished." Variations of this wording occur nine times. It originally appears in the Gospel of John, where it refers to the ways the suffering of Christ fulfills Old Testament prophecy. In this text, however, it serves as a marker for ever-greater acts of torture. The sadism implicit in the event is made apparent through references to eyes. The soldier responsible for nailing the hands to the tree is said to have "a liquid pride in his delighted eyes" (119); then he nails the right hand, "his liquid eyes sparkling like those of a jeweler inspecting the fairest pearl of his horde of preciously purloined gems" (120). The referent for the pearl is not specified; it could be the Pearl of Great Price from Matthew's gospel, the pearls that were his eyes from *The Tempest*, or the man being crucified. In any case, we are told that the jewel has been "purloined," which echoes Edgar Allan Poe's detective story.[6] Thus, despite the sanction given to the soldier's action, by both his military standing and the approval of the crowd, it is clearly considered to be illegal behavior.

The environment is represented as in league with the intensifying passion of the crowd. The narrator notes the change from rain to thunder and lightning to a darkened sky. As the tree is dropped into the hole prepared for it, it becomes more difficult to see the victim's features. Nonetheless, what is most salient are the eyes: "(Oh yes, the eyes too, yes and *especially those eyes, eyes, EYES*).... Eyes, time-telling *eyes*, seeing eyes. *Eyes*, like eyes in a rock sparkling/eyes like eyes in a mouth, yes and eyes like a womb—EYES, EYES, EYES" (121).

The narrative reverts to the action as the soldiers "inserted" their lances into the man's body, with the effect of "blood flying from his pierced sides" (122). Again, Forrest echoes and exaggerates the crucifixion story. The crowds, though they cheer the violence, seem dissatisfied, which troubles the leaders:

Now when these unlucky deeds were accomplished, the crowd cheered wildly, yet they didn't seem quite satisfied, as their leaders were soon to discover . . . as they came aggressively forward now to face each other, smartly saluting, then doing about-face motions and repeating to their respective audiences, saying almost in unison, three times:[7]
HAVE YOU ACHIEVED SATISFACTION?
And now, almost in unison, the Word coming flying frozen from both sides: NAY! NAY! NAY!
Ah, but the leaders themselves were looking wretched, yet still military as blood shot like water from the man's pierced and spread-eagled body. (122)

The triplet of NAY engages the triplet of EYES and shifts the meaning through wordplay, so that EYES become AYES. Thus, an affirmative vision represented by the victim is negated by the passionate hatred of the mobs, with the implication that the leaders may not be able to maintain control over the ritual they have initiated.

This is apparent as the violence and sadism intensify:

And there was upon the land a fierce mighty storm now, as if the skies had eyes to see and tongues to tell. . . . Because of this, yes and because the depths of their appetites were not yet satisfied, there now arose from the crowd a sense of renewed need to hurry to *roast* towards the plateau-delights of their fulfillment. . . . But their fancies labored and fluttered apparently between wish and fruition. . . . Like the starving man who knows that it is food his body needs but is unable to find the fulcrum to render his appetite fulfilled; at a certain point his wretched hunger makes him vulnerable prey for any caged-away animal within him to be reduced to its own pristine savagery, before even his ancestors walked on all fours. . . . So apparently with this crowd, this early autumn afternoon too. (122–23)

Through the comparison, Forrest turns the mob's desire into a basic hunger which it cannot find a way to satisfy. Because the people are clueless, they find themselves in a state of primeval savagery. They are now in a state that the leaders cannot control or even understand.

A man in the crowd solves the dilemma by giving the victim an identity that both ends their confusion and validates their hostility:

HE IS A NIGGER!

This thrice-spoken racist proclamation undams the pent-up emotion:

And hardly had the breath from the second nuncio-like pronouncement leapt from the man's lips before a thunderously mad trumpet did commence to blast upon the darkening early afternoon, erupting into a joy which touched interiors, which identified the cause of their broodings and heightened into bliss and vaulted towards cliffs of ecstasy. (124)

Significantly, the other side of the river does not participate in the outburst, though it does nothing to stop it. Meantime, small groups of dissenters "wash their hands" of the matter and move back to the "plantations" of the upper valley.

This passage is an allegory of the post-Reconstruction nation. With the withdrawal of federal troops, the South is able to identify a scapegoat and give license to its bloodlust. The North gives passive assent to this violence, and even those who find the behavior morally repugnant retreat to safe spaces where they may or may not express their views from a distance.

But Forrest is not satisfied with this somewhat abstract vision. He insists on providing readers with more detail, with a probing of the heart of the matter. He repeats the Biblical phrase—"Now as these things came to pass"—to introduce the next stage of the ritual. The man who had made the racial identification drags into the space an actual tree "with a life of its own, rooted in the past, frozen, and yet electric" (124). Thus, the human construction made for what appears to be a crucifixion is replaced by the "natural" object for lynching. The man bearing the tree is the epitome of American whiteness: his suit is white, his eyes are said to be "gold coin-shaped," and the word "alabaster" is three times used to refer to his appearance. The tree is presented as fecund and female:

> For the tree itself was flush, down through the leaves and to the roots of its preserved full-blown late-commencing summer pregnancy. . . . Green leaves full-blown like the ears of a woman; fruit dripping—apple ripe and luscious—throbbing like tender plumb breasts; and wild limbs and long hooking roots, making it appear now like an octopus. (125)

The description suggests a connection to Billie Holiday's rendition of "Strange Fruit," down to the designation of the tree as a poplar. The tree, which is originally figured as a tree of life, now becomes, as in the song, a tree of death. But life and death here are in a dialectical relationship: the ritual of killing is always essential to the renewal of life, even if that life in this case is the revitalization of white supremacy.

But this regeneration is not smooth; rather it is chaotic and cataclysmic. Nature itself seems to be exploding:

> And when these deeds were accomplished, the very afternoon commenced to tremble and quake and day spun into night and night began to devour its way back into day with a river-robed, gathering ferocity, across the two-hearted valley split asunder by this river, as if the stars had commenced to fall. . . .

> Now across the land there floated the odor of decaying serpents: devourers of seed and ravagers of land buds, cast ashore once upon a time and hurled into stilted barns burning, after they had also sucked up and devoured foot-long babies, frozen in the mouths of rodents; the serpents themselves possessed of breastlike stomachs pregnant/pickled and protruding stomachs like rabbits strung up by their legs in the marketplace.[8] (127)

If there is to be renewal, it will not happen in a space of purity and order, the creation of which is supposedly the goal of lynching. The ideal is a hierarchical and patriarchal society in which everyone knows his/her place and in which the categories are established at the basic level of purity of blood. Ironically, the securing of this structure is built on the occasional spilling of blood in order to guarantee compliance.

As the man is removed from the T-cross and hung from the tree, the blood starts its flow:

> And then his throbbing blood oozing; feet dangling like a puppet drooping in midair, as his neck—then ashen of face, eyes bulging and forehead sweating, bloated into one massive balloon-about-to-burst mass. . . . And the fruit of his early shredded manhood beginning to wilt, as the furnace-blasted breath in him commenced to recede and to expire . . . he was past thirty and his blood trickled from his sides, from the place just above the arch of his feet, and his hands; along his lilac lovely fingers. . . . Yet there was still an ironic dignity to the compassion scrawled upon his curling lips; nor could the bloated face in all of its apparent oneness totally distort the compassionate fury of those eyes and there was fury of those eyes and there was majesty to behold in that head, which had now finally drooped. (126)

Some elements here correspond with the traditional representation of lynching (and to some extent crucifixion). We are shown the dangling feet, the bulging eyes, the shredded manhood, and the wounds from which the blood emerges. We are given an approximate age, which matches that of the Christ. But Forrest goes beyond these markers to render this event symbolic on another level. Christ's compassion is expressed in the words, "Father, forgive them, for they know not what they do" (Luke 23:34), which not only offers forgiveness, but also bases it on the assumption of the spiritual ignorance of the offenders. In "The Vision," we are told that there was an "ironic dignity" to the victim's compassion. This phrase suggests that the scene involves a reversal: despite the assaults and insults to his body, he is not abject or vocal about his suffering; in fact, he seems to look upon his abusers with something like pity. And it may be this generosity of spirit that confuses the crowd and makes it discontent.

But Forrest does not stop here, with a superhuman (perhaps divine) attitude of kindness. Lest we think the victim is passively and calmly accepting of the situation, we have what may be the key statement of the entire narrative: "nor could the bloated face in all of its apparent oneness totally distort the compassionate fury of those eyes." If "compassionate fury" is to be understood as more than an oxymoron, then readers have to consider how recognition of the suffering of others can be linked to uncontrolled rage. What's crucial is that the two terms are grammatically tied together. In other words, this is not a condition in which one feels sympathy for those suffering and simultaneously anger at those who cause the suffering. We are asked to believe that it is possible for the victim to see the violation of his humanity that leads to lynching as a form of suffering. The violation itself is almost unspeakable, so what is apparent is the anger at what people are capable of; but the violence comes from a place of fear and self-hatred that the mob, both individually and collectively, cannot acknowledge. This dialectic would seem to provide a prescient counterstatement to the contemporary expectation that victims of police shootings and other acts of violence against racial and ethnic minorities should offer words of forgiveness regardless of the attitudes of the perpetrators of that violence.[9] Such a position implicitly claims that those who suffer have an obligation to be generous and considerate of the ones who cause the suffering; this claim carries with it the subordinate status of the one forgiving. It assumes that there is no right of retaliation or even justice.

But rather than carry this contradiction to resolution, the text explodes into a new set of images, both of the body and of the natural world. In another act of signifying on "Strange Fruit":

> And as his rail-split body swung in the darkness (although it was still early afternoon) his blood commenced to stream back back back through the many layers of the lusty foliage (richer than plant upon straw upon brick, upon robe, upon boat, upon tablet, upon toga, upon fish, upon cup bitter, upon darkness inviolate and awesome, upon machine furiously piping, upon star quaking and rocking), upon the luscious apples down down down to to where it commenced to trickle and flow, upon the massive roots, and to seep finally towards and into the waters running silently in an April running river. (126)

Forrest makes this an apple tree, thus conjuring forth the Garden of Eden (with serpents soon to appear), from which the blood is spilling everywhere, ending in the life-giving ("April running") river. We then turn to the body itself: "chest no longer heaving; loincloth blood-soaked and even caked; and his furious body like a six-foot rail split by a hypodermic nail—hanging like a sword on fire, dangling from the womb of a star, in the afflicting furnace of creation" (127). He is simultaneously the sword of Damocles, an umbilical cord, and a version of Abraham Lincoln, the rail splitter. Linked to his identity is also the oxymoronic "afflicting furnace of creation." On the one hand, the furnace is a place of purification and thus creation, as in the steel-making process; on the other, it is intended as a space of affliction, as in the biblical story of Shadrach, Meshach, and Abendego. Here we are asked to believe that the affliction is the source of creation, that the victim is transformed by his suffering into something new. His lynching would seem to make him into something different from what he was. The question for the narrative is what that "something" might be. Additionally, we must ask if he is the only one, or even the primary one who undergoes transformation. Furthermore, we cannot, in this context, assume that creation is necessarily positive.

The acts of violence so far only produce in the narrative greater demands for violence, suggesting that one aspect of the action is the creation of a nation that defines itself in terms of violence. The leaders, following traditions of lynching, now ask "SHALL WE CASTRATE HIM?" But the mob does not answer; rather the text becomes a cacophony of allusions to Greek and Biblical texts, to spirituals, and Catholic ritual. The narrator, reaching into the river, draws forth dozens of objects in a clear parallel to the eviction scene in *Invisible Man*, including such things as musical instruments, railroad whistles, false teeth, and items associated with Christianity and conjure.

The mob then turns on the leaders themselves and hang them next to the lynchee. They follow this by dismembering the man, cutting off first his arms and then his legs and kick them into the river, where they tumble toward a large rock on which some of the soldiers are gambling over his bloody tunic. The new leaders ask again their ritual question, and this time the crowd demands his head. They then engage in a war for which side will get the head. Here the narration pushes to the extreme of Civil War rhetoric—brother against brother—of internecine hostility:

> So that by noon, now, darkness once again worshiped upon the bloody havoc of the land as tear-eyed brothers slit their brothers' throats; and there was fury within the hearts of even little children, cross-eyed against their mothers, blinding them with stones, and others killing their fathers (by wrenching their necks) and then raping their blinded mothers, and late pregnant mothers—their stomachs sagging like hammocks—were seen to dash their very own burdensome bodies upon the rocks. (133–34)

The passage continues for another long paragraph as members of extended families and bloodhounds are engaged in the violence. Even efforts at ceremony are disrupted; attempts by the families to bury the hanged leaders are frustrated because the land is so thoroughly saturated with blood.

At this point, Forrest introduces an impromptu ceremony that signifies on postbellum history. To end the conflict over possession of the head, the mob demands that it be placed in the middle of the river. To accomplish this, they devise a plan in which two three-year-old children, one from each side, are chosen to sever the head. Accompanied by their parents, they climb ladders and use a saber to decapitate the body:

> This then was the union announced by the newest leadership from both war-waging sides and the many highly placed individuals (distinguishable not because of their actions but rather because of their silk and linen dress) of the few who ruled or controlled the leaders were proud of the compromise achieved, for it meant tranquility and a sweet recall of the preamble they had stated in the speeches made as a kind of prologue to the announcement of their linking, binding intentions for union amongst the peoples. (137)

The participation of the children points as well to the emergence of the plantation school of literature, which served to justify the racial behaviors of the late nineteenth and early twentieth centuries. The fictions often ended with a marriage between northern and southern white characters, symbolizing the national reunion. Here Forrest ties that happy ending to the sacrifice of black men and women, who, though constitutionally citizens, now must suffer disenfranchisement, segregation, and racial violence, all carried out with impunity.

We are also given here a parodic take on the Compromise of 1876, which enabled Rutherford Hayes to become president by agreeing to withdraw Federal troops from the South and allow white supremacists to regain control of the region, with devastating effects on the black population. Among the chief beneficiaries of this arrangement were the major manufacturers, bankers, and plantation owners in "their silk and linen dress." We see the role of greed in the tale as the soldiers wagering over the victim's tunic demand rewards from one of the lieutenants, who gives first one of his daughters, then fruit from the tree on which the man is hung, and finally pots of gold. This initiates a spree of selling and bartering of the clothing and sandals.

While all this activity is occurring, the text returns to the head, which begins swaying at the top of the pole. A voice emerges from the eyes and the mouth sings. At this moment, the man in white reappears, with an eagle on his shoulder. He sends the bird to wreak havoc on the head. The eagle is especially fascinated by the eyes, which it steadily plucks away at. Eventually, the assault is so vigorous that it causes the head to fall, with only tiny fragments of the eyes left. But they nonetheless have great power:

> Oh those eyes, my Lord and my father/my mother/EYES my Redeemer, EYES-EYES-EYES ohohoh Uncle Abraham, OHOHOH Father Frederick—EYES EYES EYES? AYEAYEAYE. . . . Stone-glazing; cunning as a mountain-blown fox's soul fleeing towards the plantation paradise—those EYES EYES, EYES. (144)

The passage blends religion and history, with the lord and redeemer whose saving role requires crucifixion linked to "Uncle" Abraham Lincoln (sacrificed for the nation) and Frederick Douglass, who envisioned the possibility of black freedom and spent his life trying to enact it.

The crowd and the man in white seek to destroy the eye, but their very efforts have the opposite effect: the more he strikes it, the more it divides and spreads: "but each time he smashed one tiny fragment of the EYE, it suddenly DIVIDED into a new—yes Lord and even Brighter—EYE (147). The terror of the eye is mitigated when they turn from destroying it to selling it, just as they did the tunic and sandals. The narrative thus suggests the cash value of black suffering. Here, Forrest may be referring to the commercialization of lynchings. Special trains were hired to bring crowds to the event; stands were set up to provide food and drink, and, specific to the image of the eye, was the practice of professional photographers recording the event and selling postcards to participants, who sent them to family and friends to boast about their presence.[10]

While the people are engaged in these mundane activities, a band of "bruised-blood" angels began gathering the body parts into a sackcloth bag, first the arms and legs floating in the river, then to the tree/cross where they add the man's trunk and his head to the bag. They transport it down the river: "And they didn't seem to expect *it* to explode, as it now did, but as the sackcloth shawl exploded—the parts and members of the man cut down did rise *Upwards* and seemed to be TOTALLY COLLECTED INTO HIS ORIGINAL FORM" (148). The Christ/lynchee figure becomes Osiris, and thus a primal resurrection figure. The conflation of Christian and Egyptian narratives grants to the black man the status of divinity and turns what had been regarded as a scapegoat into a son of God.

But Forrest carefully places this story within history. Despite the fact that the man's wings were broken, he begins to fly. We are told that the wings are "broken, storm-blasted like limb branches torn from their plantation roots, his feet bloody, his mouth twisted, his eyes bedeviled, his glorious head bloody" (148). Considerable attention is paid to the wings:

> Wretched, wrongsided, rotten rank—like the hag's rags. Yet stepladder climbing (moving on upwards, as if he heard some secret drum drum drum) with a tambourine undercurrent/a long ways from home/homeward. . . . And the wings

splattered with wine, blood, dung, rain water, snow, soot, holes, patches, icicles, grease, duck butter, sperm. (148)

This is not a transfigured Christ or even a powerful resurrected Osiris, but rather a black man who bears on his body all the damage and detritus of living in a violent white supremacist. Elsewhere in the novel, Forrest mentions the gray goose of black folklore; constantly attacked, it nonetheless always rises above its oppressors and flies away.[11] To be black in America is to be always under threat, to be caught in a history that is always being reenacted. Lynching was the most extreme expression of the racism that defines the nation, but the perspective that permitted it continues in voter suppression, incarceration, and white killings of black people. And as under lynch law, there are still seldom moral or legal repercussions to such violence. In Forrest's "Vision," then, there is a kind of divinity in the ability of African Americans to face the bigotry of their fellow citizens and continue to rise above it.

WORKS CITED

Accomando, Christina. "Troubling the 'Beat Inevitable': Brooks, Ellison, and the Cultural Logic of Lynching." *MELUS* 42.4 (2017): 113–35.

Byerman, Keith. "Angularity: An Interview with Leon Forrest." *African American Review* 50.4 (2017): 1013–24.

——. *Fingering the Jagged Grain: Tradition and Form in Recent Black Fiction.* Athens: University of Georgia Press, 1986.

Cone, James H. *The Cross and the Lynching Tree.* Maryknoll, NY: Orbis, 2011.

Forrest, Leon. *There Is a Tree More Ancient than Eden.* 1973; Chicago: Another Chicago Press, 1988.

Ellison, Ralph. "A Party Down at the Square," in *Flying Home and Other Stories.* Ed. John Callahan, 3–11. New York: Vintage Books, 1997.

Goldsby, Jacqueline. *A Spectacular Secret: Lynching in American Life and Literature.* Chicago: University of Chicago Press, 2006.

Greenway, John. "The Flight of the Gray Goose: Literary Symbolism in the Traditional Ballad." *Southern Folklore Quarterly* 18 (1954): 165–74.

Harris, Trudier. *Exorcising Blackness: Historical and Literary Lynching and Burning Rituals.* Bloomington: Indiana University Press, 1984.

Lelekis, Debbie. *American Literature, Lynching, and the Spectator: Spectacular Violence.* Lanham, MD: Lexington Books, 2015.

Lightweis-Goff, Jennie. *Blood at the Root: Lynching as American Cultural Nucleus.* Albany: State University of New York Press, 2011.

Litwack, Leon F., and Hilton Als, compilers. *Without Sanctuary: Lynching Photography in America.* Santa Fe: Twin Palms, 2005.

Mathews, Donald G. "The Southern Rite of Human Sacrifice: Lynching in the American South." *Mississippi Quarterly*, 61.1–2 (2008): 27–70.

West, Benjamin S. *Crowd Violence in American Modernist Fiction: Lynchings, Riots and the Individual Under Assault*. Jefferson, NC: McFarland Publishing, 2013.

NOTES

1. For a general study of lynching as ritual in literature, see Harris. For "The Vision" in the context of the novel, see Byerman, *Fingering*, 240–49. Other commentaries on lynching in literature include Accomando, Lelekis, West, Lightweis-Goff. Cone, Goldsby, and Mathews.

2. John Callahan, in a collection of Ellison's published and unpublished short fiction, entitles the piece "A Party Down at the Square."

3. For the 1988 edition of the novel, Forrest added a concluding section entitled "Transformation."

4. One connection here is the closing line of Gwendolyn Brooks's "The *Chicago Defender* Send s a Man to Little Rock": "The loveliest lynchee was our Lord."

5. See *Without Sanctuary* for an accounting of these public relations activities.

6. Forrest does not resist the wordplay of "pearl" and "purloined," which reinforces the idea of crime.

7. Forrest uses the number *three* repeatedly in the chapter, whether as a reference to the trinity or to African-American folk belief is not entirely clear. Given the dual nature of the man and the events, it is probably both.

8. This relatively short passage contains allusions to Hemingway ("two-hearted"), Faulkner ("barns burning"), and even Katharine Anne Porter (the skinned rabbits in the marketplace). The dominant reference, I would suggest, is to Hieronymous Bosch's paintings.

9. We have seen in recent years police and civilian killings of black men and women, attacks on Asian people, and the caging of Latin American immigrants, especially children. One could add to this assaults and murders of LGBTQ people and domestic violence. Relatively few of these end with punishment of the assailants.

10. *Without Sanctuary* offers a collection of these cards with, whenever possible, dates, places, and names of victims.

11. See Greenway, 171.

Chapter Eleven

Lynching in African-American Poetry

Toru Kiuchi

This chapter examines how lynching was described in African-American poetry. In the late eighteenth century, the definition of lynching was ambiguously "flogging or tar-and-feathering" but a hundred years later it clearly meant the execution by a mob of an individual who committed an alleged crime (Dray viii). The nation's most complete record of lynchings occurring in the United States during an 86-year period spanning 1882 to 1968 show that 4,743 people were lynched—including 3,446 African Americans and 1,297 whites.[1] Not only in the United States but in Japan, lynching of Koreans living in Japan happened about the same time on 1 September 1923 after the Great Kanto Earthquake.[2] In opposition to the monstrous violence such a political anti-lynching activist as Ida B. Wells-Barnett (1862–1931) led a fearless movement in the United States to exterminate the cruel practice in the early twentieth century and pass an anti-lynching bill. On the other hand, as almost every African-American family is said to have a lynching victim story, African-American writers continue even until today to write as a living memory lynchings and other acts of racial violence in America. Lynching is especially taken into account as a serious issue by a great number of African-American poets[3] as shown in Langston Hughes's controversial "Christ in Alabama,"[4] first published on page one in the Vol. 1, No. 13, 1 December 1931 issue of *Contempo: A Review of Books and Personalities*, beginning with the following stanza:

> Christ is a Nigger,
> Beaten and black—
> O, bare your back.

African-American poets such as Frances E.W. Harper (1824[5]–1911), Paul Laurence Dunbar (1872–1906), and Claude McKay (1889–1948) represent lynching in their poems while invoking protest against the cruel traditions of the practice. Because their poetry is basically anti-lynching, their aim to compose poetry is to awaken their readers to the need for collective action against one of the evils of long duration by employing an eloquent rhetoric in the representation of the lynching practice in their poetry. Their protest poetry is often appealing to the conscience of the readers, offering the way in order to get their readers involved in social activism. In this chapter I make a detailed explanation of the process of the composition of their poems and analyze their poetic diction, exploring the depiction of anti-lynching disposition in their poetry for discussion, especially in "The Martyr of Alabama" (1895) by Frances E.W. Harper, "The Haunted Oak" (1900[6]) by Paul Laurence Dunbar, and "The Lynching" (1920) by Claude McKay.

"THE MARTYR OF ALABAMA" BY FRANCES E.W. HARPER

"The Martyr of Alabama," whose main theme is a murder just for fun rather than lynching, was written based upon the poet's Southern experiences, probably published for the first time in her collection of poems, *The Martyr of Alabama and Other Poems* (Publisher Unknown, 1895). Harper was at the age of sixty-nine then and lived in Philadelphia when the poem was published. After the Civil War ended back in 1865, she moved to the South to teach newly freed African Americans during the Reconstruction Era. During this time, she worked with the Freedmen's Bureau encouraging many freedmen in Mobile, Alabama so that they could vote independently. She published *Sketches of Southern Life* on 1 January 1872, an anthology of poems in the form of narration by former slave Aunt Chloe. Written in African-American vernacular speech, the anthology details Harper's experience touring the South and meeting newly freed African Americans, providing a commentary on the concerns of African Americans living in the South: racism, family, education, religion, slavery, and Reconstruction: "But now we have a President, / And if I was a man / I'd vote for breaking up / The wicked Ku Klux Klan" (Harper, "Sketches" 13).

Harper is also known for her first novel, *Iola Leroy, or Shadows Uplifted* (1892) when she was sixty-seven years old, a book that "attempts to interpret the post-slavery years from a black point of view and that refers to the increasing practice of whites lynching blacks" (Bryant 71). Harper's poetry and prose were filled with racial themes and reflected her deep commitment to the cause of racial equality. As Bryant rightly notes, "It is no coincidence that Harper pays special attention to lynching, for 1892 is the year in which more blacks were lynched in the United States than ever before or since" (71). Based upon statistics provided by the Archives at Tuskegee Institute show that 299 African Americans lynched in Alabama at the fourth highest rate subsequent to Mississippi (539), Georgia (492), and Texas (352). Alone, 134 lynching cases are recorded in 1894 according to "Colored Men Lynched without Trial," a chart published in the Vol. 4, No. 3, July 1912 issue of *The Crisis*, an organ published by the National Association for the Advancement of Colored People (NAACP). Harper was probably shocked to know that almost nothing changed in the South since Reconstruction, especially in Alabama for 86 years in 1894 since "she traveled from 1864 to 1871 in thirteen Southern states at her own expense" (Sherman, *African-American Poetry* 112).

As a precedent note to "The Martyr of Alabama," Harper is disappointed but morally indignant to report calmly: "The following news item appeared in the newspapers throughout the country, issue of December 27, 1894" (147). The details of the news item follow:

> Tim Thompson, a little negro boy, was asked to dance for the amusement of some white toughs. He refused, saying he was a church member. One of the men knocked him down with a club and then danced upon his prostrate form. He then shot the boy in the hip. The boy is dead; his murderer is still at large. (147)

It is probably the *Christian Recorder*,[7] the then largest newspaper founded under the auspices of the A.M.E. Church (Jarrett 66), that reported on the murder which is most likely to escape people's attention but Harper detected the cruelty of the case quickly as Edelstein comments: "Decades later, Frances Harper similarly used poetry and fiction to rouse readers from a news-induced indifference to racial violence. . . . Poetry, she suggest, must take over after the news gives the 'facts.' Her account of the crime, juxtaposed against this brief and banal report, replaces balance and objectivity with biblical language, exclamations, and rhyme" (9).

In 1894, thirty-two years have already passed since the Emancipation Proclamation and "the first generation of black Americans who had no direct experience of slavery" had seeming audacity that unnerved white people and made them fear the loss of dominance, being reminded of the change in atmosphere (Dray 74). The imagery of an old stereotype in the minstrel show, which white people have long been in love with, is undoubtedly one of the causes why "some white toughs" asked Tim Thompson, "a little negro boy," to dance for them. Economic depression caused by a decline in cotton price the Southern states suffered from in the early 1890s underlie the motives for the racial violence.[8] Several lynching cases that drew most attention from all over the Southern states were recorded in newspapers in the early 1890s. Edward Coy, a thirty-two-year-old African-American man, was lynched and burned at the stake before a crowd of 1,000 people in Texarkana, Arkansas on 18 February 1892. Henry Smith, a retarded seventeen-year-old African-American youth, was lynched in Paris, Texas, on 1 February 1893. These two pieces of news caused Harper to write "The Martyr of Alabama," Harper must not have overlooked these two incidents but deliberately picked up such a less conspicuous case as Tim Thompson in Alabama than reported in a great scale newspapers.

"The Martyr of Alabama" is written in the form of ballad, narrated with the plot, characters, and a dramatic conclusion like *Sketches of Southern Life*. No wonder that Harper added the "little negro boy" to one of the martyrs she witnessed since she lived in the Philadelphia home of William Still (1821–1902) with Mrs. John Brown two weeks before Brown's execution in 1859, "and afterward she wrote letters and sent packages to the *martyrs* still in prison" (Sherman, *Invisible Poets* 64, emphasis added). With the martyr Harper also invokes "the God of Moses not only as a militant redeemer, but also as the scourge of men and nations who 'trample on His children'" (Sherman, "Invisible Poets" 68).

The typical ballad form uses twenty-one quatrains (four-line rhyming stanza), alternating four-and three-stresses per line (couplets of tetrameter and trimeter). In each stanza, a ballad form typically rhymes only in the second lines of the couplets, not the first, in the form of ABCB. Travelling poets used to share tales and news in ballads which were easy to remember as they used quatrains and alternating rhyme schemes. Typically composed of quatrains that follow a regular rhyme scheme, the form is often a refrain—a repeated line or stanza—like a chorus in a song.

The ballad begins with the following stanza in which Tim Thompson encounters with "some white toughs":

> He lifted up his pleading eyes,
> And scanned each cruel face,
> Where cold and brutal cowardice
> Had left its evil trace. (147)

From the second to sixth stanzas, the subject changes to the tender memories which mothers talk to boys about the birth of Jesus in Bethlehem and the Magi from the East. From the seventh to thirteenth stanzas the ballad follows the process of the murder reported in the newspaper article. The fourteenth stanza urges Christians to "behold that martyred child" while the fifteenth stanza tries to awake their religious compunction:

> Oh! Church of Christ arise! arise!
> Let crimson stain thy hand,
> When God shall inquisition make
> For blood shed in the land. (149)

If the reader does not stand up, appeals the poet, they are unqualified not only politically but religiously as the poet addressed at the Columbian Exposition in Chicago in 1893: "The hands of lynchers are too red with blood to determine the political character of the government for even four short years" ("Woman's Political Future" 244).

The sixteenth and seventeen stanzas beginning with "Take sackcloth of the darkest hue" are almost the same as first and second stanzas in Harper's another ballad, "Bible Defense of Slavery," which also represents the name of a theory built around three main scripture passages ranging from Old Testament to New Testament and is used to support slavery, such as the buying and selling of slaves as well as the Fugitive Slave Act of 1850.[9] Harper criticizes the hypocrisy of slave masters using Christianity to maintain slavery in "The Martyr of Alabama" through "Bible Defense of Slavery."

Harper puts a newspaper article and a religious poem side by side "as a site for heightening readerly sensitivity and imbuing everyday events with texture and depth" (Edelstein 10). A poet of social consciousness, Harper presents anti-lynching protest showing that lynching does not necessarily stand for a hanging execution by a mob but a frivolous murder just for fun.

In the concluding nineteenth, twentieth, and twenty-first stanzas, the poet declares, infidels "with reckless hands" are to blame, for they are sowing on their path, "The tempests wild that yet shall break / In whirlwinds of God's wrath."[10]

"THE HAUNTED OAK" BY PAUL LAURENCE DUNBAR

"The Haunted Oak" was published for the first time in *Century Magazine* 61 (2) (December 1900): 276–77. In 1897 three years before the publication of the poem, Dunbar accepted a job as a research assistant at the Library of Congress in Washington, D.C. However, his health declined, and he soon had to leave the job. Dunbar promised to devote "the rest of his life" to his wife Alice Ruth Moore's happiness if she would forgive and marry him and eloped with and married her in New York; and yet "Gloom enveloped the Dunbars on their wedding day, Sunday, March 6, 1898" (Alexandre 135, 144) for physicians diagnosed Dunbar as suffering tuberculosis. Without antibiotic medications in those days Dunbar drank heavily, developing into an alcoholic, so the Dunbars lived in Denver, Colorado, for a change from

1898 to 1899. However, it turns out that Dunbar's constant abuse of his wife due to his drinking was intensified when they returned to Washington in the spring of 1900. Especially, the Robert Charles riots[11] broke out on July 24–27, 1900 in New Orleans, Louisiana and the news reached Washington. Probably under the influence of the riot, Dunbar wrote "The Haunted Oak" around summer in 1900 and sent the manuscript to the magazine when they went to the Catskills, New York, spending a pleasant summer (Wiggins 100). At that time Dunbar's second novel *The Love of Laundry* (1900) suffered negative criticism as "raceless" due to inappreciation (Jarrett 99–100). Dunbar's desperation caused by tuberculosis, heavy drinking, his abuse of Alice and his resultant repentance, and literary society's lack of understanding is all included as an innocent man's exoneration from guilt in "The Haunted Oak":

> Using personification, Dunbar gave voice to a permanently dead tree limb, the limb from which an innocent man accused of "the old, old crime" was hanged. Dunbar evoked the suffering of the victim and the treachery and brutality of a mob that could laugh as it went about its work. There is a kind of justice portrayed in the poem. The lynchers, it says, must be troubled by their guilt. (Bruce 84)

There are double quotation marks which are put on the first stanza in the first version in *Century Magazine* but are missing from the second version anthologized in *Lyrics of Love and Laughter* (1903) and all the later versions thereafter, either. The first stanza should be enclosed with double quotation marks because they are clearly to indicate that a passerby puts a question on the narrator, namely, the bough of an oak tree, why a shudder runs over the interrogator when s/he goes through the shade the bough throws:

> Pray, why are you so bare, so bare,
> O bough of the old oak-tree;
> And why, when I go through the shade you throw,
> Runs a shudder over me?

And then the bough answers the passerby that the reason is the curse from a lynch victim

> My leaves were green as the best, I trow,
> And sap ran free in my veins,
> But I saw in the moonlight dim and weird
> A guiltless victim's pains.

The bough declares that the lynching victim is not guilty as Dunbar testifies in June 1900 just before the submission of the poem to the magazine: "Even at the North, the prejudice against the negro reverses the precedents of law, and everyone accused is looked upon as guilty until is proven innocent" ("Higher Education" 194). The victim is thrown in jail in charge of "the old, old crime" but lynchers then come to the prison to deceive a guard and take the prisoner away to the haunted oak. The judge, the doctor, the minister, and his son, all "curiously bedight," gather around the oak bough. The narrator bough feels the rope hung on and leaves thereafter never grow "from the curse of a guiltless man."

The first version of "The Haunted Oak" is seemingly a sonnet comprising fourteen four-line stanzas. The rhyming scheme is ABCB, using iambic tetrameter and trimeter, and so forth on. However, the following two stanzas, though included in all the later versions, are cut by the editor from the first version in the *Century Magazine*:

> And ever the judge rides by, rides by,
> And goes to hunt the deer,
> And ever another rides his soul
> In the guise of a mortal fear.
>
> And ever the man he rides me hard,
> And never a night stays he;
> For I feel his curse as a haunted bough,
> On the trunk of a haunted tree.

The reason for curtailment is that the last stanzas represent Dunbar's vital point: "a mortal fear." "The Haunted Oak" is based on a story Dunbar heard from an elderly formerly enslaved man who lived on the grounds of Howard University, telling him about "the branch upon which the victim hung dies in sympathy with him, never again to bear leaves" so Dunbar records a lynching legend embedded in the poem (Rice, "Introduction" 21). In "The Haunted Oak," "a mortal fear" is relevant to note that "the very conversation, which takes place between the haunted oak and the human passerby who inquires about its physical state of disrepair, enlarges the scope both of human history and natural history to include the worlds of the dead—the dead lynched victim and the dead tree" (Alexandre 75).

To further fathom the reason why the last two stanzas are omitted, it might be intriguing to know Dunbar's short story, "The Tragedy at Three Forks," included in *The Strength of Gideon and Other Stories* (1900), which is quite similar to "The Haunted Oak." Jane Hunster, a white girl, sets a house on fire, whose news spreads all over Kentucky. Two innocent African Americans are soon caught under a false accusation: "They had come over only the day before, and were passing through on the quest for work" ("Tragedy" 173). The prosecuting attorney offers them to be set free at the confession of the crime as if it were in the interests of them: "Now, I'm a friend to niggers as much as any white man can be, if they'll only be friends to themselves, an' I want to help you two all I can" (173). At their admission the mob immediately gets them out of the jail and "The ropes were around their necks and they had been let to a tree" (175). The lynch mob "jerked the negroes off their feet into eternity" while the real arsonist perpetrator Jane Hunster's boyfriend Bud Mason is also killed by Dock Heaters at their struggle for the "keepsakes" from lynch victims. An editor says in the next day's newspaper: "When the blind frenzy of a people condemn a man as soon as he is accused, his enemies need not look far for a pretext!" (176). The story warns that no one, even a white man, would be free from an instant rash lynching, which would victimize an innocent man, leaving his curse forever. Just as it is too horrible for readers of the short story concluding by evoking the blind hysteria of a mob, so the editor of the magazine ushers the readers to refrain from feeling "his [victim's] curse as a haunted bough, / On the trunk of a haunted tree" in the omitted last stanza of "The Haunted Oak."

"THE LYNCHING" BY CLAUDE MCKAY

"The Lynching" first appeared on page 55 in the Vol. 10, No. 1, Summer 1920 issue of *Cambridge Magazine*, a British literary journal edited by Charles K. Ogden (1889–1957). McKay crossed the Atlantic and arrived in London in the autumn because he wanted to avoid the "Red Summer" in 1919,[12] as in the [28 September 1919] lynching of William Brown in [Omaha] Douglas County, Nebraska (Gosciak, "Most Wanted" 89). McKay did experience the Red Summer personally, seeing violent mobs of white people while he worked for the Pennsylvania Railroad: "Traveling from city to city and unable to gauge the attitude and temper of each one, we Negro railroad men were nervous. . . . We stuck together, some of us armed, going from the railroad station to our quarters" (McKay, *Long Way* 31). McKay published "The Lynching" under such a circumstance of a critical moment.

"If We Must Die," McKay's most celebrated poem on lynching, was previously published in the Vol. 2, No. 7, July 1919 issue of *The Liberator*, a monthly magazine established by Max Eastman (1883–1969) and his sister Crystal Eastman (1881–1928). Walter Fuller (1881–1927), husband of Crystal Eastman, acted as a go-between for McKay and Ogden because Fuller was a close friend of Ogden, writing Ogden: "I am asking my friend, Mr. Claude McKay, the bearer of this letter, to call on you during his visit to London because I feel sure that you will be glad to know one another" (Fuller to Ogden, 11 November 1919, qtd. in James 74). McKay himself made contact with Ogden in February 1920, sending Ogden Fuller's letter of introduction and some of his poems: "I don't think it right to bother with business matters persons to whom one is practically a stranger" (McKay to Ogden, 18 February 1920, qtd. in James 78). Because McKay politically had much in common, Ogden responded wholeheartedly, and became good friends, offering to help get McKay's poems to be published. McKay appreciated him: "Thanks very much for devoting so much time and being so naturally nice to me" (McKay to Ogden, 7 March 1920, qtd. in James 78). Thus "The Lynching" was published and the poet was introduced by Ogden in the same issue: "Here can be found some of those peculiar qualities which rendered the visit of the Southern Syncopated Orchestra[13] so memorable last autumn, and for which we are becoming accustomed to look as the distinctive contribution of African Art in general" (Ogden, "Claude McKay Describes His Own Life" 55). Ogden further spared a lot of space for McKay's other seventeen poems[14] in the issue because he is a global translator whose international understanding is the reason why the magazine "remained the central driving force through his thirty years of work on Basic English" (Gordon 21). The original of "The Lynching" is slightly different from later versions as in *Harlem Shadows* with "cruellest" in line 2; a colon after "again" in line 3; no period after "unforgiven" in line 4; and a colon after "sun" in line 10 (Maxwell 331):

> His spirit in smoke ascended to high heaven.
> His father, by the cruelest way of pain,
> Had bidden him to his bosom once again;
> The awful sin remained still unforgiven.
> All night a bright and solitary star
> (Perchance the one that ever guided him,
> Yet gave him up at last to Fate's wild whim)
> Hung pitifully o'er the swinging char.
> Day dawned, and soon the mixed crowds came to view
> The ghastly body swaying in the sun
> The women thronged to look, but never a one
> Showed sorrow in her eyes of steely blue;
> And little lads, lynchers that were to be,
> Danced round the dreadful thing in fiendish glee.

McKay wrote the poem in iambic pentameter as a Shakespearean sonnet, using an ABAB CDCD EFEF GG rhyming pattern across three quatrains and ending with a "perfectly rhymed" couplet.[15] The poem is furthermore divided into two parts: the octave (opening eight lines) and the sestet (ending six lines). The octave presents the body of an African-American man who has been lynched though his soul ascends to heaven. The sestet presents the response of the white community to this crime: they are elated but indifferent.

The children are compared to the Devil and hell as dancing "in fiendish glee" around the body. In lines one to four, we can see the connection of "the spirit of the lynch victim" who joins his father in heaven and Christ depicted in the Gospels of the New Testament (Maxwell 331).

This leads its reader to the idea of the victim as a Christ figure, ascending to heaven in the Bible. White people do not appear to be shocked with the sight of a hanging body and "no faithful, compassionate women look on at McKay's lynch spectacle" in contrast with the Bible (Maxwell 331). "The notion of the lynching as a ritual of sacrifice, specifically as a Christian offering for the sins of a sinful society" (Dray 80) is a recurring motif in black poetry and literature.

In lines five to eight, "a bright and solitary star" represents the North Star, which used to safely guide runaway slaves to the Northern states along with the Underground Railroad stations. However, the star does not succeed in the rescue of slaves and has to give him up to the unending crime of slavery.

In lines eleven through fourteen, McKay ends his poem by mentioning the lack of white sympathy, problematic education in which children learn to be indifferent to the appalling sight. Therefore, the need for the education is urgent as exemplified by Walter White's[16] February 1935 art show in New York at the hint of Reginald Marsh's[17] picture entitled "This Is Her First Lynching" in which a mother holds up her daughter so that she can see the lynching. White parent's sons and daughters undergo the rite of passage that "establishes their superior roles as adults in the society, in the same way that the black boys in Ellison's battle royal scene in *Invisible Man*" (Harris 76). By contrast, African-American children are intimidated into silence as a would-be lynch victim as Richard Wright asserts in *Black Boy*: "I had never in my life been abused by whites, but I had already become as conditioned to their existence as though I had been the victim of a thousand lynchings" (72). In line eleven, the women who "thronged to look," not out of sympathy but only prompted by curiosity, are reminiscent of the scene where "those that thronged" to see Hester Prynne in the chapter two in Nathaniel Hawthorne's *The Scarlet Letter*.

CONCLUSION

It is necessary for us to note that the publication of poets by African Americans at that time was not only for giving their work of art to the world but also bringing about a social movement of anti-lynching as Harper "occupied a central position as a black woman in a changing society more than a hundred years ago" (Graham, "Introduction" xxxiv). Harper, who was already nationally known with *Poems on Miscellaneous Subjects* (1854), became good friends with younger and anti-lynching activist Ida B. Wells-Barnett who often visited her in Philadelphia (Giddings 209) to talk about the movement against lynching.

Dunbar broke "racial-political boundaries" (Jarrett and Morgan, "Introduction" xxxix) as America's first successful African-American author of "The Haunted Oak." Dunbar in secrecy criticizes complexities of American racial realities by presenting an innocent African-American to be lynched "very quiet and orderly," as Dr. Melville comments in Dunbar's short story "The Lynching of Jube Benson," by the judge, the doctor, and the minister, who are "curiously bedight."

McKay is "a pioneer in twentieth century in the West Indies, the United States, and Africa" (Cooper, "Preface and Acknowledgments" vii). As a pioneering black novelist and poet McKay is deeply and actively involved in the political action by condemning "racial injustices, entire social, economic, and political order" in "The Lynching" (Cooper 101).

"The Martyr of Alabama" by Frances E.W. Harper, "The Haunted Oak" by Paul Laurence Dunbar, and "The Lynching" by Claude McKay all portray an unnerving picture of a lynching and unveil much about the gloomy elements of humanity, inquiring how to maintain the human dignity through generation to generation in consideration of these conditions.

In conclusion, the violence against thousands of African Americans who have been lynched, as depicted in these poems, after the Civil War through the 1950s is a predecessor to abusive police's maneuvers against African Americans today, "a modern-day lynching," to borrow the designation of historian Arica Coleman[18] (Brown n.p.). African Americans continue to die at the hands of police and vigilantes as, according to the new study,[19] black males are about three times more likely to be killed by police than white males. Wide circulation of a cellphone video shooting the murder of George Floyd on 25 May 2020, which triggered a worldwide demonstration, is evocative of the newspapers quickly circulated throughout the country in Harper's poem; the bystander's video is suggestive of a passerby in Dunbar's poem; and the symbolization of Floyd's death is reminiscent of lynch victim's martyrization in McKay's poem. As Uche Akuta's recent poem about the murder of Floyd voices, "The agony of four centuries / [will be] Made anew in a flash" (6).

WORKS CITED

Akuta, Uche. *Black Lives Matter: Narrative Poems*. Privately published, 2021.

Alexandre, Sandy. *The Properties of Violence: Claims to Ownership in Representations of Lynching*. Jackson: UP of Mississippi, 2012.

Brown, Deneen L. "'It Was a Modern-Day Lynching': Violent Deaths Reflect a Brutal American Legacy." *National Geographic* (5 June 2020): no page. https://www.nationalgeographic.co.uk.

Bryant, Jerry H. *Victims and Heroes: Racial Violence in the African-American Novel.* Boston: U of Massachusetts P, 1997.

Cooper, Wayne F. *Claude McKay: Rebel Sojourner in the Harlem Renaissance.* New York: Schocken, 1987.

Culleton Claire A., and Karen Leick, eds. *Modernism on File: Writers, Artists, and the FBI, 1920–1950.* New York: Palgrave McMillan, 2008.

Dray, Philip. *At the Hands of Persons Unknown: The Lynching of Black America.* New York: Random House, 2002.

Dunbar, Paul Laurence. *Collected Poetry of Paul Laurence Dunbar.* Ed. Joanna M. Braxton. Charlottesville: UP of Virginia, 1993.

———. "Higher Education." In Martin and Primeau, 193–94.

———. "The Haunted Oak." *The Century Magazine* 61 (2) (December 1900): 276–77.

———. "The Tragedy at Three Forks." In Jarrett and Morgan, 171–76.

Edelstein, Sari. *Between the Novel and the News: The Emergence of American Women's Writing.* Charlottesville: U of Virginia P, 2014.

Foster, Frances Smith, ed. *Minnie's Sacrifice, Sowing and Reaping, Trial and Triumph: Three Rediscovered Novels by Frances E.W. Harper.* Boston: Beacon Press, 1994.

Francini, Antonella. "Sonnet vs. Sonnet: The Fourteen Lines in African-American Poetry." *RSA Journal* 14 (2003): 37–66. https://www.aisna.net/wp-content/uploads/2019/09/14francini.pdf

Giddings, Paula J. *Ida: A Sword among Lions: Ida B. Wells and the Campaign Against Lynching.* New York: Amistad, 2008.

Gordon, W. Terrence. *C. K. Ogden: A Bio-bibliographi Study.* Metuchen, NJ: Scarecrow Press, 1990.

Gosciak, Josh. *The Shadowed Country: Claude McKay and the Romance of the Victorians.* New Brunswick, NJ: Rutgers UP, 2006.

———. "Most Wanted: Claude McKay and 'Black Spectator' of African-American Poetry in the 1920s." In Culleton and Leick, 73–104.

Graham, Maryemma. "Introduction." In Harper, *Complete Poems*, xxxiii–lvii.

Harper, Frances E.W. *Complete Poems of Frances E.W. Harper.* Ed. Maryemma Graham. New York: Oxford UP, 1988.

———. *Sketches of Southern Life.* Philadelphia: Ferguson Bros. & Co., Printers, 1891. Electronic Text Center, University of Virginia Library.

Harris, Trudier. *Exorcising Blackness: Historical and Literary Lynching and Burning Rituals.* Bloomington: Indiana UP, 1984.

Jackson, Virginia. "Specters of the Ballad." *Nineteenth-Century Literature* 71 (2) (2016): 176–96.

James, Winston. "'A race outcast from an outcast class': *Claude McKay's Experience and Analysis of Britain.*" In Schwartz, 71–92.

Jarrett, Gene Andrew, and Thomas Lewis Morgan, eds. *The Complete Stories of Paul Laurence Dunbar*. Athens: Ohio University P, 2005.

———, ed. *African-American Literature beyond Race: An Alternative Reader*. New York: New York UP, 2006.

Martin, Woodward Herbert, and Ronald Primeau, eds. *In His Own Voice: The Dramatic and Other Uncollected Works of Paul Laurence Dunbar*. Athens: Ohio UP, 2002.

Maxwell, William J., ed. *Complete Poems: Claude McKay*. Urbana: U of Illinois P, 2004.

McKay, Claude. *A Long Way from Home*. Ed. with an introduction by Gene Andrew Jarrett. 1937; New Brunswick: Rutgers UP, 2007.

———. *Trial by Lynching: Stories about Negro Life in North America*. Translated from the Russian by Robert Winter. Ed. Alan L. McLeod. Mysore: Centre for Commonwealth Literature and Research, University of Mysore, 1977.

Rice, Anne P., ed. *Witnessing Lynching: American Writers Respond*. New Brunswick, NW: Rutgers UP, 2003.

Schwarz, Bill. *West Indian Intellectuals in Britain*. Manchester: Manchester UP, 2018.

Sherman, Joan R. *Invisible Poets: Afro-Americans of the Nineteenth Century*. Urbana: U of Illinois P, 1974, 1989.

———, ed. *African-American Poetry of the Nineteenth Century: An Anthology*. Urbana: U of Illinois P, 1992.

Tuskegee Institute Statistics Archives. "Lynching by Year and Race, 1882–1968." (http://archive.tuskegee.edu/repository/digital-collection/lynching-information/)

Wiggins, Lida Keck. *The Life and Works of Paul Laurence Dunbar*. New York: Dodd, Mead, 1907.

Wright, Richard. *Black Boy (American Hunger)*. New York: Harper Collins, 1993.

NOTES

1. "Lynching by State, 1882–1986," Tuskegee University archives.

2. At least more than 6,000 Koreans living in Japan were lynched by citizens, vigilantes, and the military when a groundless rumor spread that Koreans living in Japan poisoned the wells. The lynchings were not by hanging but stabbing to death with a bamboo spear and a fire hook.

3. To name but a few, the works about lynching by African-American poets are, according to seniority: "Out of the Shadows" (1920) by Joseph S. Cotter, Jr. (1864–1951); "Vision of a Lyncher" (1912) by Leslie Pinckney Hill (1880–1960); "The Black Finger" (1923) by Angelina Weld Grimké (1880–1958); "White Things" (1923) by Anne Spencer (1882–1975); "My Grievance" (1923) by Raymond Garfield Dandridge (1882/1883–1930); "When I Die" (1913) by Fenton Johnson (1888–1958); "Kabnis" in *Cane* (1923) by Jean Toomer (1894–1967); *Harlem Gallery* (1965) by Melvin Tolson (1898–1966); "He Was a Man" in *Southern Road* (1932) by Sterling A. Brown (1901–1989); "Hatred" (1927) by Gwendolyn B. Bennett (1902–1981); "Three Songs about Lynching" by Langston Hughes (1902–1967); "Christ Recrucified"

(1922) and "The Black Christ" (1929) by Countee Cullen (1903–1946); "Between the World and Me" (1935) by Richard Wright (1908–1960); *For My People* (1942) by Margaret Walker (1915–1998); *A Street in Bronzeville* (1945) and *Annie Allen* (1949) by Gwendolyn Brooks (1917–2000); "Gabriel" (1940) by Robert Hayden (1913–1980); *Like the Singing Coming Off of Drums* (2018) by Sonia Sanchez (1934–); *A Wreath for Emmett Till* (2005) by Marilyn Nelson (1946–); "Reflections" in *Thieves of Paradise* (1998) by Yusef Komunyakaa (1947–); "Trayvon, Redux" in *Mother Love* (1995) by Rita Dove (1952–); "The Lynching" (1993) by Thylias Moss (1954–); and "Native Guard" (2006) by Natasha Trethewey (1966–).

4. Hughes's poem might be written under the influence of Frances E.W. Harper's "The Martyr of Alabama."

5. According to Sherman's *Invisible Poets*, Harper's birth year is 1924 (p. 62) although many sources indicate 1925.

6. Virginia Jackson noted in her essay that Dunbar's poem was published for the first time in the 1901 issue of *Century Illustrated Monthly Magazine* (p. 176n1). However, according to the University of California's Online Books Page archives (https://babel.hathitrust.org), Dunbar's poem was first published on pages 276–77 in the Vol. 61, No. 2, December 1900 issue of *Century Magazine*.

7. It also printed works by Francis E.W. Harper. Her novels appeared "in approximately ten-year intervals in the *Christian Recorder*" (Foster xi).

8. The Panic of 1893 is an economic depression in the United States that began in 1893 and ended in 1897, one of the worst in American history with the ten percent unemployment rate. This might be influential upon the recklessness of jobless "some white toughs" in "The Martyr of Alabama."

9. The Fugitive Slave Act of 1850 is the one which requires that slaves be returned to their owners, even if they are in a free state such as Pennsylvania. The act made Harper have righteous indignation against slavery and lynching.

10. A Biblical quotation: "For they have sown the wind, and they shall reap the whirlwind" ("The Book of Hosea" in the *Old Testament*, 8:7).

11. After African-American worker Robert Charles fatally shot a white police officer during a quarrel, a white mob started rioting, attacking African Americans throughout the city of New Orleans. The riot began on 24 July 1900, and ended when Charles was killed on 27 July in the same year. The mob shot him more than hundred times. The events received national coverage and the news spread beyond the state, reaching Washington where Dunbar was living.

12. The first major event of Red Summer occurred in Chicago in July 1919 after a black teenager swam into a white section of Lake Michigan and was drowned by whites. During the days from April to November, more than 165 people died, thousands more injured. The violent incidents took place in Chicago, Washington, D.C., and Elaine, Arkansas while lynchings and riots spread across the country.

13. The Southern Syncopated Orchestra, an early jazz group with all black members, toured in London in 1919 and 1920. Ogden referred to the performance which he saw in fall 1919 probably at the recommendation of McKay who attended the performance in New York.

14. The other included poems in the issue are: "Flowers of Passion," "Reminiscences," "Love Song," "Sukee River," "Alfonso, Dressing to Wait at Table," "On Broadway," "North and South," "After the Winter," "The Spanish Needle," "I Shall Return," "Morning Joy," "Winter in the Country," "Dawn in New York," "The Castaways," "When Dawn Comes to the City," "Rest in Peace," "To O. E. A.," and "A Memory of June" (Maxwell 307–37).

15. For an overview of the history of the sonnet form in African-American poetry, see Francini.

16. White (1893–1955), a civil rights activist who led the National Association for the Advancement of Colored People (NAACP), traveled to the South to investigate lynchings and riots.

17. Marsh (1898–1954), an American painter, is most known for his depictions of life in New York City in the 1920s and 1930s.

18. Dr. Arica Coleman is an African-American historian and independent scholar, whose latest book includes *In the Matter of Black Lives: Womanist Prose* (Sistah Gurl Books, 2021).

19. Danielle Haynes, "Study: Black Americans 3 times more likely to be killed by police." *U.S. News* (24 June 2020). https://www.upi.com/Top_News/

Chapter Twelve

Depictions of Racial Violence in the Work of Paul Laurence Dunbar

Debbie Lelekis

Throughout his career, Paul Laurence Dunbar developed a literary voice that displayed a creative energy and power that James Emanuel refers to as "racial fire" and this was most prevalent in his works that drew attention to racial tensions, such as the stories "The Lynching of Jube Benson" and "The Tragedy at Three Forks," which I examine in this essay.[1] Biographer Felton O. Best contends that Dunbar's writing advocates covert and explicit forms of resistance and racial protest. Dunbar's "increased emphasis on race coincided with a wave of black migration to northern cities, the massive lynchings which were occurring throughout the South and Midwest, and race riots in various communities" (Best 117).[2] I argue that an analysis of Dunbar's fiction draws attention to vigilantism at the turn of the twentieth century and allows readers to better understand how African Americans in both the North and South still suffered from poverty and roadblocks to civil rights. His work is filled with protest against disenfranchisement, lynching, political manipulation, and economic exploitation. As Gossie H. Hudson asserts, Dunbar's writing is best considered as a "manifestation of the American creative genius," through which he recognized the race problem of his era and answered those social ills with poetry and fiction that promoted protest and reform (239).

Dunbar was profoundly influenced by the community of Dayton, Ohio, where he grew up in the late nineteenth century. This dynamic, cultural hub served as a solid foundation and contributed to the development of Dunbar's understanding of himself as a member of the African-American community and as a budding writer. His first attempts at writing came in the form of poetry when he was just six years old and by twelve he had written several short stories (Best 17, 21). When he attended Central High School, he was the only African American in his class, but he built a strong community of friends. He was involved with his school's literary organization, the Philomathean Society, and became the editor of the newspaper, the *High School Times*. Additionally, he started to publish some of his short stories and poems in the A.N. Kellogg Syndicate in Chicago, in his high school humor magazine *Tomfoolery*, and in the *Dayton Herald*. One of his most influential friendships was the one he developed with brothers Orville and Wilbur Wright. Before they became aviation pioneers, Dunbar published some of his work in their *West Side News* and also served as editor of their newspaper the *Dayton Tattler*, which was aimed at a primarily black audience (Best 22–23). In his literary contributions to the *Dayton Tattler*, Dunbar wanted to promote to uplift and foster community. According to Matthew Teutsch, some of Dunbar's pieces in the *Dayton Tattler* were published under pseudonyms and his four main stories, a play, and dialect poetry do not directly address racial violence. However, because the *Dayton Tattler* was a short-lived newspaper, lasting just three issues, we do not know what Dunbar intended for later works in that publication. It is clear though that he saw the *Dayton Tattler* as part of the important history of the Black Press and understood its contribution to the creation of a sense of community and collective identity.

Dunbar was unable to attend college after high school due to financial reasons, so he tried unsuccessfully to find fulltime work as a journalist in Dayton. He had to take a job as an elevator boy but continued to publish poetry and fiction in local newspapers, and in 1892, Dunbar was asked to read his poetry at the Western Association of Writers' meeting. This opportunity earned him the endorsement of James Newton Matthews and James Whitcomb Riley, two well-established authors who were impressed with his work. Dunbar was prompted to publish his first book of poems entitled *Oak and Ivy*. During the following two years, his writing gained a lot of attention, including praise from Frederick Douglass who invited Dunbar to read his poetry at the World's Columbian Exposition in Chicago in 1893. This led to more readings and publications in journals like the *Century*. When his second book *Majors and Minors* was published in 1896, William Dean Howells gave it a positive review in *Harper's Weekly*, and this further established Dunbar as a nationally known writer. Howells wrote an introduction for Dunbar's third book, *Lyrics of Lowly Life* (1896). He would reach international fame the following year during a successful trip to England. He frequently gave readings of his work and was employed by the Library of Congress for a few years.

Dunbar's work was noteworthy to both black and white readers, which made him an important figure within the African-American literary community and within the field of American literature more broadly. While interest in his writing had declined by the middle of the twentieth century, due in part to criticism over his use of dialect and his perceived passivity, Best asserts that Dunbar's writing was a form of protest itself, pushing back against the oppressive forces that attempted to narrowly define him as a "Negro writer" rather than an American writer who was black (159). Dunbar's newspaper work had laid the groundwork for his prose and poetry, and it was his series of editorships and contributions to black papers in Indianapolis, Chicago, Washington, and New York that helped him establish his point of view and commitment to depicting his community in his creative work. This is reflected in two themes that can be traced back to his journalism, including "an assertion of the worthiness of black life and an exposure of the pathology of the white denial of that worth" (Martin 30). Dunbar was part of a network of prominent black writers and leaders, including James Weldon Johnson, W.E.B. Du Bois, and Booker T. Washington. According to the account of the renowned Harlem Renaissance writer, Arna Bontemps, Dunbar's interactions with Johnson and Du Bois led to additional opportunities to share his work with large audiences. Johnson brought Dunbar to Jacksonville, Florida, for several weeks in the spring of 1900 where he gave multiple readings, and Du Bois appeared elsewhere with Dunbar two years prior at several joint lectures. Washington labeled Dunbar the "Poet Laureate of the Negro Race" and much of his poetry echoes Du Bois's notion of "double-consciousness," which was introduced in *The Souls of Black Folk* (1903) to describe the feeling of having more than one social identity and a divided sense of self. Dunbar protested racial violence in both his journalism and creative writing. His most striking depictions of racial violence in his literature appeared in two short stories, "The Lynching of Jube Benson," and "The Tragedy at Three Forks," written early in the twentieth century.[3]

Dunbar's story "The Lynching of Jube Benson" was published as part of his collection *The Heart of Happy Hollow* (1904) and "The Tragedy at Three Forks" appeared in *The Strength of Gideon and Other Stories* (1900). These stories explore how racism incites the lynchings of innocent men in each narrative. The first story contains a narrative frame that introduces the character Dr. Melville as he recounts the lynching later during a conversation with two other men, including Gordon Fairfax and an overzealous young reporter named Handon Gay. The topic is brought up by Gay because he wants to witness a lynching since his interest has been triggered by a magazine article that he had recently come across on punishments implemented without a trial. The man's callousness stands in stark contrast to the objectivity that is usually expected from a reporter. While Fairfax is not so overtly apathetic, he does still express an interest in witnessing the spectacle of a lynching.

Dr. Melville serves as a counterresponse to their insensitivity, and it is apparent that he has been deeply impacted by the lynching that he saw, which he conveys in the story of Jube that follows. Even the doctor's appearance, which makes him look much older than his actual age, transmits the profound effect that the experience has made on him. At first the younger men are critical when the doctor opposes their excitement over the prospect of witnessing a real lynching, and they question whether he is weak. Dr. Melville gravely acknowledges his role in the lynching, and it is clear that the memory of the scene still troubles him, as the young reporter takes out his notebook and pencil as the doctor begins his story. As Jean Marie Lutes points out in her article "Lynching Coverage and the American Reporter-Novelist," Dunbar never returns to the ambitious reporter at the end or explains whether or not he uses the doctor's narrative for a news story. This is unsurprising when compared to real reporting on lynchings which rarely told stories like the one that Dr. Melville describes, and Lutes argues that it was through literature that writers often took up those narratives.

Dr. Melville starts by outlining the location of the lynching, noting that it was a small, rural setting where this type of vigilantism might be more commonplace. As the area's doctor, he has established his medical practice in a rented room on the wealthy Hiram Daly's property. He becomes known in the community as a doctor who does not discriminate against potential patients due to skin color or class. He describes his fellow townspeople in contradictory terms as being "coarse and rough" while at the same time "simple and generous" (225). As the depiction of the people's kind and gentle demeanors emerge from beneath their unrefined exteriors, the narrator establishes a community that seems to be fairly welcoming and inclusive. The most noble among the people are Annie, the daughter of Dr. Melville's landlord, and Jube Benson, the well-respected black man that worked in her house. Both are characterized similarly as moral and kind. While Annie is described as beautiful, young, and possessing a "native grace" that won over all who met her; Dunbar also depicts this charming quality as a "spell" that she casts on everyone in her presence, which turns them into her "abject" slaves (225). Despite this slave imagery, Annie's external attractiveness is portrayed as mirroring her compassion and inner beauty. Jube is frequently described as trustworthy, respectful, and dependable, but his loyalty to Annie is also compared to that of a dog, which highlights his more submissive and docile characteristics. After Dr. Melville becomes romantically involved with Annie, Jube shows loyalty to him too and helps him in his courtship of the young lady. Elizabeth Young argues that Dunbar is using parody in these scenes when describing Jube to white men from a white man's perspective, and she asserts that the author might be intentionally portraying Jube as manipulating the others to his own advantage (136).

The peaceful existence of the community is disrupted when an outbreak of typhoid strikes the townspeople for over three months and even the doctor himself falls ill after tending to the others. Before the illness spread to Dr. Melville, Jube had helped him stay in contact with Annie and he had even diverted attention from other admirers away from her. Although the doctor, Annie, and Jube are generally portrayed as fair, moral, and honorable, none of them seem bothered by Jube's deceptive antics with the other suitors, and Annie seems to recognize that his actions both protect her and give Dr. Melville the advantage. The doctor jokingly labels Jube an "admirable liar" and condones the "continuance of his wrong-doing" (228). Jube remains loyal to Dr. Melville and takes care of him when the doctor falls ill. Nicole A. Waligora-Davis contends that the narrator's role as a doctor and the "backdrop of an epidemic" are key elements of the story that highlight the "historical links between law and science," a collaboration that underscores how black crime was often presented as "contingent on an assumed white and implicitly female victimization" perpetrated by a black assailant (303). Furthermore, as Waligora-Davis suggests, the "proximity of these moments—lynching as a crime of passion that occurs in the aftermath of disease" emphasizes the notion that racial tensions are part of a "social malaise" (304).

These links are especially striking when considered within the context of Dunbar's stereotypically feminine descriptions of Jube as nurse. He is characterized as gentle, caring, and emotional and compared to a mother treating a sick kitten. The depictions of Jube hovering at the doctor's bedside "weeping, but hopeful" and being sent away "weak and exhausted," further illustrate these feminine characteristics. Even though Dr. Melville has no concrete memory of these actions, he recounts his hazy vision of two contrasting figures who he calls a "black but gentle demon" and a "white fairy" (229). The black/white and dark/light dichotomy of this vision can be read as Dr. Melville's interpretations of Jube and Annie. While the connection between the color white and Annie could be a reference to her purity, the pairing of the descriptor with the figure of a fairy also aligns her with the concept of white magic, which harkens back to her the spell she was said to cast over all with her charm. Young relates the vision with an "idealization of white womanhood, albeit one whose imagery of inversion, enlargement, and dissolution suggests anxiety about the power of femininity" (137). The demon in the doctor's vision, by contrast, seems to be aligned more closely with a dark and malevolent force, especially in the minds of Christian readers.[4] These sinister connotations are softened by the adjective "gentle" which precedes the noun, and Jude is also described in the very next paragraph as a "humble ally" of the doctor.

Jube and Dr. Melville get to know each other better while the town is recovering, and Jube's devotion is described as so intense that it is "to the point of abjectness," making the doctor feel "shame at [Jube's] goodness" (230). Dr. Melville expresses love for Jube in the form of gratitude for his help during his recovery and during his courtship of Annie. Jube is a moral and generous person worthy of love and admiration but it becomes apparent that Dr. Melville conflates love and gratitude, demonstrating how his feelings for Jube are shaped by what he gets out of their alliance. This makes their relationship largely one-sided, and this is the lens through which the lynching scene can be read, particularly as Dr. Melville later refers to as "too severe a test" to their friendship (231). On the afternoon when the lynching occurs, Dr. Melville is oblivious to any of the signs of approaching doom. He arrives in town "in a particularly joyous mood and no premonition of the impending catastrophe oppressed [him]" (231). Dunbar builds up the tension by stressing the doctor's inability to recognize any signs of danger even after he sees men hastily moving through the nearly empty streets to gather in a crowd outside of his home. The look in the men's faces stirs a "sudden, sick thrill" in Dr. Melville and when he arrives at the scenes of Annie's dying words, all he hears is the incomplete uttered phrase, "That black" (232). Without any other evidence to lead them to the real assailant who attacked Annie, the townspeople accuse Jube and it is obvious that Annie's father has already determined his guilt. Waligora-Davis points to this example of the insubstantial fragment, uttered by the dying Annie and wildly misinterpreted by the white townspeople, as "the problem of evidence impacting the black body whose guilt before the law Dunbar claims is a fixed, legal presumption" (304). Due to this presumed guilt, the white townspeople automatically fill in the blanks of Annie's incomplete indictment and this sets off the actions taken against Jube. Even though Annie's final statement is unclear and unfinished, it renders any potential claims of innocence by Jube as irrelevant, merely because she is white and the accused is black. Lynchings, Sandy Alexandre argues, should be considered within the "broader questions of land, the mechanics of setting, and the emotive forces mobilized by lynching narratives" and she extends this notion of property beyond land ownership to include white Southern womanhood and honor (3). Within this context, Alexandre contends, lynching is a "spatial technology of domination that privatizes and racializes particular spaces as 'white'" (6–7).

The logical and moral Dr. Melville responds in an uncharacteristic manner after Annie's death and he seems to be driven by pure emotion as he joins up with the crowd that is quickly turning into a lynch mob, characterized by an "angry roar" and the "sudden movement of many feet" (232–33). Like the other men, the doctor is led by "intuition" and the "common consent" of the mob who have determined that Jube was the one who assaulted Annie (233). The moral character and integrity that Dr. Melville and the other townspeople admired Jube for at the opening of the story is forgotten in an instant; they interpret the word black in Annie's statement to be a reference to him despite the fact that it does not make logical sense that Jube would hurt Annie given his devotion to her and Dr. Melville. Several townspeople then claim to have seen Jube going into the woods with a "skulking air" but they had dismissed it since he was also grinning (233). These conflicting descriptions calls into question the reliability of these accounts of Jube's behavior. The act of skulking or lurking surreptitiously does not seem congruent with the description of him grinning good-naturedly. Notably, the mob never considers the possibility that Jube was going after the real criminal, which would have been more aligned with the protective, caregiver role established earlier in the story. The mob mistakenly view Jube's actions as "shrewd" and as a sign of the "diabolical reason of his slyness" (233). Jube's disappearance signifies both physical departure from the setting and, as Waligora-Davis describes, the shifting of townspeople's view of Jube as a trusted figure into a menacing one; this reimagined version of Jube causes the vision of the true person to vanish in their minds. Similarly, Young notes that the "image of the black man as loyal dog has become its inverse, the black beast" (137).

The doctor's focus on his feelings over rational thoughts dominates in this section of the narrative. He participates in the mob's search for Jube, spurred on by "a will that was half [his] own, half some more malignant power's" (234). Animal imagery is used to describe both Dr. Melville and Jube as the doctor relates his craving for vengeance to a panther's desire for blood and Jube is compared to a tiger, but neither of these depictions fits their true personalities. When Dr. Melville's mind goes blank, his predatory instincts appear to completely eclipse any of his normally rational thoughts, and when the accused man is found, he is described in terms of prey: the mob "came upon [their] quarry crouched" along a fence, and the doctor raises the cry as if part of a hunting party (234). Jube is misunderstood when he tells the white townspeople that he didn't mean any harm, and his explanation about how he had gone off to see his girlfriend Lucy was ignored. Even the doctor won't listen to the explanation and assumes Jube is lying, which fits within countless real-life examples of the "theatre of misunderstandings, misapprehensions, and misstatements circumscribing lynchings" (Waligora-Davis 305). Dunbar further develops the predator and prey metaphor in the following scene when the mob surrounds Jube like hungry beasts and terror fills his eyes like a deer about to be shot. Dr. Melville makes it clear that the mob intends to lynch Jube and refuses to protect him. In another uncharacteristic act, Dr. Melville strikes Jube, but the accused man's only response is an expression of disappointment and sadness over the doctor's unwillingness to believe his former friend.

The doctor later reflects on what led him to turn on Jube, blaming his "false education" in regards to race as the catalyst for his actions. He claims that he had been taught to associate blackness with monstrosity, believing as a child that black men would try to capture him and that that the devil was black. When he is confronted with Annie's death and the accusation of Jube's guilt, his rational knowledge of his friend's true character and integrity were surpassed by the emotional and irrational racist beliefs of his childhood. As Young argues, Dr. Melville "retroactively confesses that racism shaped his pursuit of Jube" and this mindset revolves around the "metaphorical equation of black men with monsters" (137–38). The doctor declares that he has "recovered from the sickness of that belief" but when faced with Jube's "menacing blackness," all of those racist attitudes from childhood led him to the conclusion that Jube stood for "all the powers of evil" (236). The earlier image of the black demon from the doctor's delirious dreams while he was sick with the fever aligns with the racist notions from his childhood which linked black men with a black devil. Due to the structure of the narrative being told as a frame-story by Dr. Melville, Gayle Jones, asserts that Jube Benson remains mostly invisible to the reader because he is only seen through the lens of the doctor, who has been admittedly affected by his false education about race (60). Despite the fact that Dr. Melville realizes his racist upbringing was a sickness and that he had to actively move away from those beliefs as he became an adult, he is unable to prevent those feelings from coming back to him when he finds himself in the emotionally charged lynch mob scene. He even notes that his hands were busy tying the rope as if they were detached from his rational thoughts. His emotions compel him to carry out the lynching and override his ethical and compassionate side. Even though Jube's status has been firmly established as a moral and upstanding human being who has been kind to Annie and has saved the doctor's own life, Dr. Melville still reverts back to the false stereotypes learned as a child and allows his emotions to direct his actions rather than calm, rational thoughts. He is consumed by the mob mentality at this point and loses those distinctive aspects of his character that were so carefully constructed earlier in the story in the descriptions of his moral and progressive views as a doctor who treated both blacks and whites without discrimination.

Dunbar depicts the mob as it returns with the captured Jube in a manner that is similar to other mob scenes in literature of this era, characterized most often as "orderly" and made up of prominent citizens and leaders of the community who wielded the most power and influence. The hanging is portrayed as if it is an official procedure of the law even though it is a clear example of vigilantism. The townspeople are described as possessing a stern determination, but this conviction is directed towards their desire for "a terrible vengeance" (237). It's painfully obvious that these men are not interested in real justice carried out through the legal process, but rather the spectacle of vengeance and violence without a fair trial.

They are not even moved by Jube's horrified reaction to Annie's corpse, and they never really listen to anything he says in order to determine his potential guilt or innocence. The vigilante response of the townspeople shows little respect for the law and allows emotions to rule their actions rather than reason and logic. As they frantically hang Jube from a tree with a rope hoisted up by Dr. Melville, Jube's sadness and disappointment in his former friend is highlighted again. Even the doctor who had known his true nature best was easily fooled into thinking that Jube was capable of committing such a crime. Just a few moments after his death, Jube's brother Ben drags the real criminal toward the group and proves the lynched man's innocence, though it is too late to save him. A man named Tom Skinner who was already known as "the worst white ruffian in the town" appears before the crowd disguised with a blackened face (238). This climactic scene illustrates Young's argument that the image of the black man as monster is "so fully a projection of white fantasy that it turns out to be performed by a white man himself" (138). The revelation of Skinner disguised in blackface prompts Dr. Melville to examine Annie's dead body and he finds skin beneath her fingernails and hair that belongs to a white man. Due to this new evidence, which proves Jube's innocence, the doctor realizes his mistake and he feels remorse over his role in his friend's death. His medical training should have impelled him to insist that they look for that type of evidence before the mob hunted Jube down, but his logic was surpassed by his anger. In the aftermath of his discovery of Jube's innocence he yells at the crowd, "Blood guilty! Blood guilty!" in recognition of his own shame at his participation (239).

In "The Tragedy at Three Forks," the woman responsible for the lynchings of two innocent black men is not as remorseful as Dr. Melville and the men are unnamed strangers to the community, so the story lacks the power of "The Lynching of Jube Benson," but it does explore the dire consequences of the cultural presumption of black criminal culpability. The story opens with a focus on Jane Hunster, a young white woman in Central Kentucky plotting her revenge against a female rival who she thinks has belittled her in front of others. She plans to take down the whole Williams family by burning their house and barn in order to show them what it's like to be poor. Her plan works and the family escapes the flames while everything else was completely destroyed. All of the neighbors speculate about who could have done such a thing, but soon Jane's own father incites racial violence in the community with his assertion that the fire was "the work o' niggers," claiming that he can "see their hand in it" (272). Without any evidence or even the names of specific black people who could have potentially committed the crime, the other white neighbors instantly agree and the county newspaper runs an article about the fire calling it the "most dastardly deed ever committed" in the county and placing the blame on "Negroes! Undoubtedly the perpetrators of the deed!" (273). Dunbar states that the journalist makes up the supposed facts, including the idea that some "strange negroes" had been seen sneaking around that area the day before the fire and that there was already a search party of looking for them. It doesn't take long for the article to turn into a "prophecy fulfilled" as "excited, inflamed, and misguided parties of men and boys" felt compelled to look for the supposed culprits (274).

When a pair of black men are spotted in the woods and run at the sight of a group of armed white men, their actions are interpreted as a sign of guilt. Jane witnesses the innocent men being led to the center of the village with ropes around their necks as begins to call for them to be lynched, but her only response is to turn pale as she remains silent about her own role in the fire. Like the mob in Dunbar's other story, the group that delivers the prisoners to the jailhouse is orderly, but the narrator notes that there is something "ominous in their very orderliness" as they give the accused men up to the sheriff who is described as a "scamp by the seal of Satan" (275). The idea that the men will not be much safer inside the jail than they would be outside is reinforced later in the afternoon when the prosecuting attorney visits and talks them into confessing even after they explain that they were farm-laborers from a nearby county who had just passed through the area the day before looking for work. Despite the fact that he promises that they will not be hung if they confess, a crowd begins to gather after the false declaration of their guilt gets out.

While tension over what will happen to the accused men builds, the focus is brought back to Jane who appears to be upset over the unfolding events even though she still refuses to tell anyone that she is really the guilty one. In a strange twist of fate, one of Jane's suitors named Bud Mason suddenly asks her to marry him just before getting swept up in the lynch mob that immediately follows their tender scene. The crowd literally reaches a fever pitch just as Bud kisses Jane. When he explains to her that the crowd is planning to lynch the two men who they believe burned the Williams house, Jane frantically protests that they have not been given a trial yet. Bud dismisses her concern because they have confessed. Jane, knowing that the confession is false since she is the real culprit, immediately argues that someone has forced them to do so "to git 'em hung because they're niggers" (278). Bud can see that something is wrong with Jane, but it isn't entirely clear if he knows the truth about her involvement in the fire and is trying to protect her. His warning to her is explicit though as he points out that she risks her own reputation by defending the black men: "Somebody's got to suffer fur that house-burnin'," an' it might ez well be them ez anybody else. You mustn't talk so. Ef people knowed you wuz a standin' up fur niggers so, it 'ud ruin you" (278). This is followed by a bitter exchange between Bud and a rival suitor, Dock Heaters, who is angry when he finds out that Jane has just become engaged to Bud. Set against the backdrop of the mounting tension of the lynch mob, this scene brings together the conflict over who will win Jane and the anxiety she feels bubbling to the surface in regards to the aftermath of her crime. Bud mocks

Heaters as he walks away urging him to go help with the lynching, saying that's all he's good for.

By this time the mob has set in motion and Bud jumps at the chance to be a part of it even after Jane begs him not to go. He rejects her pleas, telling her, "You don't want me to miss nothin' like that" before joining the mob. As he approaches, the two men have been taken from the jail and led to a tree with ropes already around their necks. Amongst the yells from the crowd, one man screams "Justice an' pertection," and all of the noise and lights "intoxicated [Bud] Mason, [until] he was soon the most enthusiastic man in the mob" (280–81). Just as Dr. Melville had gotten caught up in the mob, Bud similarly allows his emotions to take over any sense of reason as he pulls the rope that lifts the men off the ground. Bud has no personal connection to these men in the way that Dr. Melville did with Jube though, and he is driven further in his participation in the mob scene as he joins the others in shooting the bodies and then trying to grab a piece of the rope to keep as a souvenir. It's this last action that leads to Bud's demise as he fights over a scrap with Heaters who ends up stabbing him to death. When someone in the crowd suggests they lynch the murderer who has committed the crime right in front of their eyes, they are immediately stopped by a voice that reminds them to "Give a white man a chance for his life" (282). Heaters is taken calmly to the jail and allowed to escape later that evening. Jane watches as Bud's body is carried past her and the tragedy of losing him seems to be punishment for not speaking up and confessing her crime. The narrative ends with commentary about how the double lynching and murder was reported by the press. While some lamented the haste of the lynch mob, the assumption of guilt was still apparent when it came to black people being accused of crimes. Dunbar's final message about the results of this prejudice comes in the form of a quote by one editor who wrote "When the blind frenzy of a people condemn a man as soon as he is accused, his enemies need not look far for a pretext!" (283).

In both of the stories examined in this essay, Dunbar directly confronts and displaces the cultural presumption of black criminal culpability. While the final quote at the end of "The Tragedy at Three Forks" is compelling, Waligora-Davis asserts that Dunbar is most effective in "The Lynching of Jube Benson" through the medium of racial performance by making the real criminal a white man in blackface. Skinner's use of racial parody further underscores Dunbar's critique and his depiction of racial prejudice as a social disease.

Unlike the commentary by the newspapers at the end of "The Tragedy at Three Forks," the framing device that closes "The Lynching of Jube Benson" brings the reader back to the doctor's retelling of the lynching narrative. Dr. Melville's guilt and remorse remain, and they are reinforced in the final line which repeats the doctor's unwillingness to witness any more lynchings.

Young suggests that "despite its exposure of racism, Melville's story still makes for good copy, which the journalist will eagerly market," so perhaps by not returning to that potential journalistic account, Dunbar is condemning the "voyeurism of Melville's listeners [and] of the readers of the journalist's future story" (139). In the late nineteenth century, journalists began to be seen as professionals, like doctors and lawyers, predominantly due to the development of objectivity as a key element of reporting, and Lutes argues that an emphasis on objectivity shaped both journalism and realist fiction. A detached sense of objectivity is a complicated matter within the context of a lynching, as expressed succinctly by W.E.B. Du Bois in his *Autobiography* when he wrote that "one could not be a calm, cool, and detached scientist, while Negroes were lynched, murdered, and starved" (222).[5] Lutes asserts that while journalism often failed to adequately represent mob violence, literature could do so more effectively through the use of other professional figures like doctors to explore these racial scenes. Famous examples can be found in the depictions of doctors in works by Dunbar, Stephen Crane, and Charles Chesnutt.[6] Each of these works of fiction were inspired by actual lynchings and they exhibit the problematic nature of objectivity in lynching narratives.

Stories that revolve around lynching, as Lutes asserts, are "emotionally laden and politically complex, structured by an ongoing, often explicit, struggle between detachment and intimacy" that transform observers, "however unwilling, into participants" (473). "The Lynching of Jube Benson" is one of Dunbar's most overtly anti-racist texts, which, as Young observes, "explod[es] the myth of the black rapist central to turn-of-the-century lynching" (135). It is through this reversal that Dunbar is able to confront the notion of the legal presumption of guilt associated with the black body, and challenge readers to question cultural traditions. While writers like Dunbar valued the role of the press for its ability to educate, inform, expose hypocrisy and fraud, and supply citizens with the facts on which they could establish their involvement in political and social issues, there were also notable limits to traditional journalism, particularly when it came to certain subjects like lynching. These narratives were often presented in a superficial, formulaic manner that failed to inspire readers to think for themselves. These limitations were apparent to Dunbar, and so it was in his poetry and fiction that he most effectively drew attention to vigilantism and racial violence. Through stories like "The Lynching of Jube Benson" and "The Lynching of Jube Benson," Dunbar was able to engage the reader's thoughts and emotions in ways that journalism often could not accomplish.

WORKS CITED

Alexandre, Sandy. *The Properties of Violence: Claims to Ownership in Representations of Lynching*. Jackson: University Press of Mississippi, 2012.

Best, Felton O. *Crossing the Color Line: A Biography of Paul Laurence Dunbar 1872–1906*. Dubuque, IA: Kendall/Hunt, 1996.

Bontemps, Arna. "The Relevance of Paul Laurence Dunbar." *A Singer in the Dawn: Reinterpretations of Paul Laurence Dunbar*. Ed. Jay Martin. New York: Dodd, Mead & Company, 1975. 45–53.

Dunbar, Paul Laurence. "The Haunted Oak." *Lyrics of Love and Laughter*. New York: Dodd, Mead & Company, 1903.

____. "The Lynching of Jube Benson." *The Heart of Happy Hollow*. New York: Dodd, Mead & Company, 1904.

____. "The Tragedy at Three Forks." *The Strength of Gideon and Other Stories*. New York: Dodd, Mead & Company, 1900.

Emanuel, James A. "Racial Fire in the Poetry of Paul Laurence Dunbar." *A Singer in the Dawn: Reinterpretations of Paul Laurence Dunbar*. Ed. Jay Martin. New York: Dodd, Mead & Company, 1975. 75–93.

Hudson, Gossie H. "The Crowded Years: Paul Laurence Dunbar in History." *A Singer in the Dawn: Reinterpretations of Paul Laurence Dunbar*. Ed. Jay Martin. New York: Dodd, Mead & Company, 1975. 227–42.

Jones, Gayl. *Liberating Voices: Oral Tradition in African American Literature*. Cambridge: Harvard University Press, 1991.

Lelekis, Debbie. *American Literature, Lynching, and the Spectator in the Crowd: Spectacular Violence*. Lexington Books, 2015.

Lutes, Jean Marie. "Lynching Coverage and the American Reporter-Novelist." *American Literary History* 19.2 (2007): 456–81.

Martin, Jay, ed. "Forward: Paul Laurence Dunbar: Biography Through Letters." *A Singer in the Dawn: Reinterpretations of Paul Laurence Dunbar*. New York: Dodd, Mead & Company, 1975. 13–35.

Pantelia, Maria, Dir. *Thesaurus Linguae Graecae: A Digital Library of Greek Literature*. Online Liddell-Scott-Jones Greek-English Lexicon. University of California, Irvine. 2011.

Rice, Anne P., ed. *Witnessing Lynching: American Writers Respond*. New Brunswick: Rutgers University Press, 2003.

Teutsch, Matthew. "Paul Laurence Dunbar, Racial Uplift, and Collective Identity." *Black Perspectives*. African-American Intellectual History Society. 19 February 2019. https://www.aaihs.org/paul-laurence-dunbar-racial-uplift-and-collective-identity/

Waligora-Davis, Nicole A. "Dunbar and the Science of Lynching." *African-American Review* 41.2 (2007): 303–11.

Young, Elizabeth. Black Frankenstein: The Making of an American Metaphor. New York: New York University Press, 2008.

NOTES

1. In *Witnessing Lynching: American Writers Respond*, Anne P. Rice describes Dunbar as the first native-born African-American writer to attain recognition both nationally and internationally for his body of work which included four novels, four short story collections, and six volumes of poetry.

2. Best's historical biography, *Crossing the Color Line: A Biography of Paul Laurence Dunbar 1872–1906* (1996), lays out Dunbar's family background, based on information from the Ohio Historical Society. Dunbar's parents, Matilda and Joshua were in Kentucky during their time as slaves and met after the end of the Civil War in Dayton, Ohio, where Paul was born in 1872.

3. In addition to these two short stories, Dunbar also deals with lynching in powerful poem entitled "The Haunted Oak," which was first published in *Century Magazine* in 1900 and later appeared in the collection *Lyrics of Love and Laughter* (1913). My chapter on Dunbar in *American Literature, Lynching, and the Spectator in the Crowd: Spectacular Violence* (2015) includes a reading of this poem, which features the tree itself as the narrator and spectator of the story of the lynching of an innocent man by a judge, doctor, and pastor. I also examine the role of the doctor in "The Lynching of Jube Benson" as a spectator of violence.

4. The words "dæmon" and "daimōn" are Latinized versions of the Greek "δαίμων," which translates roughly to "godlike power, fate, god," according to the Thesaurus Linguae Graecae and the Online Liddell-Scott-Jones Greek-English Lexicon created by the University of California, Irvine. These earlier versions do not carry the negative connotations we now associate with the term, as they were seen as benevolent or benign spirits. The term wasn't associated with a spirit that is considered dangerous or evil until Plato's ideas which were later absorbed into Christian writing.

5. Du Bois was profoundly affected by the news of a lynching in 1899 that drew 4000 spectators; he wrote a letter to the *Atlanta Constitution* but on the way to deliver it to the newspaper, he found out that the man had already been lynched. This experience inspired a lynching situation in *The Souls of Black Folk* (1903) and impacted his leadership in the African-American community at the turn of the century.

6. These works consist of "The Lynching of Jube Benson" (1904), *The Monster* (1897), and *The Marrow of Tradition* (1901), respectively.

Index

Absalom, Absalom! (Faulkner), 70–71
Accomando, Christina, 149n1
Adventures of Huckleberry Finn (Twain), 31
African-American Poetry of the Nineteenth Century (Sherman), 153
"After the Winter" (Dunbar), 165n14
Aftermath (Burill), 90n16
Ainslee's Magazine, 1–3, 22, 24, 26–27, 29n2, 30n6, 44n3, 49
Akuta, Uche, 161
Alabama, 70–71
Alexandre, Sandy, 157, 172
"Alfonso, Dressing to Wait at Table" (Dunbar), 165n14
Alford, Bessie C., 66, 68
American Literature, Lynching, and the Spectator in the Crowd: Spectacular Violence (Lelekis), 6, 9, 180n3
An American Tragedy (Dreiser), 2, 26, 28, 55–57, 58–59, 118, 122–33
Anderson, Sherwood, 44n9
Annie Allen (Brooks), 164n3
Apel, Dora, 51
"Aria Con Amore" (Faulkner), 70
Armwood, George, 90n16
The Art of the Novel: Critical Prefaces (James), 2, 83

Association of Southern Women for the Prevention of Lynching (ASWPL), 66–69
Atkinson, Michael, 95
Attaway, William, 85–86
The Autobiography of an Ex-Colored Man (Johnson), 90n16
The Autobiography of W. E. B. Du Bois (Du Bois), 178

Bagnal, Robert, 90n16
Baldwin, James, 34, 48, 117, 119, 126, 132
Barnes, Djuna, 20n3
Barnes, Solon, 53
Barrineau, Nancy, 54
"The Battle Hymn of the Republic," 82
"Battle Royal" (Ellison), 92
Bayam, Nina, 6
Beasley, Maurine H., 8
Belknap, Alvin, 58
Bennett, Gwendolyn B., 163n3
"The Berkshire Tragedy," 50
Best, Felton O., 167
The Best Short Stories of Theodore Dreiser, 30n10
"Between the World and Me" (Wright), 76–77, 164n3
"Bible Defense of Slavery," 155

"Big Boy Leaves Home" (Wright), 37–38, 74–76, 79–86, 91–94, 96, 100, 101n1, 137
Billy Bud (Melville), 109, 118
"Biography of a Bolshevik, Notes on David Poindexter" (Wright), 84
Black Boy (Wright), 75, 83, 93, 96–97, 114, 122, 160
"The Black Christ" (Cullen), 164n3
"Black Confession" (Wright), 83
"The Black Finger" (Grimké), 163n3
Black Nationalism, 109
"A Black Woman Speaks" (Gore), 59
Blotner, Joseph, 65, 70
Bly, Nellie (Elizabeth Jane Cochrane), 8, 20n3
Blythe, Hal, 92
Boni, Albert, 79
Boni, Charles, 79
Bontemps, Arna, 169
A Book About Myself (Dreiser), 22, 29n2, 30n3, 49, 97
Book-of-the-Month Club, 116
Booker, Perry, 80
Bosch, Hieronymous, 149n8
Bradley, Adam, 108
Bradley, Patricia, 7, 20n4
"The Brooch" (Faulkner), 70
Brooks, Cleanth, 107
Brooks, Gwendolyn, 149n4, 164n3
Brown, Billy, 54
Brown, Deneen L., 161
Brown, Ed, 80
Brown, Joe, 80
Brown, Sterling A., 90n16, 116, 163n3
Brown, William, 158
Brown vs. Board of Education, 109
Brundage, Fitzhugh, 68–69
Bryant, Jerry H., 152
Buckner, John, 49, 58
The Bulwark (Dreiser), 27–28, 53
Burdett, Samuel, 41–42
Burill, Mary Powell, 90n16
Burke, Edmund, 37, 39, 44n2
Butler, Robert, 75

"By the Book: The Legal Executions of Kentucky Blacks" (G. Wright), 57
Caldwell, Erskine, 83
Callahan, John, 149n2
Calvin, Floyd J., 90n16
Cane (Toomer), 90n16, 163n3
"Capital Punishment as Legal Lynching?" (Kaufman-Osborn), 57
Cash, Wilbur, 68
"The Castaways" (Dunbar), 165n14
The Castle (Kafka), 109
Cather, Willa, 20n3
Charles, Robert, 164n11
Chesnutt, Charles, 178
The Chicago Race Riots, July 1919 (Sandburg), 90n16
Chopin, Kate, 19
"Christ in Alabama" (Hughes), 90n16, 151
"Christ Recrucified" (Cullen), 90n16, 163n3
Christian Recorder, 153
Civil War, 1, 31, 69, 73, 82, 94, 103, 114, 130, 145, 152, 161, 180n2
"Claude McKay Describes His Own Life" (Ogden), 159
Coleman, Arica, 161, 165n18
Coleman, Lindsey, 77
The Collected Plays of Theodore Dreiser (Newlin and Rusch), 51
Columbian Exposition in Chicago, 155, 168
Compromise of 1876, 146
Cone, James H., 149n1
Connors, Julia, 51
Conversations with Richard Wright (Kinnamon and Fabre), 37, 44n9
Cooper, Wayne F., 161
Costigan, Edward P., 78
Cotter, Joseph S., Jr., 163n3
Cowley, Malcolm, 119
Coy, Edward, 154
Craft, Mabel, 7
Crane, Stephen, 6, 42, 178

Crime and Punishment (Dostievsky), 118
Crossing the Color Line: A Biography of Paul Laurence Dunbar 1872–1906 (Best), 180n2
Cullen, Countee, 90n16, 164n3

Davis, Frank Marshall, 86
Dawn (Dreiser), 26
"Dawn in New York" (Dunbar), 165n14
Dead Souls (Gogol), 109
"A Death-Drag" (Faulkner), 70
"Delaware's Blue Laws" (Dreiser), 1
Dies, Harold J., 29n1
Dostoievsky, Fyodor, 44n9, 103
Douglass, Frederick, 147, 168
Dove, Rita, 164n3
"Down by the Riverside" (Wright), 77
Dray, Philip, 73–75, 80, 151, 153, 160
Dreiser (Swanberg), 30n6
Dreiser, Helen, 126
Dreiser, Paul, 54
Dreiser, Theodore, 1–3, 21–29, 29n2, 30nn3–4, 30n6, 30n8, 31–32, 34, 37–39, 41–43, 44n2, 44nn4–5, 44n7, 44n9, 47–59, 90n16, 91, 96–100, 122
Dreiser on Scottsboro (ILD), 57
Driscoll, Marjorie, 7
"Dry September" (Faulkner), 65, 71, 111n1
Du Bois, W.E.B., 74, 137, 169, 178, 180n5
Duffy, Richard, 29n2
Dunbar, Joshua, 180n2
Dunbar, Matilda, 180n2
Dunbar, Paul Laurence, 2, 82, 152, 155–57, 161, 164n6, 164n11, 167–78, 180nn1–3
Durant, 54

Eastman, Crystal, 158
Eastman, Max, 158
Edelstein, Sari, 7, 18–19, 153, 155
Elias, Robert H., 21, 29n2
Eliot, T. S., 110

Ellington, Yank, 80
Ellis, Robert, 83
Ellison, Ralph, 74, 92, 103–5, 108–10, 138, 160
Emanuel, James, 167
Emerson, Ralph Waldo, 31, 33, 37, 44n6
Estelle, Faulkner, 70
"The Ethics of Living Jim Crow" (Wright), 92–93
"An Extravagance of Laughter" (Ellison), 104–5

Fabre, Michel, 37, 73, 76, 80–81, 83–86
Fadiman, Clifton, 122
Fahs, Alice, 8–9, 18, 20n2
Farnsworth, Robert M., 86
Farrell, James, 86
"The Fascination of Fan Tan" (Michelson), 6
"Father and Son" (Hughes), 90n16
Faulkner, William, 2, 44n9, 61, 64–71, 72n2, 103–5, 107–10, 111nn1–2, 132, 137, 149n8
Ferber, Edna, 20n3
"Fire and Cloud" (Wright), 77
Fitzgerald, F. Scott, 110
"Flag Salute" (Popel), 90n16
"The Flowers" (Walker), 138
"Flowers of Passion" (Dunbar), 165n14
Floyd, George, 161
For My People (M. Walker), 164n3
Forrest, Leon, 137–44, 146–48, 149n3, 149nn6–7
Foster, Frances S., 164n7
Francini, Antonela, 165n15
Frank, Leo, 50, 54
Frank, Waldo, 83
Franklin, John Hope, 51
Free and Other Stories (Dreiser), 22, 32, 44n3, 49, 52, 96
From Lynch Mobs to the Killing State: Race and the Death Penalty in America (Ogletree and Sarat), 57
Front-Page Girls (Lutes), 6

From Slavery to Freedom: A History of African Americans (Franklin), 51
Fruscione, John, 110
"The Fugitive Slave Act of 1850," 155, 164n9
Fuller, Walter, 158

"Gabriel" (Hayden), 164n3
Gates, Henry Louis, Jr., 110
The Gay Woman, 115, 120, 127
The "Genius" (Dreiser), 30n8
Gibbons, Shelia J., 8
Gillette, Chester, 55–56, 123, 126
Gilman, Charlotte Perkins, 19
Go Down, Moses (Faulkner), 71
Gogol, Nikolay, 109
Going to the Territory (Ellison), 104
"Goldie" (Grimké), 90n16
Goldsby, Jacqueline, 41–43, 49, 149n1
Gordon, W. Terrence, 159
Gore, Dayo F., 59
Gosciak, Josh, 158
Graham, Maryemma, 160
the Great Flood of 1927, 77
the Great Kanto Earthquake, 151
Grimké, Angelina Weld, 90n16, 163n3

Hakutani, Yoshinobu, 38–39, 41, 44n4, 44n8, 86
Hall, Jacquelyn Dowd, 66, 68
The Hand of the Potter (Dreiser), 51–53
Harlem Gallery (Tolson), 163n3
Harlem Shadows (McKay), 159
Harper, Frances E. W., 152–55, 160–61, 164nn4–5, 164n7, 164n9
Harris, Carlisle, 54
Harris, M. Cooper, 109
Harris, Trudier, 149n1, 160
Harrison-Kahan, Lori, 5–7, 19
"Hatred" (Bennett), 163n3
"The Haunted Oak" (Dunbar), 152, 155–58
Hawthorne, Nathaniel, 23, 160
Hayden, Robert, 164n3
"He Was a Man" (S. Brown), 90n16

"Hearst Headline Blues" (Wright), 78
The Heart of Happy Hollow (Dunbar), 90n17, 169
Hemingway, Ernest, 2, 44n9, 103, 149n8
Henry, Arthur, 22
Hey Rub-a-Dub-Dub (Dreiser), 22, 28, 54
"Higher Education" (Dunbar), 157
Hill, Karlos, 82, 86
Hill, Leslie Pinckney, 163n3
Hill, Rebecca, 57
Holiday (Frank), 83
Holiday, Billie, 43, 142
"Honors Are Easy" (Michelson), 6, 9, 14
A Hoosier Holiday (Dreiser), 50–51
Hoskins, Margaret, 89n6
Hoskins, Silas, 76, 89n6
"The Hound" (Faulkner), 70
"How 'Bigger' Was Born" (Wright), 45n10, 123, 125, 129
Howe, Irving, 113
Howe, Russell, 64, 71
Howells, William Dean, 168
Howley, Haviland, and Company, 54
Hudson, Gossie H., 167
Hughes, Langston, 78, 90n16, 151, 163n3, 164n4
Hurston, Zora Neale, 81

"I Am a Red Slogan" (Wright), 78
"I Have Seen Black Hands" (Wright), 78
"I Investigate Lynchings" (White), 77
"I Shall Return" (Dunbar), 165n14
"If We Must Die" (McKay), 90n16
"In Chy Fong's Restaurant" (Michelson), 5
In the Bishop's Carriage (Michelson), 7
In the Matter of Black Lives: Womanist Prose (Coleman), 165n18
"Indians Built a Fence" (Faulkner), 70
International Labor Defense (ILD), 57
Intruder in the Dust (Faulkner), 71

Invisible Man (Ellison), 104, 108–9, 145, 160
Invisible Poets (Sherman), 154, 164n5
Iola Leroy, or Shadows Uplifted (Harper), 152
Irving, Washington, 23

Jackson, Blyden, 94
Jackson, Virginia, 164n6
James, Henry, 2, 9, 44n9, 83
James, W. H., 61–64, 66–69, 70, 71
James, Winston, 158–59
Jarrett, Gene, 153, 156, 161
"John Brown's Body," 82
John Reed Club, 78–79
Johnson, Fenton, 163n3
Johnson, Florence, 120
Johnson, James Weldon, 43, 77, 90n16, 137, 163n3, 169
Jones, Casey, 90n14
Jones, Gayl, 174
Jordan, Bill, 86
Jordan, Dick, 80
Journalism (Dreiser), 49–50
Joyce, James, 110, 118, 137
Joyce, Joyce Ann, 118, 122

Kafka, Franz, 109
Kaufman-Osborn, Timothy V., 57
Kazin, Alfred, 29
Kearns, Edward, 119
Kennedy, John F., 109
Kennedy, Robert, 109
King, Martin Luther, Jr., 109
Kinnamon, Keneth, 115, 120
"Kneel to the Rising Sun" (Caldwell), 83
Komunyakaa, Yusef, 164n3
Kreymborg, Alfred, 79

Lady Godiva, 96
Lancaster, Guy, 89n6
Lanier High School, 80
"Laughter and Tears" (Wright), 81
Lawd Today! (Wright), 78

Lelekis, Debbie, 149n1
Lewis, John, 74
Light in August (Faulkner), 71, 104, 106, 108, 110, 111n1
Lightweis-Goff, Jennie, 149n1
Like the Singing Coming Off of Drums (Sanchez), 164n3
Lincoln, Abraham, 145, 147
Lingeman, Richard, 57
"The List of Bassett's" (Michelson), 18
London, Jack, 6
"Long Black Song" (Wright), 114
The Long Dream (Wright), 114
A Long Way from Home (McKay), 158
The Love of Laundry (Dunbar), 156
"Love Song" (Dunbar), 165n14
Loving, Jerome, 42
Lutes, Jean Marie, 6, 9, 11, 14, 17–18, 20n3, 170, 178
Lynch, Charles, 73
Lynch, John R., 73
"The Lynching" (McKay), 152, 158–59, 161
"The Lynching" (Moss), 164n3
"Lynching Coverage and the American Reporter-Novelist" (Lutes), 170
The Lynching Files (Tuskegee), 61
"The Lynching of Jube Benson" (Dunbar), 82, 161, 167, 169, 175, 177–78, 180n3
"The Lynching of Nigger Jeff" (Dreiser), 22, 26, 44n3, 44n7
Lyrics of Love and Laughter (Dunbar), 156, 180n3
Lyrics of Lowly Life (Dunbar), 168

The Madigans (Michelson), 6
Majors and Minors (Dunbar), 168
Malcolm X, 109
Malraux, André, 44n3, 103
"The Man Who Killed a Shadow" (Wright), 116
"The Man Who Saw the Flood" (Wright), 77
Margolies, Edward, 132

Markovitz, Johnathan, 47–48
The Marrow of Tradition (Chesnutt), 180n6
Marsh, Reginald, 160, 165n17
Martin, Jay, 169
Martin, Lawrence, 86
Martinsville Seven, 59
"The Martyr of Alabama" (Harper), 152–55, 161, 164n4, 164n8
The Martyr of Alabama and Other Poems (Harper), 152
Mason, Orville, 58
The Master of Light: A Biography of Albert A. Michelson (Livingston), 20n1
Mathews, Donald G., 149n1
Matthews, James Newton, 168
Matthiessen, F. O., 126
Maxwell, William J., 159–60, 165n14
"McEwen of the Shining Slave Makers" (Dreiser), 32
McGee, Willie, 59
McKay, Claude, 90n16, 152, 158–60, 164n13
McMillen, Neil R., 66, 68–69, 111n1
Melville, Herman, 109
"A Memory of June" (Dunbar), 165n14
Men, Mobs, and Law: Anti-Lynching and Labor Defense in U. S. Radical History (Hill), 57
Metamorphoses (Ovid), 94
Michelson, Miriam, 5–9, 11, 14, 16, 18–19, 20n1
Miller, James, 78, 82
"Miriam Michelson's Yellow Journalism and the Multi-Ethnic West" (Harrison-Kahan and Skinazi), 6
Moby Dick (Melville), 118
Modern Tragedy (Williams), 50
Moers, Ellen, 29
Monro, Harold, 79
Monroe, Harriet, 79
The Monster (Crane), 42, 180n6
Moore, Alice Ruth, 155
Morgan, Thomas Lewis, 161

"Morning Joy" (Dunbar), 165n14
Morrison, Toni, 110
Moss, Thylias, 164n3
"Most Wanted: Claude McKay and 'Black Spectator' of African American Poetry in the 1920s" (Gosciak), 158
Mother Goose, 79
Mother Love (Dove), 164n3
Mounger, Dwyn M., 69
Mumford, Lewis, 79
"My Grievance" (Dandrigde), 163n3
The Mysterious Stranger (Twain), 109

Nagel, James, 120
National Association for the Advancement of Colored People (NAACP), 58, 70, 72nn1–2, 74, 77–78, 153, 165n16
"Native Guard" (Tretheway), 164n3
Native Son (Wright), 37, 74, 78, 93, 113–17, 119, 121–34
"Nature" (Emerson), 31, 37
"A Negro Lynched" (Dreiser), 2
Nelson, Marilyn, 164n3
"Neurotic America and the Sex Impulse" (Dreiser), 54
The New Caravan (Kreymborg, Mumford, and Rosenfeld), 79, 101n1
Newlin, Keith, 51–53
Newton, Jane, 85
Nicholas, Grover, 77
"Nigger Jeff" (Dreiser), 2, 21–22, 24–29, 29–30n2, 30n8, 30n10, 31–33, 35, 37–38, 40–42, 44nn3–4, 44n7, 47–50, 52, 58, 90n16, 91, 96–100
Norris, Frank, 128
"North and South" (Dunbar), 165n14
Nostwich, T. D., 49
Nutt, Howard, 79

Oak and Ivy (Dunbar), 168
"Obsession" (Wright), 78
The Octopus (Norris), 128

Ogden, Charles K., 158–59, 164n13
"The Old South: For Richard Wright" (Kreymborg), 79
"On Broadway" (Dunbar), 165n14
"Out of the Shadows" (Cotter), 163n3
Out on Assignment: Newspaper Women and the Making Modern Public Space (Fahs), 20n2
The Outsider (Wright), 94, 116
Ovid, 94

"A Party Down at the Square" (Ellison), 104–5, 149n2
Patterson, Nan, 54
Patton, Nelse, 72n2
Peeping Tom, 96
The Philomathean Society, 168
Philosophical Enquiry into the Origin of Our Ideas of the Sublime and Beautiful (Burke), 37
Pizer, Donald, 32, 38, 44n3, 44n5, 96
Podhoretz, Norman, 110
Poe, Edgar Allan, 140
Poems on Miscellaneous Subjects (Harper), 160
Poindexter, David, 84
Polk, Noel, 111n1
"The Pollexfen Story" (Michelson), 9
Popel, Esther, 90n16
Porter, Katherine Anne, 149n8
"The Present South" (Calvin), 90n16
"The Prophet," 54
Pudd'nhead Wilson (Twain), 31

Quinn, Dennis, 53

Rampersad, Arnold, 103, 109–10, 115
Ray, David, 86
"Recent Directions for the Study of Women's History in American Journalism" (Beasley), 8
Reconstruction, 1–2, 31, 49, 61–62, 64, 67, 69, 73, 142, 152–53
"The Red Summer of 1919," 76, 158, 164n12

Reed, Mac, 65
"Reflections" (Dreiser), 54
Reilly, John M., 135n6
Remembering Scottsboro: The Legacy of an Infamous Trial (Miller), 78, 82
"Reminiscences" (Dunbar), 165n14
"Rest in Peace" (Dunbar), 165n14
Revolutionary War, 1, 69, 73, 116
Rice, Anne, 157
Richard Wright's Art of Tragedy (Joyce), 135n11
Riley, James Whitcomb, 168
the Robert Charles riots, 156
Robinson, Carl T., 76
Robinson, Ray "Chunky," 76
Roggenkamp, Karen, 7
Roosevelt, Franklin D., 20n1
Rosenfeld, Paul, 79
Rowley, Hazel, 76
Rusch, Frederic, 51–53

Sanchez, Sonia, 164n3
Sanctuary (Faulkner), 65, 70
Sandburg, Carl, 90n16
The Scarlet Letter (Hawthorne), 160
Schwenk, Katrin, 75
the Scottsboro Case, 57, 78, 82
Scottsboro Limited: Four Poems and a Play in Verse (Hughes), 78
"Self-Reliance" (Emerson), 44n6
Shadow and Act (Ellison), 103
Shakespeare, William, 104
Sherman, Joan R., 153–54, 164n5
Shields, Henry, 80
Siegel, Paul N., 119
"Silt" (Wright), 77
Sister Carrie (Dreiser), 2, 22, 26, 27, 131–32
Sketches of Southern Life (Harper), 152, 154
Skinazi, E. H., 5–7, 19
Smith, Hal, 70
Smith, Henry, 41, 154
Smith-Robertson Public School, 80

"Some Aspects of Our National Character" (Dreiser), 54
The Souls of Black Folk (Du Bois), 169, 180n5
Southern Horrors (Wells), 2
Southern Road (Brown), 163n3
the Southern Syncopated Orchestra, 159, 164n13
"The Spanish Needle" (Dunbar), 165n14
Special Laughter (Nutt), 79
A Spectacular Secret (Goldsby), 49
Spencer, Morgan, 62
the Spingarn Medal, 74
"Spread Your Sunrise!" (Wright), 81
St. Louis Republic, 2, 21, 29n2, 49
Steinbeck, John, 132
Stevens, Ethel Featherston, 66, 68
Still, William, 154
Stone, Phil, 65
"Strange Fruit" (Holiday), 43, 142, 144
A Street in Bronzeville (Brooks), 164n3
The Strength of Gideon and Other Stories (Dunbar), 157, 169
"Sukee River" (Dunbar), 165n14
Swanberg, W. A., 21, 30n3, 30n6
Swartz, Nathan, 51
Sweet, Charlie, 92

Tanner, Laura E., 117–18
Taub, Allan, 78
The Tempest (Shakespeare), 140
"The Terror of Quarantine to an Unsophisticated Chinese Lady" (Michelson), 6
A Test of Lynch Law (Burdett), 42
Teutsch, Matthew, 168
Thaw, 54
Their Eyes Were Watching God (Hurston), 81
Theodore Dreiser Encyclopedia (Newlin), 51
"Theodore Dreiser's 'Nigger Jeff': The Development of an Aesthetic" (Pizer), 101n7

There Is a Tree More Ancient Than Eden (Forrest), 137–38
Thieves of Paradise (Komunnyakaa), 164n3
"This Is Her First Lynching" (Marsh), 160
Three Days before the Shooting (Ellison), 104–10
"Three Songs about Lynching" (Hughes), 163n3
Till, Emmett, 59
"*Time*: an era of lynching, Jim Crowism" (Wright), 79
Tin Pan Alley publishers, 54
"To O. E. A." (Dunbar), 165n14
Tolson, Melvin, 163n3
Toomer, Jean, 90n16, 137–38, 163n3
Trader Horn, 115, 127
"The Tragedy at Three Forks" (Dunbar), 157, 167, 169, 175, 177
"Transcontinental" (Wright), 78
Trethewey, Natasha, 164n3
Turner, Mary, 90n16
Tuskegee Institute, 1, 61, 72n1, 73, 88nn2–3
Twain, Mark, 6, 31, 109
"Two Million Black Voices" (Wright), 79

Uncle Tom's Children (Wright), 37, 91–99
the Underground Railroad, 160
The Unfinished Quest of Richard Wright (Fabre), 37
"The Unquenchable Fire" (Bagnal), 90n16

"A Victim of Justice" (Dreiser), 21–24, 27, 29, 44n3, 44n7, 96
"Vision of a Lyncher" (Hill), 163n3

Wagner, Robert F., 78
the Wagner-Costigan bill, 80
Waligora-Davis, Nicole A., 171–73, 177
Walker, Alice, 138

Walker, Margaret, 81, 86, 92, 164n3
Washington, Booker T., 169
Wells-Barnett, Ida B., 2, 20n3, 43, 57, 68, 137, 151, 161
Wharton, Edith, 19
"When Dawn Comes to the City" (Dunbar), 165n14
"When I Die" (Johnson), 163n3
White, Sallie, 21
White, Walter, 77, 160, 165n16
"White Things" (Spencer), 163n3
Whitfield, Stephen, 51
Wiggins, Lida, 156
Williams, Mack, 90n16
Williams, Raymond, 50
Williamson, Joel T., 69
"Winter in the Country" (Dunbar), 165n14
"With the Nameless Dead" (Dreiser), 21
Without Sanctuary: Lynching Photography in America (Allen), 149n10

Witnessing Lynching: American Writers Respond (Rice), 180n1
Women Writers of the American West, 1833–1927 (Bayam), 6
A Wreath for Emmett Till (Nelson), 164n3
Wright, Ella, 76
Wright, George C., 57
Wright, Orville, 168
Wright, Richard, 37–40, 43, 44n9, 45n10, 73–86, 89n6, 89n8, 91–100, 101n1, 103, 113–27, 129–30, 132–33, 135, 137, 160, 164n3, 168
Wright, Wilbur, 168

A Yellow Journalist (Michelson), 5–7, 9, 14, 18–19
Young, Elizabeth, 170, 173–74
Young Dreiser (Hakutani), 44n4, 44n8

About the Contributors

Robert Butler is professor of English at Canisius College in Buffalo, New York. He has written and edited many books, including *The Critical Response in Japan to African American Writers* (coeditor 2003); *The Critical Response to Ralph Ellison* (2001); *Contemporary African American Literature: The Open Journey* (1998); *The Critical Response to Richard Wright* (1995); *The City in African American Literature* (coeditor 1995).

Keith Byerman is professor of English at Indiana State University. Aside from numerous essay contributions on African-American literature, he is author of *The Life and Work of John Edgar Wideman* (2013); *The Art and life of Clarence Major* (2012); and others. He is also coeditor of *Critical Essays on John Edgar Wideman* (2006).

Yoshinobu Hakutani taught in the English department at Kent State University in Ohio, where he was also a university distinguished scholar. His recent books include *Jack Kerouac and Haiku* (2018); *East-West Literary Imagination: Cultural Exchanges from Yeats to Morrison* (2017); *Richard Wright and Haiku* (2014); and *Haiku and Modernist Poetics* (2009).

Toru Kiuchi taught as professor of English at Nihon University in Japan. He is the author or editor of many books on American literature, including *American Haiku: New Readings* (2017); *Richard Wright: A Documented Chronology, 1908–1960* (coauthor, 2014); *The Critical Response in Japan to African American Writers* (coeditor, 2003); among others. He is also a Japanese translator of many works in American literature, including Wright's *The Long Dream* (2017); Wright's *Haiku: This Other World* (co-translator, 2007), and *A Langston Hughes Reader* by Hans Ostrom (2006).

Debbie Lelekis is associate professor of English, School of Arts and Communication at Florida Tech University. She is author of *American Literature, Lynching, and the Spectacular in the Crowd: Spectacular Violence* (2015), which examines literary depictions of the witnessing and reporting of racial violence.

Neil R. McMillen is an American historian, and professor emeritus at the University of Southern Mississippi. He has authored and edited many works including *Remaking Dixie* (editor 1997); *Dark Journey: Black Mississippians in the Age of Jim Crow* (1990).

Kiyohiko Murayama taught at Hitotsubashi University, Tokyo Metropolitan University, and Toyo University in Japan. He is a leading scholar on American Literature and wrote a book on Theodore Dreiser and Edgar Allan Poe. He is now retired from academic teaching but continues writing.

Donald Pizer, the Pierce Butler Professor of English Emeritus, Tulane University, is the author of many books on American Literature and Naturalism, in particular. Works include *American Naturalism and the Jews: Garland, Norris, Dreiser, Wharton, and Cather* (2008); *The Cambridge Companion to American Realism and Naturalism: Howells to London* (2002).

Noel Polk was a professor of English at the University of Southern Mississippi, a Faulkner scholar, and editor of the *Mississippi Quarterly* and *The Southern Quarterly*. His publications include *Children of the Dark House: Text and Context in Faulkner* (1996); *Faulkner and Welty and the Southern Literary Tradition* (2010).

Michael Sanders is associate professor of English at Kent State University in Ohio, and the author of the forthcoming *Theodore Dreiser's Encounter with American Romanticism and Realism*.

www.ingramcontent.com/pod-product-compliance
Lightning Source LLC
Chambersburg PA
CBHW020744020526
44115CB00030B/921